WORKING WITH USERS AND GROUPS:

DSPACE (*)
View and change users' disk-space limitations on the file server (and directory limitations in NetWare 3.*x*).

SYSCON (*)
Add and delete users and groups, view information about users and groups, set account restrictions, and create login scripts.

USERLIST (♦)
List all users who are currently logged in, their addresses, login times, and connection numbers.

WHOAMI (♦)
View your username and connection information, such as your group assignments, login time, and trustee rights.

WORKING WITH NETWARE SECURITY:

ALLOW (♦)
In NetWare 3.*x* only, view and change a directory's or file's Inherited Rights Mask.

FILER (*)
View and change a directory's or file's Rights Mask, attributes, and trustee assignments.

FLAG (♦)
View and change file attributes.

FLAGDIR (♦)
View and change directory attributes.

GRANT (♦)
Grant trustee rights to users or groups.

NDIR (♦)
List files and subdirectories and view information about their attributes, Rights Masks, effective rights, and so on.

REMOVE (♦)
Remove a user or group from the trustee list of a directory (or file in NetWare 3.*x*).

REVOKE (♦)
Take away some or all of a user's or group's trustee rights to a directory (or file in NetWare 3.*x*).

RIGHTS (♦)
View your effective rights in a directory.

SECURITY (♦)
Identify possible network security violations.

SETPASS (♦)
Change your password.

SYSCON (*)
View and change trustee assignments, Rights Masks, passwords, and login scripts.

TLIST (♦)
List the trustees of a directory (or file in NetWare 3.*x*).

TALK TO NOVELL PRESS AND SYBEX ONLINE.

JOIN THE SYBEX FORUM ON COMPUSERVE®

- Talk to Novell Press and SYBEX authors, editors and fellow forum members.

- Get tips, hints, and advice online.

- Download shareware and the source code from SYBEX books.

If you're already a CompuServe user, just enter GO SYBEX to join the SYBEX Forum. If you're not, try CompuServe free by calling 1-800-848-8199 and ask for Representative 560. You'll get one free month of basic service and a $15 credit for CompuServe extended services—a $23.95 value. Your personal ID number and password will be activated when you sign up.

Join us online today. Enter GO SYBEX on CompuServe. You can also find out about a wide variety of Novell Inc. forums by entering GO NOVLIB. If you're not a CompuServe member, call Representative 560 at 1-800-848-8199.

(outside U.S./Canada call 614-457-0802)

 CompuServe®

SYBEX
Shortcuts to
Understanding

Novell's® Guide to

MANAGING SMALL
NetWare® Networks

▶

KELLEY J. P. LINDBERG

Novell Press, San Jose

Publisher: Peter Jerram
Editor-in-Chief: Dr. R. S. Langer
Series Editor: David Kolodney
Acquisitions Editor: Dianne King
Program Manager: Rosalie Kearsley
Developmental Editor: David Kolodney
Editor: Marilyn Smith
Project Editor: Abby Azrael
Technical Editors: Dan Tauber and William Harding
Production and Layout Artist: Ingrid Owen
Technical Illustrators: John Corrigan and Cuong Le
Screen Graphics: John Corrigan
Typesetter: Suzanne Albertson
Proofreader/Production Coordinator: Catherine Mahoney
Indexer: Kelley Lindberg
Cover Designer: Archer Design
Novell Press Logo Design: Jennifer Gill
Cover Photographer: Kelley Lindberg
Screen reproductions prodiced with Collage Plus

Collage Plus is a trademark of Inner Media Inc.

SYBEX is a registered trademark of SYBEX Inc.

Novell Press and the Novell Press logo are trademarks of Novell, Inc.

TRADEMARKS: SYBEX and Novell have attempted throughout this book to distinguish proprietary trademarks from descriptive terms by following the capitalization style used by the manufacturer.

Every effort has been made to supply complete and accurate information. However, neither SYBEX nor Novell assumes any responsibility for its use, nor for any infringement of the intellectual property rights of third parties which would result from such use.

Library of Congress Card Number: 93-83421
ISBN: 0-7821-1238-2

Manufactured in the United States of America
10 9 8 7

For Andy

Acknowledgments

This is the part where I get to sit back, breathe a sigh of relief, and thank everyone who helped make this book happen.

First, I would like to thank the good people at SYBEX for pulling it all together: Dianne King, Abby Azrael, John Corrigan, Marilyn Smith, Dan Tauber, and especially David Kolodney for convincing me that this book was a good idea and that I was the writer for the job.

I would also like to thank Rose Kearsley and Peter Jerram for making me part of the Novell Press team.

More thanks go to Novell, Inc., for allowing me to pursue this project, and for producing the best networking software in the world.

A special thank you belongs to William Harding, who made sure everything I wrote was really true, and who merely laughed the day I set his disk space to zero and then went home.

Wild appreciation goes to Louise and Mel Pollard for their unfailing encouragement and for Louise's watchful editorial eyes.

Of course, I want to express my gratitude to all my family and friends, who still have the grace to feign interest when they smile and ask, "So, how's the book going?"

Above all, I want to thank my husband Andy for everything. Without him, royalties wouldn't be nearly as much fun.

And finally, I would like to send a noisy standing ovation to all the terrific people in Novell's Provo Technical Publications Department, with whom I toil every day.

CONTENTS AT A *Glance*

TABLE OF *Contents*

. . . .

CHAPTER 7 *Making Life Easy for Your Users* 165

CHAPTER 8   *Routine Network Maintenance*
and Troubleshooting   *213*

CHAPTER 11 *Using NetWare Version 3.12*   *281*

Introduction

These days, chances are good that if you work in an office that uses computers, you're using a network. In this era of information overload, a tight economy, and a widespread desire for instant gratification, computer networks are growing in importance. They have become the standard for efficiently sharing information, expensive hardware, and costly software. Networks are the information backbone of businesses ranging from small law offices to major television networks, and from universities to preschools.

The networking software that is running on the majority of those computer networks is NetWare. NetWare, from Novell, Inc., is the leading networking software in the world. Its power, features, and flexibility are unmatched in the networking industry.

If you are the network supervisor of a small NetWare version 2.2 or 3.x network, this book will help you find the most efficient and practical ways to run your network. This book also contains a chapter about using NetWare for Macintosh, another Novell product that allows you to connect Macintosh workstations to your NetWare network.

Who Manages the Network?

With the spread of computer networks has come the need for people who know how to run them.

For large companies with huge networks, network administration often becomes the domain of a team of full-time, dedicated, well-trained computer gurus. These full-time network supervisors have their hands full, optimizing each aspect of their company's enormous internetwork, connecting their network with various other resources such as mainframes and global internetworks, training hundreds of new employees, and so on.

However, not all networks are sold to huge conglomerations that can afford to hire full-time network supervisors. In these smaller environments, network supervision is often tacked onto the end of someone's job description as an afterthought, euphemistically known as a "special project." All over the world, dentists, accountants, lawyers, sales representatives, technicians, teachers, and office administrators are struggling to keep their networks running smoothly while continuing to perform their regular jobs.

This can look like an unattainable goal at times. You're faced with the dizzying array of features built into NetWare, not to mention the daunting number of technical manuals that come with the software. Fortunately, it's not nearly as bad as it looks.

Who Should Read This Book?

This book is designed to simplify your life as the supervisor of a small NetWare version 2.2 or 3.x network. A "small" network has one or two file servers, one or two printers, and fewer than 100 workstations.

NetWare designers recognized that not all their customers are supervisors of massive networks. For many of NetWare's features, you'll find that default settings, straightforward procedures, and real-world examples are all that you need to get your small network running efficiently and your fellow employees working together. However, isolating these simplified goals from all the more complicated options is often difficult and time-consuming. This book will help you determine which features you need to use and which ones you can ignore. Then you can get on with your "real" job as account representative, reporter, music director, fund-raising coordinator,....

What Do You Need to Know before Using This Book?

Most supervisors of small networks get the job because they already know something about computers. Before trying to use this book to run a NetWare network, you should be familiar with the operating systems that run on your workstations. If you have PCs on your network, study the manufacturer's documentation to learn how to install and run DOS, OS/2, or Windows on a computer. For example, you should know how to create, copy, and delete files and directories. If you have Macintoshes, you should know how to set them up and how to create, copy, and delete Macintosh files, too.

This book provides the basic information, guidelines, and examples you need to install and run a NetWare network. However, you should keep at hand a set of the NetWare documentation that came with your network, because you may need to refer to the documentation for more specific information about your particular situation, as well as for detailed installation instructions.

What Does This Book Contain?

The ten chapters in this book take you from the basics of networking to routine maintenance and troubleshooting:

- ▶ Chapter 1 provides information about how a NetWare network operates and which tasks you can expect to perform as a network supervisor.

- ▶ Chapter 2 explains how to install your network, including the file server, workstations, and peripheral devices.

- ▶ Chapter 3 describes how to organize your network files and directories for maximum efficiency and security.

▶ Chapter 4 is about managing network users and covers setting restrictions, adding users, and creating groups.

▶ Chapter 5 explains how network printing works and how to set up for printing.

▶ Chapter 6 covers the important topic of network security and includes information about how trustee rights work and how to manage those rights.

▶ Chapter 7 describes how you, as a network supervisor, can make your network users' jobs easier by creating login scripts and menus.

▶ Chapter 8 summarizes the routine tasks that are necessary to maintain a network and provides guidelines and suggestions for troubleshooting network problems.

▶ Chapter 9 explains how network file backups are your insurance against data losses and how to create and manage your backups.

▶ Chapter 10 is about Novell for Macintosh, the software product that allows Macintosh computers to run on a PC-based network.

▶ Chapter 11 describes the new features offered in NetWare 3.12 and explains how to use them.

The Glossary that follows Chapter 11 provides definitions of the terms used in this book.

What Are the Differences between NetWare Versions 2.2 and 3.x?

NetWare versions 2.2 and 3.x are currently the most widely used versions of Net-Ware. NetWare version 2.2 is a solid workhorse designed for workgroup networks, such as those found in departments or small businesses. NetWare version 3.x is a faster, more powerful version of NetWare, designed for networks that require all the features of NetWare version 2.2, plus more advanced features, such as support for different types of networking protocols, Remote Console (which lets you control the file server from your workstation), and SBACKUP (an enhanced backup program).

To add functionality to your NetWare version 2.2 file server, you can load programs called Value-Added Processes (VAPs) onto the server. VAPs can be added to a file server only if you shut down the file server and reboot it.

To add functionality to your NetWare version 3.x file server, you load programs called NetWare Loadable Modules (NLMs). NLMs are especially convenient because you can add them to your file server while the server is running.

This book describes how to manage both versions of NetWare networks.

What Are NetWare's Hardware Requirements?

To run the NetWare network operating system, your file server must meet the following requirements:

▸ It must be a DOS-based personal computer. NetWare version 2.2 runs on 80286, 80386, or 80486 computers. NetWare version 3.x runs on 80386 or 80486 computers.

▸ It must have enough RAM (random-access memory). NetWare version 2.2 requires a minimum of 2.5 MB (megabytes) of RAM. NetWare version 3.x requires a minimum of 5 MB of RAM. You may need additional RAM depending on the features and applications you use.

▸ It should have a hard disk for storing network applications and files. You can also add external hard disks to the file server for extra storage.

▸ It must have a network board installed that supports the network protocol that your workstations are using, such as Ethernet, Arcnet, or Token Ring.

A PC workstation on a NetWare network must meet the following requirements:

- ► It must be an IBM PC AT, PS/2, PC XT, or compatible computer, running DOS or OS/2. (DOS workstations may also run Windows.)

- ► It must have a minimum of 512K of memory, although you may need more depending on the type of applications that will run on the workstation.

- ► It must contain a network board that matches the network board installed in the file server (such as Ethernet, Token Ring, or Arcnet).

Macintosh workstations on a NetWare for Macintosh network must be running the following software:

- ► System version 6.0 or above

- ► Finder version 6.1 or above

- ► AppleShare workstation software version 2.0 or above

CHAPTER 1

Taking the Network Reins

You're the supervisor of a small NetWare network. Perhaps it's not your only job responsibility; perhaps it is. Whatever the rest of your job entails, at least part of your time will be spent managing the network. What exactly are you in for?

Knowing what each part of a network does and how it's supposed to work will help you understand your job as a network supervisor. You will be able to determine if a network element is functioning properly, if it needs to be upgraded, or if you can happily leave it alone. This chapter explains the elements that make up a NetWare network. It also describes some of the tasks you may perform as a network supervisor.

Getting Oriented

If you're relatively new to NetWare networks, your first question is probably "What is a NetWare network?" A *network*, sometimes called a *LAN* (local area network) is a group of computers connected together so that users can share the same files, applications, printers, and other resources. NetWare is the software that allows the computers to be connected and work together.

Few networks look exactly alike, but they are all formed from the same set of basic elements. Networks consist of physical components, such as computers, printers, modems, and other types of hardware. Networks also have software elements, which are what NetWare provides. The software elements connect the physical components and allow them to communicate with each other.

WHAT ARE THE PHYSICAL COMPONENTS OF A NETWORK?

The physical (hardware) components of a network are the easiest to identify and describe. They are the building blocks of your network. Any NetWare network has some combination of the same components. Figure 1.1 illustrates the physical components of a simple NetWare network: workstations, file server, network boards, network cabling, printer, and peripherals.

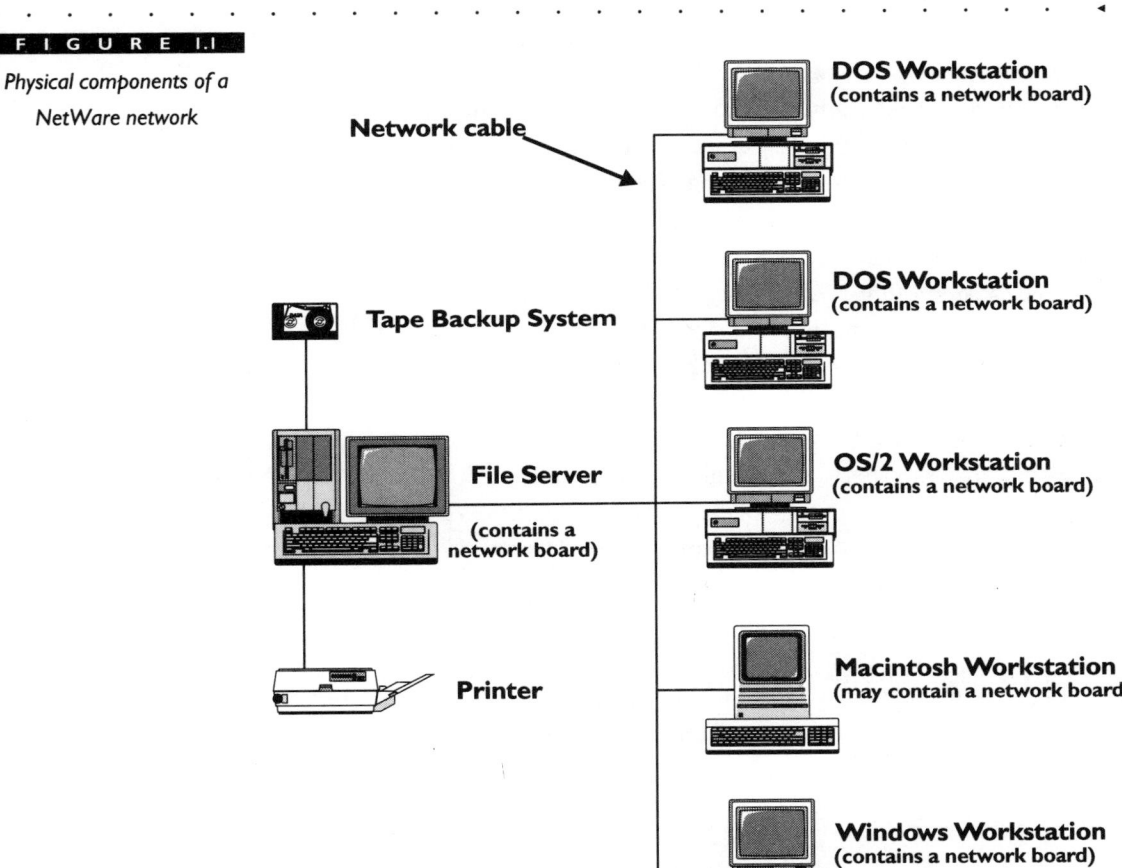

*Physical components of a
NetWare network*

Network cable

DOS Workstation
(contains a network board)

DOS Workstation
(contains a network board)

Tape Backup System

File Server
(contains a
network board)

OS/2 Workstation
(contains a network board)

Macintosh Workstation
(may contain a network board)

Printer

Windows Workstation
(contains a network board)

Workstations

Workstations are the computers (PCs or Macintoshes) that sit on network users' desks. Workstations are where users do their daily work: writing memos, creating spreadsheets, sending electronic mail, and so on.

When you buy a computer and turn it on, the software that brings the computer to life and controls how you work with it is called an *operating system*. On personal computers such as IBM PCs, this operating system can be DOS or OS/2. You may also be running Windows on a DOS computer. On Macintoshes, the operating system is called System. Any computer running one of these operating systems can be a workstation on a NetWare network.

To users, working on a computer that happens to be attached to a NetWare network doesn't appear to be much different from using the computer by itself (called a *stand-alone computer*). This is because NetWare takes care of the workstation's communications with the rest of the network without affecting how the computer's own operating system works. Therefore, users can work with files—open files, run applications, save files, and so on—in the same way they would if the computer weren't attached to a network.

What makes a network-connected workstation different from a stand-alone computer is the fact that users can access applications and files that are stored on the network in addition to files stored on their own disks. Workstation users can also share those applications and files with other users through the network, eliminating the search through the office for the floppy disk that holds the Jones report.

Because workstations are attached to the network and can use the network's services, workstations are sometimes called network *clients*.

File Server

The *file server*, also called a *network server*, is the computer that controls the entire network. A single file server can control a network of up to 250 workstations.

The file server does not need to be a special type of computer; it is simply a DOS-based personal computer that happens to be running special NetWare software. However, to avoid slow network communications, you will probably want to use the most powerful computer you can afford as the file server.

You will probably want your file server to be at a least a 386 computer (a requirement for NetWare version 3.11), run at a speed of at least 16 Megahertz, and have at least 5 Megabytes of RAM (random-access memory). Its hard disk should be as large as possible, because it will store files from all your network users, as well as all your applications. If necessary, you can connect additional hard disks to your file server for more storage space.

In NetWare version 3.x, the file server computer is dedicated to being a file server. This means that you cannot use that computer as a workstation to run applications or perform other work. The file server's sole function is to run the network.

In NetWare version 2.2, the file server can be either dedicated or nondedicated. A nondedicated file server can be used as both the file server and a workstation. The file server operations will run quietly in the background, controlling the network without interfering with the user's normal, everyday work with that workstation. This is often an ideal setup for small companies that cannot afford to dedicate a computer to being a full-time file server.

The drawback to using a nondedicated file server is that the network may run a little slower. Also, if a user accidently turns off that machine, or if an application the user is working with suddenly hangs, the entire network shuts down.

Networking Hardware: Boards and Cables

Network boards and cabling physically connect workstations and file servers. *Network boards* (also called *network interface cards*) are specialized circuit boards that must be installed in every workstation and file server on the network. On one edge of each board is a connector to which a cable can be fastened. The network boards are installed so that their connectors protrude from the back of the computer. After the boards are installed, you connect the network cables to them. This way, each workstation becomes attached to the network. Figure 1.2 illustrates a network board and cable installed in a workstation.

The exact process for connecting the network cables and boards depends on the type of cabling you use, such as coax, twisted-pair, or fiber-optic cabling.

The type of cabling you choose depends on your networking requirements. A reseller or consultant can help analyze your particular needs and recommend the best cabling for your network.

Your file server and workstations must have the same type of network board installed. For example, if you install an Ethernet board in your file server, you need to install Ethernet boards in all your workstations and use Ethernet cable

Network board installed in
a computer

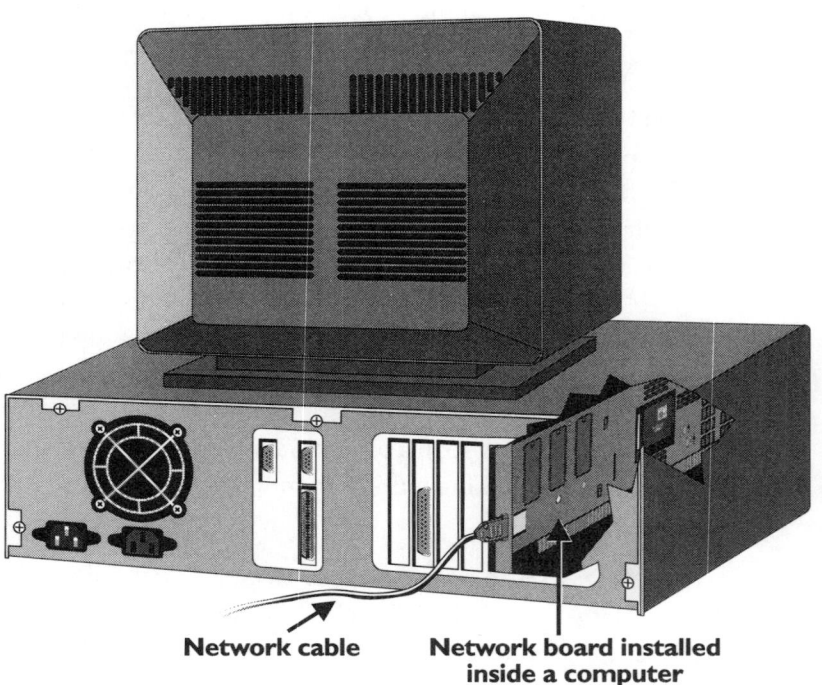

Network cable   **Network board installed inside a computer**

to connect them all. The boards do not need to come from the same manufacturer, but they must all be of the same type.

However, if your workstations have different types of network boards installed, you can still use them with the same file server by installing more than one network board in that file server. For example, you can install one Ethernet board in the file server and connect several Ethernet workstations to that board. Then you can install an Arcnet board in the same file server and connect several Arcnet workstations to that board. In essence, you end up with two separate networks, both being controlled by the same file server.

Printers

One of the main reasons small companies invest in networks is to allow their employees to share printers easily. With a network, employees do not need to borrow the computer that has the printer attached, or move the cable and printer over to their own computer. The company does not need to buy a laser printer for the accounting office and another one for the sales office, because workers in those two offices can share the same printer. Of course, there's still the debate about which office the laser printer sits in—even networks can't solve that problem.

Miscellaneous: Everyone's Favorite Category

Just as networks make it easier to share printers, they also make it easier to share other types of resources, such as modems, tape backup systems, and CD-ROM players. These types of hardware products are often called *peripherals*. NetWare supports a wide variety of peripherals. To find out if your peripherals can be shared on a network, consult your reseller or the product documentation.

WHAT ARE THE SOFTWARE ELEMENTS OF NETWARE?

The networking software ties all the hardware together. The NetWare network operating system is the core of NetWare and of the network itself. The other software elements are the NetWare shell, drivers, the print server, the router, and NetWare utilities.

The NetWare Network Operating System

The network operating system does for the network what DOS and System do for PCs and Macintoshes. The NetWare network operating system is the set of software programs that turn a computer into the file server. This software controls how the hardware components communicate across the network, how files are stored on the network, how security is enforced, how printers are shared, and so on.

Shells

Physically connecting computers to the file server with cables isn't enough to turn them into network workstations. Each workstation computer must also have the special software called the *NetWare shell*. The shell determines whether a given task should be handled by the workstation's operating system (DOS, OS/2, or System) or by the network. If the task should be handled by the computer's operating system, the shell doesn't interfere. If the task should be performed by the network, the shell directs the task to the network, bypassing the computer's own operating system.

Anything that is handled by the computer's own operating system rather than by the network is called *local*. For example, *local drive* refers to either the floppy disk or hard disk installed in your workstation; *network drive* refers to the file server's hard disk. Similarly, a local task is any task performed by the workstation's operating system rather than by the network.

Drivers

Drivers are software programs that allow particular pieces of hardware to communicate with the operating system. For example, a LAN driver allows a network board to transmit information between the computer it is installed in and the network.

Each file server and workstation on the network must have a LAN driver in order for its network board to communicate with the rest of the network. The type of LAN driver you need to install in every computer depends on the network board each computer contains. Each type of network board (Ethernet, Arcnet, and so on) requires a different type of LAN driver. In addition, boards of the same type but from different manufacturers might require different LAN drivers.

NetWare provides LAN drivers for some network boards. If the driver required by your network board isn't in your NetWare package, check the software that came with the network board; most manufacturers include their own LAN driver with the board.

Other hardware devices have their own drivers. For example, print drivers allow your printer to accept information from the network. Tape backup systems have drivers that let them receive network data. Hard disks that you install in (or add to) your file server have disk drivers that let the file server communicate with those hard disks. Some of these types of drivers are provided by NetWare, and others are provided by the manufacturer. Although NetWare can support more varieties of hardware than any other networking system, never assume that any piece of hardware will work on your network; always check with your reseller or the hardware manufacturer.

Print Servers

Print servers allow network printers to be shared by network users. A print server is a software program that can be installed either in the file server or in a workstation. If you install print server software in a workstation, that workstation becomes a dedicated print server and cannot be used for any other purposes.

Whenever a network user wants to print a file, that print job is sent to the print server first. The print server takes the print job and temporarily stores it in a special directory called a *print queue* until the printer is ready for the job. This means that users do not need to wait until the actual printing is done before resuming work on their workstations. Figure 1.3 illustrates a print job's path from a workstation to the print queue to the printer.

As new print jobs come in from users all over the network, those jobs are also stored in the same print queue in the order they arrive. Then, one by one, the print server takes the print jobs from the queue and sends them to the printer. In this way, the print server prevents printing from developing into a network traffic jam. Without a print server, a user would need to wait for all the previous print jobs to finish before his or her workstation could finally get its print job to the printer.

Routers

A *router* is software that allows two networks to communicate with each other. For example, suppose that you install an Ethernet board and an Arcnet board in the same file server, and then attach Ethernet workstations to the Ethernet board and Arcnet workstations to the Arcnet board. You now have two

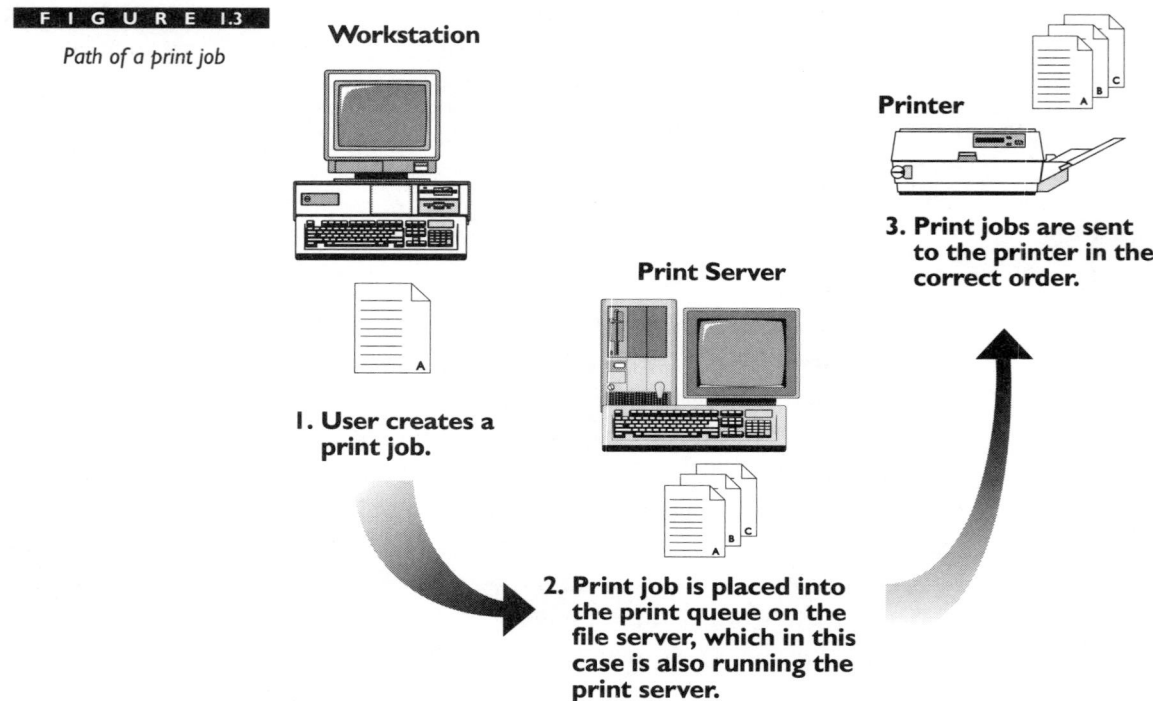

FIGURE 1.3

Path of a print job

Workstation

Printer

Print Server

1. User creates a print job.

2. Print job is placed into the print queue on the file server, which in this case is also running the print server.

3. Print jobs are sent to the printer in the correct order.

separate networks, both controlled by the same file server. The router software in the file server connects the two network boards, allowing the two networks to communicate with each other.

Router software in the file server works automatically; after you load the LAN drivers for each board, the router immediately connects the two networks. This is called *internal routing*, because it all happens inside the file server. Figure 1.4 illustrates two networks connected through the file server's internal router.

You can also install two network boards in a workstation, turning that workstation into a router between two networks. This type of router is called an *external router*, because the routing is going on outside the file server. To use a workstation as an external router, you must install extra software in that

FIGURE 1.4

Internal router

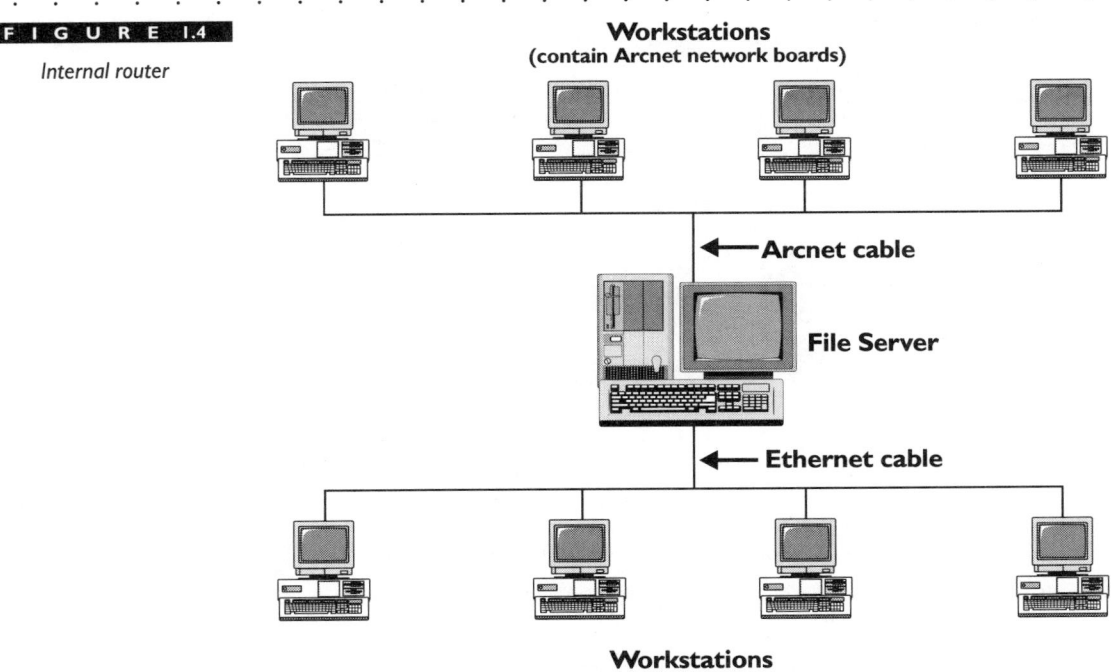

Workstations
(contain Arcnet network boards)

◄— **Arcnet cable**

File Server

◄— **Ethernet cable**

Workstations
(contain Ethernet network boards)

workstation and dedicate that workstation to being a router. No one can use the router workstation for any other tasks.

Figure 1.5 shows how an external router can connect two halves of the same network, with one half running on Ethernet and the other half running on Arcnet. By using an external router this way, you can get around the requirement that all workstations contain the same network hardware as the file server. Figure 1.6 illustrates an external router connecting two separate networks, each with its own file server.

FIGURE 1.5

*External router connecting
an Arcnet segment to an
Ethernet network*

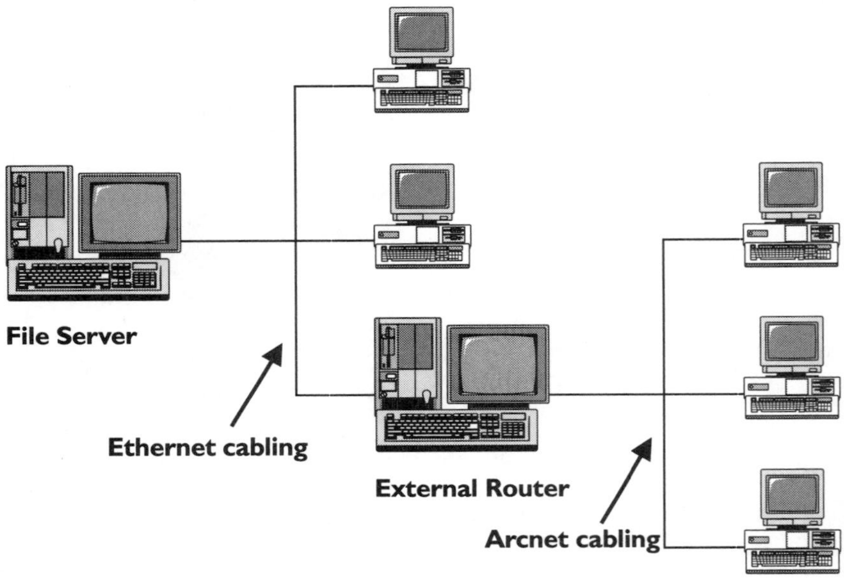

File Server

Ethernet cabling

External Router

Arcnet cabling

Utilities

Once you've got all the elements of a network installed, you will run NetWare utilities to manage, change, monitor, and use the network. NetWare *utilities* are individual programs that you use to perform network tasks. NetWare provides two sets of utilities: workstation utilities and server utilities.

Workstation utilities are run from workstations. Most of these utilities are tools for working with user accounts, files, directories, security, and so on. *Server utilities* (also known as *console commands*) must be run on the file server. You use them to change the way the file server and the network operate. Many workstation utilities can be used by both network users and the network supervisor. Server utilities are usually used only by the network supervisor.

NetWare version 3.11 introduced a new feature called *Remote Console*, which allows you to control the file server from a workstation by turning your

F I G U R E 1.6

External router connecting
two separate networks,
each with its own file server

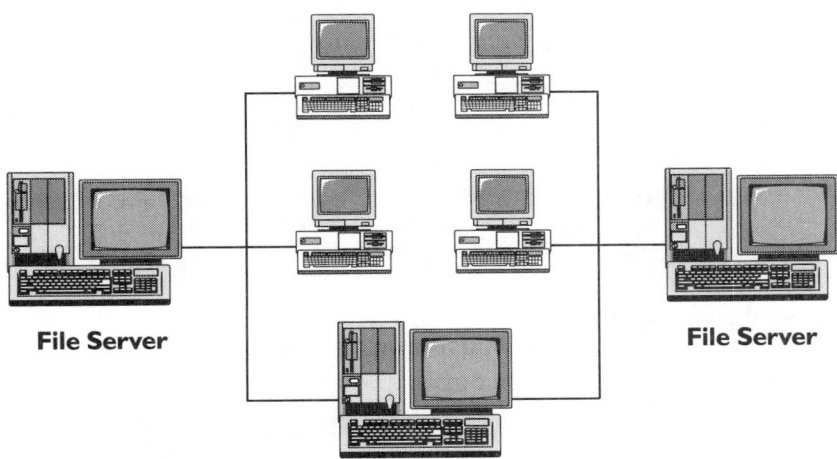

File Server **File Server**

External Router

workstation's screen and keyboard into the file server's screen and keyboard. (Remote Console is not included in NetWare version 2.2.) By running Remote Console on your workstation, you can use server utilities from that workstation. The data is sent to the real file server, but your workstation's keyboard and screen become a long-distance connection to the server.

Both workstation and server utilities come in two different styles: command line and menu. You run a command line utility by typing a command. To use a menu utility, you type the name of the utility to see a menu of options, and then you select the option you need to accomplish a network task.

Many workstation utility tasks can be performed by both a command line and a menu utility, so you can often use whichever style you prefer. With server utilities, however, you usually do not have a choice of which style to use. There are only a few menu utilities for the server, and they do not accomplish the same tasks as the command line server utilities.

YOU ARE HERE...

A NetWare network pulls all the hardware and software elements together into a unified source of information and communication. Figure 1.7 shows how the pieces fit together. Once each element is installed correctly, the network itself ceases to be a jumble of different hardware and software products thrown into a room together and becomes a seamless background for the work that everyone in the office does every day.

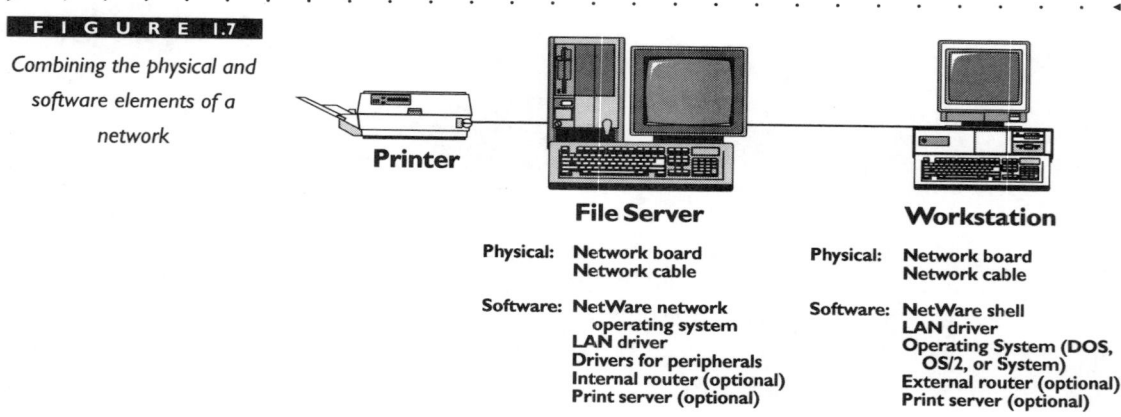

FIGURE 1.7

Combining the physical and software elements of a network

Printer

File Server

| Physical: | Network board |
| | Network cable |

Software:	NetWare network
	operating system
	LAN driver
	Drivers for peripherals
	Internal router (optional)
	Print server (optional)

Workstation

| Physical: | Network board |
| | Network cable |

Software:	NetWare shell
	LAN driver
	Operating System (DOS,
	OS/2, or System)
	External router (optional)
	Print server (optional)

What Does a Network Supervisor Do?

As the network supervisor, your primary job is to get the network running smoothly and keep it that way. The important thing to remember about a network is that everyone in the group is more productive and efficient than they were without it.

Many network supervisors find that the more time their users spend trying to figure out how to use the network, the less time they spend doing their "real" job.

Obviously, this was not the reason management decided to buy a network. Therefore, network supervisors across the globe have a common goal: Set up the network so that users don't need to know it's there in order to benefit from it. The second most common goal of network supervisors is to set up the network so that they themselves don't need to worry about it.

Novell's Technical Support division can tell stories about customers who have called Novell to find out how to change the supervisor's password. When one such customer was asked why he wanted to change the password, he answered that the network supervisor had died two years before, and no one had needed to do anything to the network since. Now, two years later, they wanted to add a new user to the network, but no one knew how.

The moral of this story is that running a small NetWare network doesn't need to take up all your time. However, neglecting the network completely for two years probably isn't the wisest course either (although no one would dispute that the deceased network supervisor had a reasonable excuse).

For most network supervisors, managing a small NetWare network requires some careful initial planning, periodic housekeeping, routine maintenance, and occasional reassessment of network needs. With a little care and some ability to organize, these tasks can be kept to a minimum so that they don't interfere with any other duties you have.

What specifically will you be expected to do as a network supervisor? The following tasks usually fall into the supervisor's domain:

- ► Maintaining the hardware (replacing broken cables, adding new printers and workstations, adding memory to computers, tracking down and replacing faulty network boards, and the like)

- ► Maintaining the software (installing a new word processing application on the network, deleting old files that are just taking up space, upgrading the graphics package, and so on)

- ► Adding and deleting users from the network as people move in or out of your group

▶ Ensuring network security (preventing users from reading payroll records, insulating the network from viruses, keeping users from pirating copies of your applications for their friends, and so on)

▶ Backing up files on a regular basis (by keeping backups of files, you can restore a file that a user accidently deletes, for example, or you can retrieve an earlier copy of a database file that this morning's power outage destroyed)

▶ Keeping records (registering software and hardware for warranties, recording serial numbers for inventory, documenting network information about each workstation, justifying new purchases of software and hardware to management, and so on)

▶ Troubleshooting (answering questions from users and solving problems)

Of all these duties, the most difficult to anticipate is the last one: troubleshooting. The only way to minimize the amount of time you'll spend troubleshooting your network is to try to stay on top of the other aspects of your network supervisor duties. The more you understand how the network operates and the more organized you are about routine maintenance and record keeping, the better off you and your users will be.

Review

A NetWare network is made up of both physical components and software components that work together. Workstations (or clients) are attached to the network and can use the network's services. File servers (or network servers) control the network and provide access to network resources. Network boards (or network interface cards) and cabling physically connect workstations and file servers together. The printer and peripherals (modems, CD-ROM players, and so on) are hardware that can be shared through the network.

The network software allows the physical components to communicate. The NetWare network operating system installed in the file server controls how the network operates. The NetWare shell determines whether tasks are handled by the computer's own operating system or by the network. Through drivers, the network operating system can communicate with the hardware attached to the network. Print servers allow users to share the printers attached to the network. Your network may also use a router so that two networks can communicate with each other. To perform network tasks, you use the NetWare utilities.

As a network supervisor, your primary responsibility is to make sure the network runs smoothly so that your users don't need to interrupt their normal workday activities. To accomplish this, you will find yourself handling these tasks:

► Maintaining the hardware

► Maintaining the software

► Adding and deleting users from the network

► Ensuring network security

► Backing up files on a regular basis

► Keeping records

► Troubleshooting network problems

Now that you understand what a network is and what your job as network supervisor entails, you are ready to begin to set up your network. The next chapter describes the first step: installing the network.

Installing the Network

Before you install your NetWare network, you should prepare your location for the network. Then you can proceed to install the file server, the workstations, and the peripheral devices (printers, backup systems, and so on).

The precise procedures for installing a network depend on your version of NetWare, the type of workstations you use, and the brand of network boards and cables you have. This chapter provides basic guidelines for setting up your network. For complete step-by-step instructions, refer to the Novell documentation for your version of NetWare and to the manufacturers' documentation for computers, peripherals, and other hardware. If your network is already up and running, you can refer to this chapter when you need information about adding items to your existing setup.

Preparing for the Network

As with most ventures, the proverbial ounce of prevention is worth a pound of network cures. The time for making sure your office is equipped to handle a network of computers is before the power company sends a huge power spike your way, not after. So before you start stringing network cables and plugging in workstations, take stock of your office situation. There are several ways you can protect your company's investment, your users' files, your users' health, and of course, your own peace of mind.

PROTECTING THE NETWORK FROM ELECTRICAL PROBLEMS

One problem that often plagues networks is fluctuations in the power that is delivered to the site. Even if you have the most reliable power supplier, a rare surge in power can still crackle through the lines and zap your network, or an outage can shut down your database in the middle of a transaction. In the worst case, hardware can be fried, volumes of data can be corrupted, and many days' or even weeks' worth of work can be lost.

To protect your network, you should invest in an *uninterruptible power supply* (*UPS*) for your file server. A UPS has its own battery, which allows it to keep the file server (not all the workstations and peripherals) running during a power outage. When the UPS's battery begins to run down, the UPS tells the file server to close all its open files and shut itself down. By allowing the server time to shut itself down properly, the UPS can prevent excessive damage to the network files.

If your budget allows, you can also get a UPS for each workstation. In some offices, the wiring that the network (including the file server and all the workstations) is running on is connected to a huge UPS that keeps the entire wiring system going during a power outage. Usually, the office has two sets of wiring: one for the computer systems and the other for general office needs (such as lights, photocopiers, radios, and so on).

Even if your company has a limited budget, you should at least purchase surge suppressors for each workstation. *Surge suppressors* help smooth out the power peaks that occasionally come through the line. Although surge suppressors can't handle big power problems, they can provide some protection.

No one is safe from power problems. One network supervisor was telling me how reliable his NetWare network had been. It had been running for more than a year without any problems at all—well, "except for the one time we had a power outage." I asked him, "Didn't you have your file server hooked up to a UPS?" "No," he replied, "We're a power company. It never occurred to me that we might lose our own power."

PROTECTING THE NETWORK CABLING

You need to protect your network cabling from damage. Don't string network cables across the floor where people will step on them, run over them with mail carts or chairs, and so on.

To keep cables off the floor, you can run the cables through the walls and ceilings. However, take care to keep the cables away from other wiring or lighting fixtures that can emit electrical interference. For example, if your network cable runs within a few inches of a fluorescent light, the light fixture may cause interference with the network data that is traveling through the network cable.

PROTECTING THE NETWORK FILE SERVER

Not all network problems are caused by electricity and wayward office furnishings. One of the most important things you can do to protect your network is to lock up the file server. Find a room, a closet, or anywhere else with a locking door and put the file server in it. Then hide the key where only you and your backup supervisor can find it.

Locking up your file server protects it from both malicious and accidental tampering. Malicious tampering is more theatrical: disgruntled employees trying to derail projects when they get fired, competing employees tampering with each other's files to get an advantage, corporate spies trying to steal the plans for Project X.

Accidental tampering is less worthy of attention from movie script writers, but a lot more common: a curious employee typing commands at the file server console "to see what happens," another employee tripping and pulling the file server plug out of the wall socket, the custodian turning the file server off over the weekend because he thought no one was using it. By locking the file server in its own room, you can prevent many problems.

PROTECTING YOUR USERS

News stories and magazine articles about office hazards are becoming more and more frequent. With the rise in desktop computing has come a rise in related illnesses and injuries. Unfortunately, not every company can afford to establish entire ergonomically designed workspaces for each user. However, there are a few simple steps you can take (or suggest to management) that may help reduce the number of computer-related maladies your network users are subjected to.

First, position workstations so that the back of the monitors point away from users. While the debate over whether monitors emit dangerous levels of radiation continues, most experts will concede that whatever radiation is being emitted is strongest at the back of the monitor. Therefore, do not allow any user to spend a significant amount of time within two feet of the back of a monitor. (Older monitors are supposedly the worst offenders.)

Second, determine if you need to supply your users with glare-reducing or polarizing screens for your workstations. Some monitors may be difficult to read in certain lighting. Providing glare-reducing screens can reduce the eyestrain and headaches your users may be suffering.

Third, train your users to give their eyes, necks, backs, and wrists a break at least once an hour. There are a variety of quick and simple exercises that users can do in their offices to stretch their muscles and ease their eyes. Talk to a doctor or check out a book on surviving the workplace to find exercises that your users can adopt. It's not only relaxing for the users, but it might even help cut down on your company's health insurance costs.

Finally, do what you can to prevent your users from getting Carpal Tunnel Syndrome or its precursor, Forearm Overuse Syndrome. Both of these syndromes are a result of an aggravated nerve in the user's wrist, usually caused by repetitive motion. Many people are suffering from these injuries as a result of prolonged use of computer keyboards and mice. You can take several steps to help users avoid getting (or aggravating) these syndromes:

- Supply users with padded keyboard wrist-rests, which should be placed directly in front of the keyboard. Wrist-rests help keep the wrist straighter, lessening the pressure on the carpal nerve.

- If your keyboards have movable feet that allow the top of the keyboard to be elevated, encourage your users to avoid using the feet. Propping up the top of the keyboard exaggerates the angle of the wrist, which can contribute to the Carpal Tunnel and Forearm Overuse syndromes. Keep the keyboards as flat as possible.

- Purchase movable keyboard trays. These trays attach to the desktop but can be lowered or elevated to suit the user. When typing on the keyboard, the user's forearms should form a right angle with the upper arms.

Figure 2.1 illustrates the positioning and equipment that can help protect users' health.

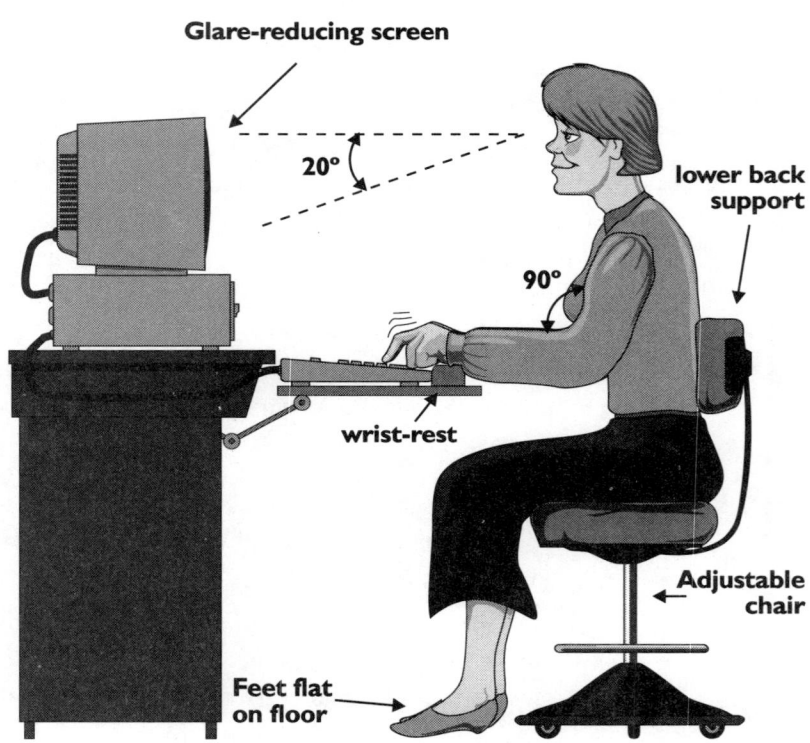

FIGURE 2.1

Proper positioning and some equipment can protect a user from health problems

Glare-reducing screen

20°

90°

lower back support

wrist-rest

Adjustable chair

Feet flat on floor

Installing the File Server

After you've prepared your location for the network, your next step is to install the file server. The exact procedure you use to install your file server depends on whether you are installing NetWare version 3.*x* or 2.2 and whether you are installing the software on the file server for the first time or upgrading from a previous version of NetWare. However, some decisions and tasks are common to all the file server installation procedures. Knowing ahead of time what choices you will make and what you need to do will save you time during the installation.

Before you install NetWare on your file server, you should take the following preliminary steps:

1 · Install the network board in the file server before you try to install NetWare, because the installation program will ask you what settings are used on the board.

If all your workstations use the same type of network boards (such as Ethernet), you will probably install only one network board in your file server. If your workstations use two or more types of network boards, such as Ethernet, Arcnet, and Token-Ring, you will need to install one of each of those boards in your file server so that the server can communicate with each group of workstations. If you install more than one network board in your file server, make sure that the board settings, such as interrupts, do not conflict with each other. Check with the board manufacturer's documentation to see how to set the board.

2 · Install any external hard disks and their corresponding controller boards in the file server.

3 · Decide whether you want to use disk mirroring (or disk duplexing) to protect the file server's disks.

Disk mirroring and disk duplexing are methods of duplicating your network files on two identical disks, so that if one disk goes bad, the other disk still has the current files, and users can continue to work on the network as usual. If the two disks run from the same disk-controller board, it's called *disk mirroring*. If the two disks run from two different disk-controller boards, it's called *disk duplexing*. Disk duplexing is more secure than disk mirroring because it protects files even if one of the disk-controller boards goes bad. Disk mirroring and disk duplexing are good methods of protecting your network files, although they do require the extra investment for additional disks.

4 · Write down information about all the file server's hardware. Record the network board settings, the type and size of hard disks, and other configuration data. See Chapter 8 for more information about documenting your network.

5 · Make working copies of all the NetWare diskettes that came in your NetWare package. That's a lot of diskettes and a lot of copying, but it will be worth it if one of the diskettes gets corrupted somewhere along the line.

6 · If the computer you're going to turn into a file server has important files on its hard disk, make backup copies of those files because they will be deleted during the installation or upgrade process.

7 · If you are upgrading a file server from one version of NetWare to another, make two backup copies of all network files to ensure that they aren't lost if something goes wrong.

8 · (NetWare version 3.x only) Decide whether you want the server to boot from a floppy diskette or from a hard disk.

If you boot from a diskette, you do not need to create a DOS partition on the file server hard disk, and you can store the boot diskette in a secure location away from the file server. If you boot from a hard disk, the boot files will be less subject to accidental deletion (than they are on a diskette), you can store other files on the DOS partition, and the booting process will be faster.

9 · (NetWare version 2.2 only) Decide if you want your file server to be dedicated or nondedicated.

Nondedicated means that the file server can also be used as a workstation. However, a nondedicated server has several disadvantages: it tends to be slower than dedicated servers, it increases the risk of the network being shut down accidentally if the user turns off that computer or an application on that computer hangs, and some applications won't run on a nondedicated server because of memory requirements.

10 · Decide how many volumes you want.

Every file server must have at least one volume, called SYS:. The SYS: volume contains all the files that NetWare needs to operate, including the *bindery*, which is the database of network information that NetWare uses to run the network. You should reserve SYS: for NetWare's own files and create at least one additional volume for your other files. See Chapter 3 for more information about volumes and NetWare's directory structure. If you are using NetWare for Macintosh, you may want to create a separate volume just for your Macintosh files. See Chapter 10 for more information about using NetWare for Macintosh to connect Macintosh workstations.

II • (NetWare version 3.*x* only) If you are using NetWare for Macintosh or OS/2 and its High Performance File System (HPFS) on your network, you will need to load a software program called a *name space module* on your file server. Macintosh and OS/2 both support longer file names than DOS does. The name space modules tell NetWare that these operating systems are running on workstations on the network, so NetWare should allow these long names to be stored.

When you are ready to install NetWare on your file server, follow the detailed instructions in your NetWare documentation.

Installing the Workstations

After you install the file server, you can begin installing workstations. Once you get the first workstation running on the network, you can begin creating user accounts, directories, and so on, or you can install the rest of the workstations.

The installation of a workstation involves two stages: installing the network hardware (the board and cables) and copying the necessary files to a disk where the workstation can get to them. The following sections discuss the procedures for installing DOS- and Windows-based workstations. Chapter 10 contains information about setting up Macintosh workstations.

CHOOSING A NETWORK DRIVER

NetWare 2.2, 3.1, and 3.11 include two different types of drivers that can be used with DOS and Windows workstations. The first step in installing a workstation is to choose which type of driver you want your workstation to use: a *dedicated IPX driver* or an *ODI driver*. NetWare 3.12 only uses ODI drivers.

The main difference between dedicated IPX drivers and ODI drivers is the type of protocols they support. A *protocol* is a format for sending and receiving data across the cable. NetWare uses the IPX protocol for communication between LAN drivers and the network.

Dedicated IPX (Internetwork Packet eXchange) drivers understand only the IPX protocol. ODI (Open Data-Link Interface) drivers can handle more than one type of protocol. In addition, ODI drivers can handle different types of Ethernet. (Ethernet comes in different varieties, called *frame types*.) In most small networks, either type of driver will work. If you need to use different protocols, or if you are using two different Ethernet frame types, you should use the ODI drivers. The procedures for installing an ODI workstation are similar to those for installing a dedicated IPX workstation.

BASIC STEPS FOR INSTALLING A DOS OR WINDOWS WORKSTATION

Each workstation that you will install must have its own network board and its own legal copy of DOS and the DOS manual. Each Windows workstation should have its own legal copy of Windows and the Windows manual. (The manuals are your proof that the software isn't pirated.)

The following steps outline the basic procedure for installing a workstation using either an ODI or IPX driver and NetWare's NETX file. For information about using VLM files, see Chapter 11. For detailed installation instructions, see your NetWare documentation.

1 · Before adding network hardware and software to a workstation,
   set up the workstation by itself and boot it with DOS to make sure the
   workstation is working properly. If this is a Windows workstation,
   install and run Windows. When you are satisfied that the workstation
   is functioning correctly, turn it off.

2 · Configure and install a network board in each workstation. Refer to the board's documentation for instructions on how to configure its interrupt, base I/O address, and so on.

You can probably use the default configuration setting for each board. Usually, the only time you need to change a board's default setting is when two boards will be installed in the same computer (to form a router between two networks), because those two boards will conflict with each other. Boards installed in different computers will not conflict.

3 · Write down each board's configuration setting so that you will have a record of this information. Also record which workstation the board is being installed in and other pertinent information. See Chapter 8 for details on documenting your network.

4 · Connect each workstation's network board to the network cabling. Make sure you use the correct hardware for your type of cabling. For example, you may need to use hubs, terminators, connectors, and so on. Check with your reseller or with the documentation that came with the cabling.

5 · (Dedicated IPX drivers only) Boot DOS on any computer (it doesn't need to be connected to the network yet), and then run NetWare's WSGEN program to create the IPX.COM file.

The IPX.COM file allows the network board's LAN driver to communicate with the network. Each type of network board has its own type of LAN driver, so it will also require its own IPX.COM file. If two workstations have different brands of network boards, you will need to use the WSGEN program to create two different IPX.COM files. You can create several different IPX.COM files from the same workstation; the WSGEN program lets you select the LAN driver you need for any network board.

6 · Decide which version of the shell file each workstation will use.

NETx is the basic shell file for use with ordinary workstation memory. If your workstations have expanded or extended memory, you can use one of the other versions of the shell file: EMSNETx for expanded memory or XMSNETx for extended memory. These versions save the workstations' base memory for other applications.

In earlier versions of NetWare, the x is replaced by a number that corresponds to the version of DOS (NET2, NET3, and NET4). The most recent versions of the shell files (shipped after NetWare version 3.11 and 2.2 were released) are called NETX, EMSNETX, and XMSNETX, and they work with any version of DOS. You can get these new shell files in the NetWare Workstation for DOS product, from your reseller, or from Novell's NetWire bulletin board on Compu-Serve. They are also included in DR DOS 6.0.

7 · Make a boot disk for each workstation. The boot disk can be either a floppy diskette or the workstation's hard disk.

The boot disk contains the files necessary for booting the workstation with DOS and attaching the workstation to the network. Even if the workstation is diskless, you must still create a boot diskette. Using diskless workstations is discussed later in this chapter. The following section describes how to create a boot disk.

8 · (Windows workstations only) Run Windows, and then run the NetWare utility called NWSETUP, which is included in the NetWare Workstation for Windows kit. This utility sets up your Windows workstation to function on the network. You may also need to install NetWare task-switching files. Refer to the NetWare and Windows documentation for more information.

Creating a Boot Disk

When a user turns on his or her workstation, several processes must take place before that user can begin working on the network:

1 · When the power switch is turned on, the workstation boots up with DOS.

2 · The workstation's DOS environment may need to be configured to run correctly.

3 · Several NetWare files, such as the protocol driver, the LAN driver, and the shell file, must be loaded onto the workstation.

4 · The workstation's NetWare environment may need to be configured to run correctly.

5 · With the NetWare files loaded, a network drive, usually drive F:, is mapped to the SYS:LOGIN directory on the network. The user changes to that drive.

6 · Finally, the user logs in to the network by typing LOGIN, a username, and a password.

To set up the workstation so that it accomplishes all these steps, you create a *boot disk* for the workstation. The boot disk can be either a floppy diskette or the workstation's hard disk. The boot disk contains the files necessary for booting the workstation with DOS, configuring the workstation's environment, loading the NetWare shell files, and logging the user into the network.

CHOOSING WHERE TO BOOT FROM

The first step in creating a boot disk for a workstation is to decide whether you want the workstation to boot from its hard disk or from a diskette. If you choose to boot from a hard disk, you will copy all the necessary boot files onto the hard disk, usually drive C:.

If you want to boot from a floppy diskette, format a blank diskette using the DOS FORMAT command with the /S parameter so that the DOS system files are copied to that diskette. Insert the diskette in floppy disk drive A: and type

FORMAT A: /S

(If the diskette is in drive B:, replace the A: with B:.) Then you will copy the necessary NetWare files to the root directory of this diskette.

Even if you intend for your workstation to run DOS from the network, the DOS system files must be on the workstation's boot disk in order for it to boot. The DOS system files on the boot disk must be the same version as the DOS that the workstation will access from a network directory.

DECIDING WHICH FILES TO INCLUDE ON THE BOOT DISK

The next step in creating a boot disk is to determine which files to include. Some are files that you copy from NetWare diskettes; others are files you create using a text editor. The files you may need to create yourself are CONFIG.SYS, SHELL.CFG, NET.CFG, and AUTOEXEC.BAT. These files are described later in this chapter.

The files you need on the boot disk depend on whether the workstation is using a dedicated IPX driver or an ODI driver.

Boot Files for IPX Workstations

If the workstation will be using a dedicated IPX driver, you will include the following files on your boot diskette:

- ▶ **DOS System Files:** These files are located on your DOS diskette. Their purpose is to boot DOS on the workstation.

- ▶ **CONFIG.SYS (optional):** This file is created when you install DR DOS 6.0 or MS DOS 5.0, or you can create (or edit) it with a text editor. It configures the DOS environment on the workstation.

- ▶ **AUTOEXEC.BAT:** This file is created when you install DR DOS 6.0 or MS DOS 5.0, or you can create (or edit) it with a text editor. It is a batch file that automatically loads the NetWare files and logs the user in to the network. It can also include other commands.

▸ **SHELL.CFG:** You also create this file with a text editor. It configures certain options in NetWare files (similar to the NET.CFG file in ODI workstations).

▸ **LAN Driver:** The driver file, such as NE2000.COM, is located on the NetWare workstation software diskette. It allows the network board to communicate with the network.

▸ **IPX.COM:** This file will be generated on the NetWare workstation software diskette. It allows the LAN driver to communicate with NetWare's IPX protocol.

▸ **NETx, EMSNETx, or XMSNETx:** The NetWare shell file is located on the NetWare workstation software diskette. Use the file for the type of memory the workstation has available: NETx for ordinary memory, EMSNETx for expanded memory, or XMSNETx for extended memory. Updated shell files are available in the NetWare's Workstation for DOS Kit, from your reseller, from NetWire, or in DR DOS 6.0.

▸ **NETBIOS.EXE (optional):** This file is located on the NetWare workstation software diskette. Use it only if you have applications that require NetBIOS.

▸ **INT2F.COM (optional):** This file is located on the NetWare workstation software diskette. Use it only if you have applications that require NetBIOS.

▸ **ROUTE.COM (optional):** This file is located on the NetWare workstation software diskette. Use it only if your workstations are on a Token-Ring network that is using source routing.

▸ **LANSUP.COM (optional):** This file is located on the NetWare work station software diskette. Use it only if your workstations are using the IBM LAN Support program. You load LANSUP.COM from the CONFIG.SYS file.

Boot Files for ODI Workstations

If the workstation will be using an ODI driver, you will include the following files on the boot diskette:

- ▸ **DOS System Files:** These files are located on your DOS diskette. Their purpose is to boot DOS on the workstation.

- ▸ **CONFIG.SYS (optional):** This file is created when you install DR DOS 6.0 or MS DOS 5.0, or you can create (or edit) it with a text editor. It configures the DOS environment on the workstation.

- ▸ **AUTOEXEC.BAT:** This file is created when you install DR DOS 6.0 or MS DOS 5.0, or you can create (or edit) it with a text editor. It is a batch file that automatically loads the NetWare files and logs the user in to the network. It can also include other commands.

- ▸ **NET.CFG:** You also create this file with a text editor. It configures certain options in NetWare files (similar to the SHELL.CFG file in dedicated IPX workstations).

- ▸ **LSL.COM:** This is the Link Support Layer file, which is located on the NetWare workstation software diskette. It allows the workstation to communicate with different protocols.

- ▸ **LAN Driver:** The driver file, such as NE2000.COM, is located on the NetWare workstation software diskette. It allows the network board to communicate with the network.

- ▸ **Protocol Driver:** The protocol driver file, such as IPXODI.COM, is located on the NetWare workstation software diskette. It allows the LAN driver to communicate with various protocols.

- ▸ **NET*x*, EMSNET*x*, or XMSNET*x*:** The NetWare shell file is located on the NetWare workstation software diskette. Use the file for the type of memory the workstation has available: NET*x* for ordinary memory, EMSNET*x* for expanded memory, or XMSNET*x* for extended memory. Updated shell files are available in the NetWare's Workstation for DOS Kit, from your reseller, from NetWire, or in DR DOS 6.0.

▶ **NETBIOS.EXE (optional):** This file is located on the NetWare workstation software diskette. Use it only if you have applications that require NetBIOS.

▶ **INT2F.COM (optional):** This file is located on the NetWare workstation software diskette. Use it only if you have applications that require NetBIOS.

▶ **ROUTE.COM (optional):** This file is located on the NetWare workstation software diskette. Use it only if your workstations are on a Token-Ring network that is using source routing.

▶ **LANSUP.COM (optional):** This file is located on the NetWare workstation software diskette. Use it only if your workstations are using the IBM LAN Support program. You load LANSUP.COM from the CONFIG.SYS file.

▶ **RPLODI.COM:** This file is located on the NetWare workstation software diskette. Use it only if you are creating this boot disk for a diskless workstation.

CREATING THE CONFIG.SYS FILE

The *CONFIG.SYS file* is a DOS file that allows you to customize the DOS environment for a workstation so that certain applications run more efficiently under DOS. If you are using DR DOS 6.0 or MS DOS 5.0, this file was created when you installed DOS. You can create your own CONFIG.SYS file or edit an existing one by using a text editor or any word processing application that lets you create and save a file as an ASCII text file. The many different commands you can put in your CONFIG.SYS file are described in detail in the DOS manual. Most of these commands do not affect how the workstation operates with NetWare.

This is an example of a typical CONFIG.SYS file:

```
DEVICE=ANSI.SYS
BUFFERS=20
FILES=30
SHELL=C:\COMMAND.COM /P /E:1024
```

This example includes the most common CONFIG.SYS file commands. Each of these common commands is explained in the following sections.

The DEVICE Command

The DEVICE= command tells the computer to look for a device driver or another software program. For example, if the workstation is using extended memory or Windows, you can use this command to tell the workstation to load the necessary files.

In the sample CONFIG.SYS file above, the command

DEVICE=ANSI.SYS

tells the workstation to look for the ANSI.SYS device driver. The ANSI.SYS driver enables the workstation to use features such as an enhanced standard input and output device driver. If you use this command, you must make sure the ANSI.SYS file is also on your boot disk. See your DOS documentation for details.

The BUFFERS Command

The BUFFERS= command allows a workstation to store a larger amount of data in dynamic memory so that file access is faster. When you increase the number of buffers, more information from large files on the workstation's hard disk can be stored in these buffers. For example, when the workstation accesses a large database, more records will go into the buffers. Accessing data from a workstation's buffers is faster than accessing data from a disk.

On the down side, the more buffers you specify, the less memory will be available to applications. Therefore, use only the number of buffers you need. You probably will need to increase the number of buffers only if you are using applications such as large databases that appear to be running too slowly. Generally, you will set the number of buffers to between 10 and 25. The CONFIG.SYS file shown earlier sets the number of buffers to 20:

BUFFERS=20

The BUFFERS= command in the CONFIG.SYS file is different from the CACHE BUFFERS= command that is used in the SHELL.CFG or NET.CFG file. That command is described later in this chapter.

The FILES Command

The FILES= command specifies how many files applications running locally in DOS can have open at a time. Many applications open numerous files at a time in order to complete a task, even though it may seem that you have only a single file open. For example, if you open a word processing file and begin to work in it, the word processing application may open several temporary files, the spelling and thesaurus files, and so on.

In many cases, you will not need to increase the number of files that can be opened. If you get error messages indicating that there are not enough files (or *file handles*) available, you can increase the number of files with the FILES= command. Also check to see if the documentation that came with the application specifies the number of files to allow in the CONFIG.SYS file. Usually, allowing between 20 and 50 files is adequate. The CONFIG.SYS file shown earlier allows 30 files:

FILES=30

The FILES= command in the CONFIG.SYS file is similar to the FILE HANDLES= command that is used in the SHELL.CFG or NET.CFG file. Usually, both commands in the CONFIG.SYS file and SHELL.CFG (or NET.CFG) files should be set to the same number of files. The SHELL.CFG and NET.CFG files are described later in this chapter.

The SHELL Command

The SHELL= command can be used to tell the workstation where the DOS file COMMAND.COM is located. *COMMAND.COM* is the DOS command processor. In most cases, you will not need to use this command. If the workstation will be running DOS from the network, you should use the COMSPEC command in the login script instead, to tell the workstation that DOS is located in a network directory. See Chapter 7 for information about using the COMSPEC command in login scripts. If the COMMAND.COM file is located in the root directory of the workstation's boot disk, you do not need to use this command.

One reason you may need to use this command is to increase your DOS environment size. The /E:*xxxx* part of the SHELL= command specifies how large you want the DOS environment to be. In simplified terms, the DOS environment size controls how many SET commands you can specify for your DOS workstation. Even if you just want to set the DOS environment size, you must still include the default path to the COMMAND.COM file (C:\) and the /P option, which will store COMMAND.COM in memory. The CONFIG.SYS file shown earlier sets the DOS environment size to 1024 bytes (in this example, COMMAND.COM is located on the hard disk drive):

C:.SHELL=C:\COMMAND.COM /P /E:1024

See the DOS manual for more information about using the SHELL= command.

CREATING THE AUTOEXEC.BAT FILE

The *AUTOEXEC.BAT file* is a *batch file*, which is a file that executes several commands automatically for the user. This file is important mainly because of its convenience for the user. The AUTOEXEC.BAT file can take care of several startup steps, including loading the necessary NetWare shell files, changing to the network drive, and executing the LOGIN command with the user's name. Every user should have an AUTOEXEC.BAT file.

If you are using DR DOS 6.0 or MS DOS 5.0, this file was created when you installed DOS. You can create your own AUTOEXEC.BAT file or edit an existing one by using a text editor or any word processing application that lets you create and save a file as an ASCII text file. The commands you include in the AUTOEXEC.BAT file depend on the specific needs of the workstation user. The commands for a workstation with a dedicated IPX driver vary slightly from those for one with an ODI driver.

This is an example of a typical AUTOEXEC.BAT file for a workstation with a dedicated IPX driver:

```
NE2000
IPX
NET3
PROMPT=$P$G
F:
LOGIN PHOTO/MEL
```

The first two commands load drivers: NE2000 loads the LAN driver that matches the workstation's network board, which in this case is the NE2000 board; IPX loads the NetWare IPX protocol driver.

The next command, NET3, loads the NetWare shell for DOS 3.*x*. The number varies with the version of DOS. If the workstation is using DOS 4.0, you would load NET4 instead. If you have NETX, which works for all versions of DOS, you would load NETX instead.

The PROMPT=PG command changes the DOS prompt to display the current directory path.

The F: command changes the current drive to F:, which is the first network drive.

The final LOGIN command logs user MEL in to the file server called PHOTO.

This is an example of an AUTOEXEC.BAT file for a workstation with an ODI driver:

```
LSL
NE2000
IPXODI
NET3
PROMPT=$P$G
F:
LOGIN PHOTO/MEL
```

The first command, LSL, loads the Link Support Layer. The third command, IPXODI, loads the NetWare IPXODI protocol driver. The rest of the commands are the same as those in the sample AUTOEXEC.BAT file for a dedicated IPX workstation.

You can also set DOS paths and DOS environment variables in the AUTOEXEC.BAT file. For example, you might include commands similar to the ones shown below in addition to the normal commands for loading the NetWare files:

PATH C:\WINDOWS

This command sets a DOS path to the Windows directory.

SET TEMP=C:WINDOWS\TEMP

This command sets the Windows TEMP setting to the correct subdirectory.

C:\MOUSE1\MOUSE

This command indicates the directory that contains the correct mouse driver.

SET EMAILUSER=LSNOW

This command sets the user's name to be used with the Da Vinci electronic mail program.

SET WP="/U-LKS/B-5"

This command sets the user's environment variables for WordPerfect.

CREATING THE SHELL.CFG FILE

The *SHELL.CFG file* allows you to customize the NetWare environment on a dedicated IPX workstation. (For an ODI workstation, you create a NET.CFG file instead, as described later in this chapter.) With SHELL.CFG, you can set parameters that help the workstation run on a network.

To create SHELL.CFG, use a text editor or any word processing application that will let you create and save a file as an ASCII text file. This is an example of a typical SHELL.CFG file:

```
LOCAL PRINTERS=0
LONG MACHINE TYPE=COMPAQ
SHORT MACHINE TYPE=CMPQ
CACHE BUFFERS=20
FILE HANDLES=30
SHOW DOTS=ON
```

This example includes the most common SHELL.CFG file commands. Each of these common commands is explained in the following sections.

The LOCAL PRINTERS Command

The first command in the sample SHELL.CFG file is

```
LOCAL PRINTERS=0
```

It tells the workstation that it is not directly attached to a local printer.

For each workstation that does not have a local printer, you should create a SHELL.CFG file with at least this one command in it. Otherwise, when the workstation user presses the Shift-PrintScreen key combination, the workstation may hang because it is looking for a printer attached directly to its ports.

The SHELL.CFG file for any workstation that *is* attached to a local printer should *not* include the LOCAL PRINTERS= command at all. NetWare can determine that there is a local printer attached.

The LONG MACHINE TYPE Command

You may need to use the LONG MACHINE TYPE= command in a SHELL.CFG file if the workstation is running DOS from the network instead of from a local disk. If you decide to run DOS from the network, you will create different directories for each DOS version you have, as explained in Chapter 3. These directories are named with the brand of workstation you are using. For example, IBM and Compaq have slightly different versions of DOS. Therefore, if you have some IBM workstations and some Compaq workstations, you may have one directory named IBM_PC and one named COMPAQ.

The LONG MACHINE TYPE= command in the SHELL.CFG file tells the workstation which DOS directory it needs to access. The default value for this command is IBM_PC, so if you are using IBM's version of DOS, you don't need to include this command. However, if you are using Compaq's version of DOS, include the command

LONG MACHINE TYPE=COMPAQ

so that the workstation can find the Compaq DOS directory.

The SHORT MACHINE TYPE Command

The SHORT MACHINE TYPE= command is similar to the LONG MACHINE TYPE= command, in that they both tell the workstation the type of computer and the type of information it needs to access on the network. The SHORT MACHINE TYPE= command specifically tells the workstation to use one of two files that control how monitors display the NetWare menu utilities. IBMs use the file IBM$RUN.OVL. Other computers, such as Compaqs and AT&Ts, use the file CMPQ$RUN.OVL. Both files are located in SYS:PUBLIC. The default short machine name is IBM.

If the NetWare menu utilities are unreadable on your non-IBM workstation's monitor, try using the command

SHORT MACHINE TYPE=CMPQ

The CACHE BUFFERS Command

The CACHE BUFFERS= command increases the number of buffers that the workstation can use to manage incoming and outgoing network data. Increasing the number of buffers may improve the workstation's communications with the network. This command is different from the BUFFERS= command in the CONFIG.SYS file, which is described earlier in the chapter.

Most likely, you won't need to increase the number of cache buffers unless your workstation seems to be running too slowly on the network. The SHELL.CFG file shown earlier sets the number of cache buffers to 20:

CACHE BUFFERS=20

The FILE HANDLES Command

The FILE HANDLES= command specifies how many files applications can have open at a time. This command is similar to the FILES= command in the CONFIG.SYS file. You should have the two commands in the CONFIG.SYS and SHELL.CFG files set to the same number of files.

In the SHELL.CFG file shown earlier, the command

FILE HANDLES=30

specifies that 30 files can be open at the same time.

The SHOW DOTS Command

The SHOW DOTS= command is important if the workstation is running Windows. Include the command

SHOW DOTS=ON

in the SHELL.CFG file for any workstation that is running Windows. Without this command, users won't be able to see the parent directories when they move around in subdirectories.

CREATING THE NET.CFG FILE

The *NET.CFG file* allows you to customize the NetWare environment on a workstation that is running ODI drivers. For a dedicated IPX workstation, use the SHELL.CFG file instead, as described in the previous sections.

To create NET.CFG, use a text editor or any word processing application that will let you create and save a file as an ASCII text file. The NET.CFG file can contain the same commands as the SHELL.CFG file. This is an example of a simple NET.CFG file:

```
LOCAL PRINTERS=0
FILE HANDLES=30
SHOW DOTS=ON
```

But a NET.CFG file can go beyond the SHELL.CFG file because it can also contain commands to configure several other files on the boot disk, such as NET*x*, IPXODI, NETBIOS, and the LAN driver. If you have a simple network setup and use the default configuration settings on the workstation's network board, you may not need to include the commands for configuring the other shell and driver files.

The NetWare documentation explains how to add commands to the NET.CFG file to configure the shell and driver files. If you must use these commands, be sure to format them correctly. List the file you are configuring, then indent the commands that affect that file. For example, to configure the NE2000 LAN driver, you might include the following commands in the NET.CFG file:

```
LINK DRIVER NE2000
   INT 3
   PORT 300
   FRAME ETHERNET_802.3
   FRAME ETHERNET_II
   PROTOCOL IPX 0 ETHERNET_802.3
```

In this example, the line that is flush left indicates that the following commands will affect the NE2000 LAN driver. Then the next two commands specify configuration options for the driver that vary from the default values. The last three lines establish the frame types and protocol that the LAN driver will use.

The following example shows a NET.CFG file for a more complex setup:

```
LOCAL PRINTERS=0
LONG MACHINE TYPE=COMPAQ
SHORT MACHINE TYPE=CMPQ
CACHE BUFFERS=20
FILE HANDLES=30
SHOW DOTS=ON
```

```
LINK SUPPORT
  BUFFERS 8 1500
  MEMPOOL 4096

LINK DRIVER NE2000
  INT 3
  PORT 300
  FRAME ETHERNET_802.3
  PROTOCOL IPX 0 ETHERNET_802.3
```

Remember, if your network is fairly simple, you won't need to use any of these specialized configuration commands. But if you do need to create a more complex NET.CFG file, refer to the NetWare documentation for detailed information about the options. See Chapter 11 for information about using NET.CFG with VLM files.

Installing Diskless Workstations

Using diskless workstations is sometimes an attractive option for smaller networks. Users can't insert a disk infected with a virus, nor can they pirate network applications by copying them to diskettes and taking them home.

An ordinary workstation boots DOS and runs NetWare files from a local boot disk—either a floppy diskette or the workstation's own hard disk. A diskless workstation obviously cannot boot from a local disk, because it doesn't have one. Therefore, it must be able to find all the necessary DOS and NetWare files on the file server and boot from there. This method of booting diskless workstations from the network instead of from a local disk is called *remote booting*, or *remote reset*. Figure 2.2 illustrates how a diskless workstation boots DOS.

If you decide to use diskless workstations, keep in mind that you must have one workstation with a floppy disk drive available, at least until you get all your applications copied onto the network and the rest of the workstations installed. You can then remove the workstation with the floppy drive.

To put the files onto the network and allow a diskless workstation to find them, you run a NetWare utility called DOSGEN. The following are the basic

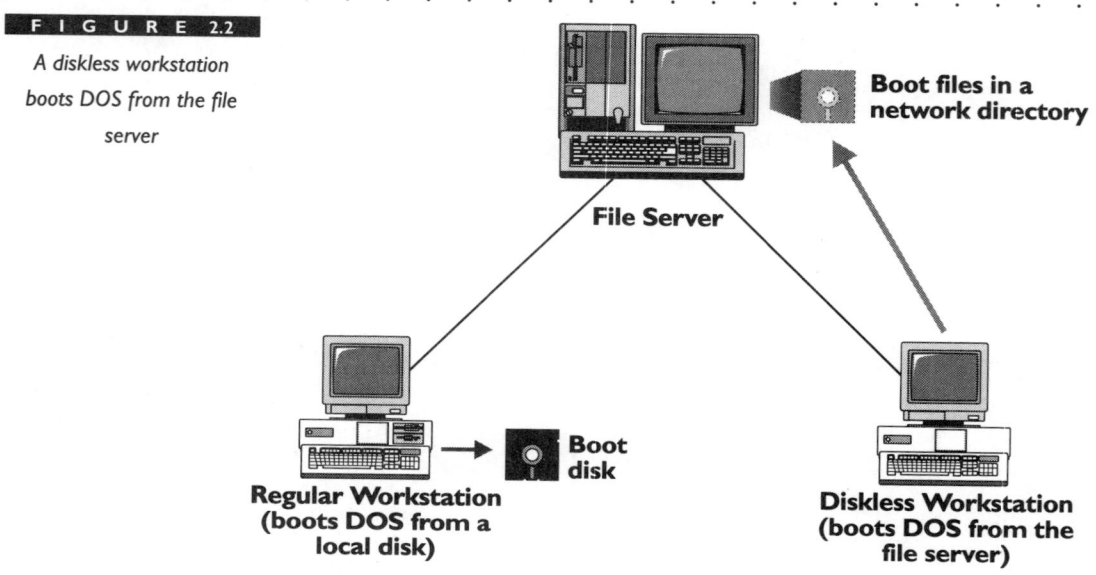

F I G U R E 2.2

A diskless workstation
boots DOS from the file
server

Boot files in a
network directory

File Server

Boot
disk

Regular Workstation
(boots DOS from a
local disk)

Diskless Workstation
(boots DOS from the
file server)

steps for installing a diskless workstation. For more detailed instructions, refer
to the NetWare documentation.

1 · Make sure the workstation has a network board and a Remote Reset
PROM chip installed. (A PROM chip is a special memory chip.)
Some diskless workstations come with the board and PROM already
installed.

2 · Connect each workstation's network board to the network cabling.
Make sure you use the correct hardware for your type of cabling.
For example, you may need to use hubs, terminators, connectors,
and so on.

3 · (NetWare version 3.*x* only) If your diskless workstations are running on
a Token Ring network, load the TOKENRPL.NLM loadable module on
your file server. Then you must bind the TOKENRPL protocol to the
Token Ring LAN driver in your server. To load the module and bind the

protocol, type the following commands at the file server's console:

```
LOAD TOKENRPL
BIND TOKENRPL TOKEN
```

You can add these commands to the file server's AUTOEXEC.NCF file so that they will be executed whenever the server is rebooted.

4 · (For dedicated IPX drivers only) Boot DOS on the workstation that has a floppy disk drive, and then run NetWare's workstation software program to create the IPX.COM file. As explained earlier in this chapter, if you have two workstations with different brands of network boards installed, you need to use the workstation software program to create two different IPX.COM files.

5 · Decide which version of the shell file each workstation will use: NET*x*, NETX, EMSNET*x*, or XMSNET*x*. (The shell file versions are described earlier in this chapter.)

6 · Make a boot diskette for each diskless workstation, following the instructions given earlier in this chapter. This seems like an odd step, since the diskless workstation can't use a diskette. However, the DOSGEN utility will copy this boot diskette into a network directory, so it is important to make the boot diskette.

7 · Follow the instructions in the NetWare documentation for running DOSGEN. If you are creating remote boot files for only one workstation, the DOSGEN procedure is simple. If you are creating remote boot files for several diskless workstations, you may need to change several file names and copy different versions of the files to various directories before you can run DOSGEN. The NetWare documentation explains these steps in detail.

8 · If you created multiple remote boot files, create a BOOTCONF.SYS file in the SYS:LOGIN directory. This file tells the workstation which remote boot files to use.

9 · Give the users who will be using the diskless workstations the correct rights for accessing the directories where the remote boot files are stored.

10 · Load DOS into a network directory so the diskless workstations can run DOS from the network after they've booted. See Chapter 3 for instructions for running DOS from a network directory.

After you finish running DOSGEN to put the remote boot files in a network directory, the diskless workstations will be able to boot from the network.

Installing Peripheral Devices

Installing additional hardware devices, such as printers, modems, and tape backup systems, usually involves two steps:

▸ Physically connect the device to the network cabling

▸ Load the software on the file server (or occasionally a workstation)

The software you load allows the device to communicate with the network. Often, you must specify particular settings that will make the device compatible with NetWare. Each peripheral should come with its own instructions for installing it on a network. Chapter 5 explains how to set up network printers.

Review

To prepare for installing your network, you need to make sure you take steps to protect your network:

▶ Protect the network from electrical problems by putting the file server on a UPS (uninterruptible power supply) and the workstations on surge suppressors.

▶ Protect the network cabling by keeping it out of harm's way and by making sure it doesn't come too close to other wiring or lighting fixtures that can cause electrical interference.

▶ Protect the file server by locking it in a secure room.

▶ Protect the users by taking simple steps to prevent eyestrain, wrist strain, and so on.

After you prepare your office for the network, you install the file server, the workstations, and peripheral devices.

When installing workstations, you must decide whether to use dedicated IPX drivers or ODI drivers, because this decision will affect the files you need to include on the workstations' boot disks. Dedicated IPX drivers work with only the NetWare IPX protocol. ODI drivers can handle several protocols at a time, as well as multiple Ethernet frame types.

For each workstation, you need to create a boot disk, which contains all the drivers, shell files, and configuration files that allow the workstation to operate on the network. Some of these files are copied from a NetWare disk. You will need to create other files, such as the CONFIG.SYS, SHELL.CFG, NET.CFG, and AUTOEXEC.BAT files.

You can install diskless workstations on the network. Diskless workstations do not have boot disks; they boot from files located on the file server.

To install peripheral equipment, follow the manufacturer's instructions for connecting the equipment to the network cabling and for loading software drivers and configuration programs that allow the device to communicate with the network.

After your network is installed, you can begin adding directories and users. The next chapter describes how to set up network directories and files. Chapter 4 describes how to add users to the network.

CHAPTER 3

Organizing Files and Directories on the Network

One of the powerful features of NetWare is that it allows users to share files. On a NetWare network, everyone's files and applications can be stored on the file server's hard disk so that all network users can access them. To make it easier to store, find, and protect files, NetWare organizes them in a filing system called the *directory structure*, or *directory tree*.

This chapter explains how to use NetWare's directory structure to organize and protect your network files. It also describes how to manage your network directories.

What Is a Directory Structure?

In an office filing system, files are stored in a filing cabinet. The filing cabinet contains drawers, in which you divide your files into a few general areas. Each drawer might contain many hanging folders, which sort the files into more specific subjects. The hanging folders can hold one or more manila folders, which contain the individual files—letters, memos, reports, drawings, charts, and so on.

NetWare's directory structure organizes network files in a similar fashion. On a network, files are stored on your file server's hard disk, which is like the office filing cabinet. The server's hard disk is divided (figuratively speaking) into *volumes*, which correspond to the drawers in the filing cabinet. Each file server must have at least one volume, called SYS: (for system), which contains all the files required to run NetWare. In addition, you may want to create additional volumes on your file server. It's usually a good idea to reserve the SYS: volume for NetWare's own files and create a second volume for your regular working files and applications.

To organize files within the file server's volumes, you create directories. A *directory* is a collection of files, just as a folder in your drawer is a collection of files. (In fact, in the Macintosh world, directories are actually called *folders*.) Directories can contain both files and other directories. If a directory contains other directories, it is referred to as a *parent directory*. The directories within a parent directory are called *subdirectories*. Parent directories and subdirectories are both groups of files; the terms merely explain where you are in the directory structure.

For example, suppose you write a project status report every Monday and a budget report every Friday. To organize these files, you could create a directory called REPORTS, then create two additional directories under REPORTS: one called STATUS and one called BUDGET. You would store all your project status reports in the STATUS directory and all your budget reports in the BUDGET directory.

Figure 3.1 illustrates the NetWare directory structure. In the example, REPORTS is the parent directory, and BUDGET and STATUS are subdirectories. If BUDGET contained a subdirectory called MONTHLY, BUDGET would be the parent directory of MONTHLY.

To specify where a directory is located in the directory structure, each directory has a path. The *path* lists the parent directory, its parent directory, and so on, all the way up to the volume name. For example, this is the directory path for our example subdirectory MONTHLY:

SYS:REPORTS\BUDGET\MONTHLY

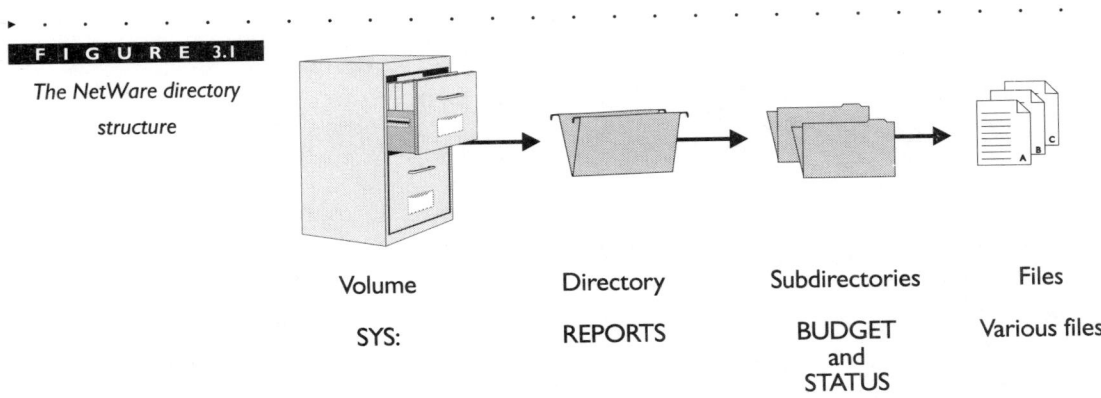

FIGURE 3.I

The NetWare directory structure

| Volume | Directory | Subdirectories | Files |
| SYS: | REPORTS | BUDGET and STATUS | Various files |

The directory path starts with the volume, which is separated from the directories by a colon. A backslash separates each parent directory from its subdirectory.

Making the Most of Your Directory Structure

In planning your directory structure, you need to consider the security of network files, as well as how to make it easy for users to find files. The key to setting up a directory structure is to determine which users need access to which network files.

With NetWare, you can establish how each user can access different network files and directories. By assigning rights, you determine whether a user can open files, read them, change them, delete them, or not even see them.

As you design your network's directory structure, consider how you want users to use the directories:

> ▶ Will your users run DOS or Windows from the network or from their own workstation?

> ▶ Should any of your applications be accessible to some users but not to others?

> ▶ Where do you want your users to store their daily work files: in personal directories, project-specific directories, or in some other directory structure?

By considering these questions, you can simplify your job as a network supervisor. For example, suppose you group all the payroll files beneath a single directory called PAYROLL. You can restrict everyone but the appropriate payroll employees from accessing those files by giving only the payroll employees rights to the PAYROLL parent directory. If users can't get into the PAYROLL directory, they won't be able to get into any subdirectories beneath PAYROLL either. If the payroll files were scattered among several different directories, you would need to spend more time setting up similar access rights in those individual directories. Setting up users' rights to directories is explained in Chapter 6.

If you already have a directory structure in place but realize you would rather have done it a different way, you can change the structure easily. NetWare allows you to create, delete, move, and copy directories at anytime, as described later in this chapter. Although it's easier and less time-consuming when you set up your directories appropriately from the beginning, if you don't get it right the first time, you're not alone.

Before you begin planning how to organize your network files, you should know which directories are created automatically when you install NetWare.

Directories Created Automatically

When you install NetWare on a file server, four directories are created automatically in the SYS: volume:

▶ The SYSTEM directory contains the NetWare network operating system, the drivers, and the server utilities. This directory is used primarily by you, the network supervisor. Other network users generally do not have access to the SYSTEM directory.

▶ The PUBLIC directory contains all the NetWare workstation utilities. Since all the network users may need to use these utilities, everyone usually has access to this directory.

▶ The MAIL directory contains a separate subdirectory for each user. Each subdirectory is named with a user's ID number (which is assigned when the user account is created), and it contains that user's login script. A *login script* is a file that executes when a user logs in to the network, as explained in Chapter 7.

▶ The LOGIN directory contains a few essential NetWare utilities that allow users to log in to the network.

These four directories contain all the files necessary to run the network, so you should not delete or rename any of them.

Planning the Directories You Will Create

You will create directories to contain your network applications and files. Because network users need to access these directories on a regular basis, it is important that you organize them efficiently. The following sections describe some types of directories you might want to set up: home, DOS, Windows, application, and work directories. You will find suggestions for organizing these directories, but the directory structure that is most suitable for your network depends on your own situation.

A HOME DIRECTORY FOR EACH USER

A home directory can be a storage place for any files that a network user creates for his or her own use. Although your users may store their project-related files in specific project directories, it is sometimes convenient to give each user a home directory to store files such as first drafts, memos, or personal files.

Whenever you add a new user to the network, you can have NetWare create a home directory for that user automatically. Home directories are named with the user's name. For example, if you create a user named Andy, his home directory will also be called ANDY. By default, NetWare creates home directories as subdirectories directly under the SYS: volume, but you can specify a different parent directory on a different volume.

DIRECTORIES FOR DOS AND WINDOWS

Each workstation on a network runs its own operating system. Macintosh workstations always run System from their local disk. DOS workstations can run

DOS from either their own local disks (floppy disks or hard disks) or from a network directory. Windows can also be run from either local disks or network directories.

Allowing workstations to run DOS and Windows from network directories offers some advantages:

▸ You can upgrade all workstations to a new version of DOS or Windows at the same time by updating the files in one directory instead of changing the files on each individual workstation.

▸ You can prevent users from accidently deleting DOS or Windows from their local disks.

▸ You can buy diskless workstations for your users.

You must place network directories that contain DOS and Windows under the PUBLIC directory on the SYS: volume. The following sections describe how to plan the directories for DOS and Windows.

Planning Directories for DOS

To load DOS into a network directory, create specific subdirectories under the PUBLIC directory, and then copy the DOS files into those subdirectories. If all your DOS workstations are the same type of computers (all IBM or all Compaq, for example) and are running the same version of DOS, you need only one DOS directory for the network. However, if you have different brands of computers on your network, or if any of the computers are using different versions of DOS, you must create several DOS directories.

First, list the types of computers and the versions of DOS that each uses. For example, suppose you have the following workstations on your network:

▸ Four IBMs running DOS 3.3

▸ Two IBMs running DOS 5.0

▸ Five Compaqs running DOS 5.0

▸ One AT&T running DOS 3.3

This list shows that you need four different DOS directories on your network, because you have four different types of DOS running on your workstations.

Whether you have one DOS directory or several, you must create a specific path to each one using the following format:

SYS:PUBLIC*machine name*\\MSDOS*DOS version*

Replace *machine name* with the computer type and *DOS version* with the version number for the machine's operating system. For the workstations listed above, you would need to create four directories:

SYS:PUBLIC\\IBM_PC\\MSDOS\\3.3
SYS:PUBLIC\\IBM_PC\\MSDOS\\5.0
SYS:PUBLIC\\COMPAQ\\MSDOS\\5.0
SYS:PUBLIC\\ATT\\MSDOS\\5.0

After you create your DOS directories, complete the following steps to allow your users to run DOS from the network:

1 · Copy the DOS files into the last subdirectory (the one named with the version number of DOS, such as 5.0).

2 · Protect the DOS files by assigning the directory attributes Read Only (so that users cannot copy, change, or delete the DOS files) and Shareable (to allow users to share the files with other users) to the directory that contains the DOS files. Chapter 6 explains how to assign attributes to a directory.

3 · Map a search drive to the DOS directory in the system login script. Mapping search drives is described later in this chapter. Login scripts are described in Chapter 7.

4 · Use the COMSPEC command in the login script to tell the workstation where to find the DOS command processor. Using the COMSPEC command in login scripts is described in Chapter 7.

5 · Put the correct machine name, such as IBM_PC, COMPAQ, or ATT, in each workstation's SHELL.CFG or NET.CFG file. This way, the workstation will find its machine name in the SHELL.CFG or NET.CFG file and know which DOS directory it should look for on the network. The SHELL.CFG and NET.CFG files are discussed in Chapter 2.

If you plan to use diskless workstations, you must also create remote boot files so that the workstations can boot from the network. See Chapter 2 for more information about diskless workstations.

Planning Directories for Windows

Generally, the most efficient way to set up workstations to run Windows from the network is to store the Windows program files in a directory that can be accessed by all the network users, and then copy the Windows user files into a separate directory for each individual user. However, you should use a permanent swap file on each workstation's hard disk.

If you prefer, you can store only the Windows program files in a network directory and store the user files on each user's local disk. However, you may find that it's easier for you to manage the network if all the Windows files are in network directories.

DIRECTORIES FOR NETWORK APPLICATIONS

In addition to directories for workstation operating systems, you need directories for network applications, such as word processing and spreadsheet programs, so that all your users can access them. If you've reserved volume SYS: for NetWare's own files, you can place your application directories in the second volume.

One way to further organize your application directories is to group them under a parent directory. For example, suppose you have WordPerfect, Lotus Notes, and Microsoft Project, and you want to install all of them on volume

VOL1. You could create a directory called APPS in VOL1, then create subdirectories for each application, as shown in Figure 3.2.

By grouping application directories under a parent directory, you save yourself a few steps in protecting those applications. You can set access rights once for the parent directory, and all the subdirectories beneath it will automatically get the same protection. If your applications were installed in various directories, you would need to set access rights individually for each directory to ensure that users could see and execute the application without being able to copy, change, or delete it.

Many manufacturers sell one version of their applications for stand-alone computers and another version for networks. The stand-alone version is designed to be accessed by a single user; the network version can be accessed by multiple users at the same time. Other manufacturers have developed a single version of their application that can be used either on a stand-alone computer or on a network. Before installing an application on the network, check the manufacturer's documentation (or check with your reseller) to see if there is a specific network version or if you need to follow special instructions to install the product on a NetWare network.

In many cases, you can install a stand-alone version of an application on a network without any technical problems. However, make sure you do not violate the licensing agreement you made with the manufacturer when you opened the software's packaging. If the software is designed to be used by a single user, it's wise to honor that agreement; software piracy lawsuits are becoming more and more frequent.

Some applications must be installed at the root of a volume. If you are concerned about security and would rather install the application in a subdirectory,

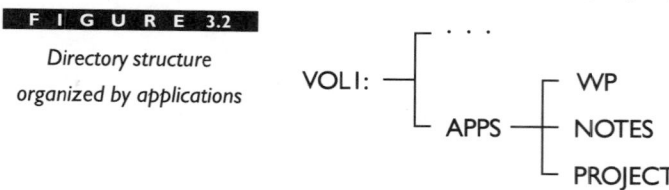

FIGURE 3.2

Directory structure organized by applications

VOL1: ┌ ・・・
      └ APPS ─┬ WP
              ├ NOTES
              └ PROJECT

you can get around this restriction. NetWare versions 2.2 and 3.*x* allow you to designate a subdirectory to be a "fake root." For more information about creating a fake root, see Chapter 6.

WORK DIRECTORIES

After you've planned where you want your applications to be installed, you need to decide where to store the files your users create in their daily work. The best location for these files depends on the types of files your network users create. You might place users' files in project-specific directories, in personal directories, in application-specific directories, or in some combination of these.

If the users' files relate to projects, project directories could be a logical choice. For example, for a project team that is designing new fingerprint-resistant camera lenses, you might create a directory called LENSES, with subdirectories beneath it called RESEARCH, TESTS, and RESULTS. Then everyone on the Lenses team can store research logs, test plans, and result reports in those directories and share them with each other. Figure 3.3 illustrates this type of directory structure.

On the other hand, you might prefer to have your users store their files in their own personal directory rather than in a project-specific one. For example, Louise, who happens to be working on the Lenses project team, could have a personal directory called LOUISE. Beneath that directory could be subdirectories called PERSONAL, REPORTS, SHUTTERS, and LENSES. Under LENSES, Louise might create yet more subdirectories called RESEARCH, TESTS, and RESULTS, in which she keeps her individual reports about the Lenses project. Figure 3.4 shows the setup for this personal directory.

▶ · ◀

FIGURE 3.3

Project-specific directory structure

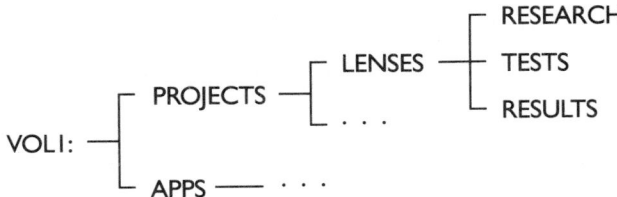

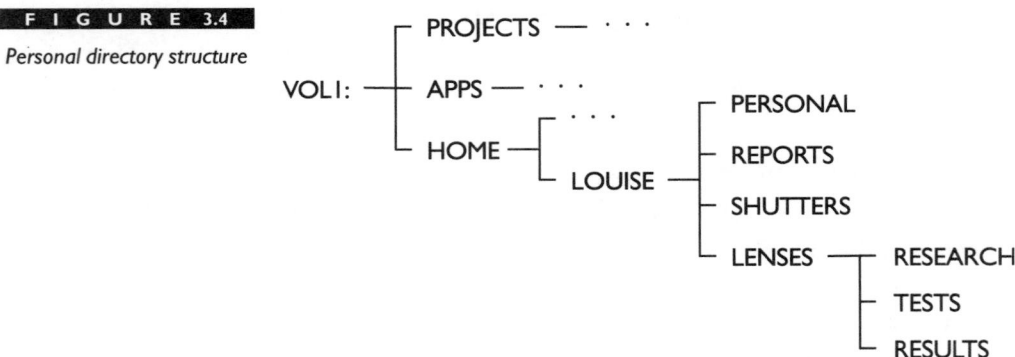

FIGURE 3.4

Personal directory structure

Another way to organize users' work files is to group them by the application they were created with, regardless of who created them or what project they relate to. For example, you could store all word processor files in a directory called WORDS and all spreadsheet files in a directory called SPREADS.

These are just a few of the many ways that you can organize work directories. For your own network, you may use a combination of project, personal, and application work directories, or an entirely different structure. Your main objectives are to ensure that users can find their files easily and that you can manage network security efficiently.

EXAMPLES OF NETWORK DIRECTORY STRUCTURES

When you put all the pieces of your plan together, you will have a blueprint of your network directory structure. Figures 3.5 and 3.6 show examples of two different network directory structures.

An example of a directory structure for a medical office's network

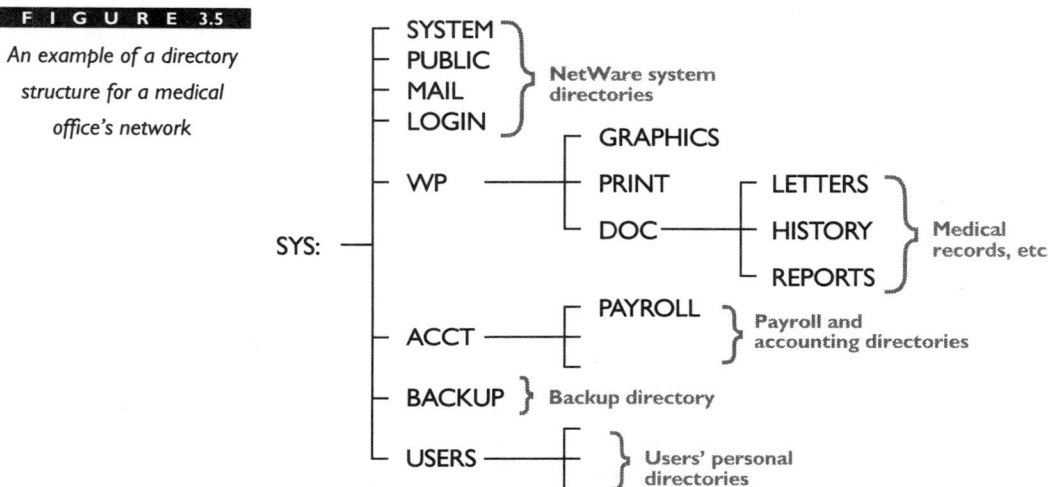

Creating Directories

After you've planned your directory structure, you're ready to create the directories. You can create directories for the network by using the DOS MD command or the Windows File Manager, just as you create directories for stand-alone computers. Or, if you prefer to use menus, you can create directories through NetWare's FILER utility.

FILER is a NetWare menu utility for managing files. To create a directory with FILER, follow these steps:

1 · Start the FILER utility from your workstation by typing FILER and pressing the Enter key.

2 · Use the arrow keys to move to the Directory Contents option on the Available Topics menu, and then press the Enter key to select it. A list of the files and subdirectories in your current directory appears.

FIGURE 3.6

An example of a directory structure for a CPA office's network

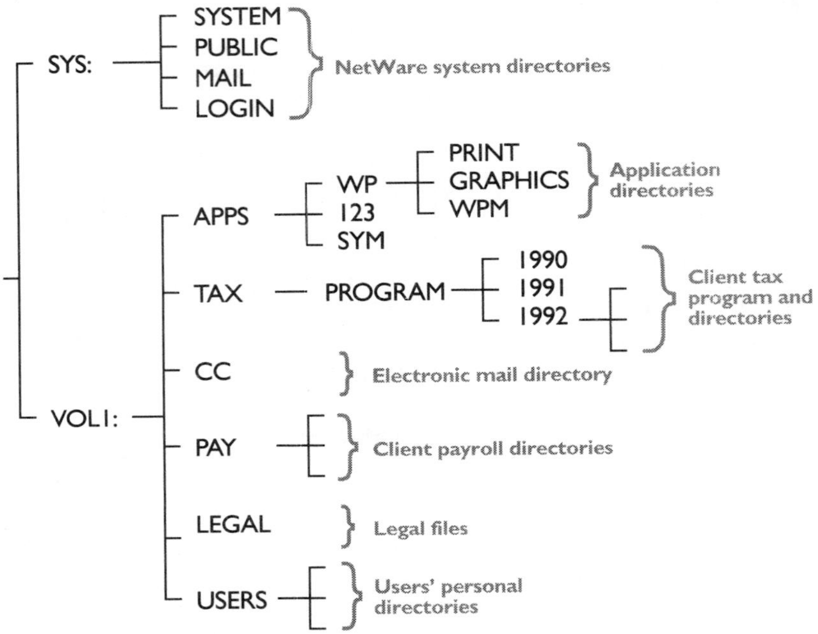

3 · Move to the directory under which you want to create a new directory if you aren't already there. For example, to place a directory under the PUBLIC directory, you must first change to the PUBLIC directory.

The top bar of the FILER utility screen shows the current directory. To move to a different directory, press the F2 key. In the window that appears, type the path of the parent directory (such as SYS:PUBLIC) and press the Enter key. Alternatively, you can press the Ins key from the window, choose the directory path from lists of volumes and directories, and then press the Esc key to return to the directory path window.

4 · To create the new subdirectory, press the Ins key.

5 · In the window that appears, type the name of the new subdirectory you want to create and press the Enter key. For example, to create a directory called APPS for your applications, type APPS.

The new subdirectory now appears in the Directory Contents list. You have successfully created a directory.

6 · To exit FILER, press the Esc key several times until you are asked if you want to exit, and then choose Yes.

Deleting Directories

To delete directories, you can use the DOS RD command or the Windows File Manager. You can also use the FILER utility to delete directories.

To delete a directory with the FILER utility, follow these steps:

1 · Start the FILER utility from your workstation by typing FILER and pressing the Enter key.

2 · Select the Directory Contents option from the Available Topics menu.

3 · Use the arrow keys to move up and down the Directory Contents list until you highlight the directory you want to remove.

4 · Press the Del key. A menu appears asking if you want to delete only the files in the directory you selected or if you want to delete both the files and the directory itself.

5 · Choose to delete the directory and then choose Yes when you are asked to confirm the deletion.

The directory disappears from the Directory Contents list, and you have successfully deleted a directory.

6 · To exit FILER, press the Esc key until you are asked if you want to exit, and then choose Yes.

Taking the Shortcut to Your Directories: Mapping Drives

You are probably familiar with how DOS uses drive letters. Drive letter A: refers to the local floppy disk drive in your workstation, so it points to whatever diskette you happen to insert in that drive. Drive B: usually points to the second floppy disk drive in your workstation. However, if you've worked on a computer with only one floppy disk drive, you probably noticed that you can use either A: or B: to point to the same drive. Drive C: usually points to a hard disk.

Drive letters don't refer to a particular diskette; in some cases, they don't even refer to a particular disk drive. They are simply pointers, and you can control which diskette they point to.

On a NetWare network, you also have drive letters that you can control, but NetWare drive letters point to *directories* instead of to diskettes. You specify which drive letter refers to which directory. DOS usually reserves letters A: through E: for local drives (floppy disk drives, hard disks, and external hard disks). NetWare gives you F: through Z:.

For example, if Mel has a home directory that he uses all the time, he can assign a NetWare drive letter to point to that directory. Then, instead of typing out the entire directory path (VOL1:HOME\MEL) every time he wants to indicate that directory, he can type just the drive letter assigned to that directory (such as F:).

USING THE MAP UTILITY TO MAP DRIVES

Assigning a drive letter to a directory is called *mapping a drive*. To map a drive to a network directory, you use the NetWare MAP utility. For example, to map drive F: to his home directory, Mel would type the following command from his workstation:

MAP F:=VOL1:HOME\MEL

When you use the MAP utility to map a drive to a directory, that mapping is temporary. It is in effect only until you change it or log out of the network. When you log out of the network, the mapping disappears, and you will need to remap the drive the next time you log in. You can make a drive mapping permanent by putting the MAP command into a login script. Chapter 7 explains how to map drives permanently.

You can also use the MAP utility to find out which drives have already been mapped for your workstation. Type

MAP

and you will see a display similar to the one shown in Figure 3.7. This display shows that the first four drive letters are currently mapped to the user's local disks. Drives F: and G: are mapped to Mel's home directory and his project directory, respectively. The last two drives are search drives, which are described in the next section.

USING SEARCH DRIVES TO FIND APPLICATIONS

Search drives are a slightly different type of drive mapping. They are especially useful for mapping network drives to application directories.

FIGURE 3.7

The MAP utility's current drive mappings display

```
Drive  A:    maps to a local disk.
Drive  B:    maps to a local disk.
Drive  C:    maps to a local disk.
Drive  D:    maps to a local disk.
Drive  E:    maps to a local disk.
Drive  F: = SERVER\VOL1:  \HOME\MEL
Drive  G: = SERVER\VOL1:  \PROJECTS\LENSES
       -----
SEARCH1:  = Z:. [SERVER\SYS:  \PUBLIC]
SEARCH2:  = Y:. [SERVER\VOL1:  \APPS\WP]
```

Normally, when you type the command to execute an application, that command will look for the application in the directory you are currently working in. If the application isn't located in the current directory, it won't run.

When you map a search drive to a directory that contains an application, you can execute that application no matter where you are in the directory structure, without first changing to its directory. The system searches through your current directory, then through all directories that have search drives mapped to them to find that application.

You use the MAP utility to map a search drive to a directory, but instead of indicating a drive letter, you specify a number preceded by an S. The search drive will assign its own letter. (Search drives assign drive letters in reverse order, starting with Z: and working backward.) For example, to map your first search drive to the PUBLIC directory, which contains the NetWare utilities, type the following command from your workstation:

MAP S1:=SYS:PUBLIC

Then, every time you want to execute a NetWare utility (such as MAP or FILER), you can type the utility's name from anywhere in the directory structure, and NetWare will find the utility in the PUBLIC directory.

You can have up to 16 search mappings. Like other drive mappings you assign through the MAP utility, your search mappings are in effect only until you log out of the network, unless you put the MAP command in a login script.

Copying Files and Directories

You can copy files and directories in three ways:

- ► Use the DOS COPY or XCOPY command or the Windows File Manager.

- ► Use FILER, a NetWare menu utility.

- ► Use NCOPY, a NetWare command line utility.

COPYING FILES AND DIRECTORIES WITH NCOPY

When you use the NCOPY command line utility to copy a file, the file's attributes are also copied. The owner of the copy of the file will be changed to the user who copied it.

To copy files and directories using the NCOPY command line utility, type the command in the following format:

NCOPY *drive:original-file drive:new-file*

Substitute the drive letter and file name of the original file for *drive:original-file*, and the destination's drive letter and file name for *drive:new-file*. For example, to copy the file MEMO.3A from drive F: to drive G:, type this command:

NCOPY F:MEMO.3A G:MEMO.3A

To copy MEMO.3A to drive G: and rename it to NEWMEMO at the same time, add the new file name to the command:

NCOPY F:MEMO.3A G:NEWMEMO

To copy a directory, specify the drive letter that is mapped to the directory, without entering a file name. For example, to copy the directory that is mapped to drive L: to the directory that is mapped to drive M:, type this command:

NCOPY L: M:

If the directory that is mapped to drive L: contains subdirectories and you want to copy the subdirectories as well, add /S (for subdirectories) at the end of the command:

NCOPY L: M: /S

NCOPY Shortcuts

You can use shortcuts with the NCOPY command to eliminate some typing. For example, if you are not changing the name of the file, you can omit the *new-file* name. This means that instead of typing this command:

NCOPY F:MEMO.3A G:MEMO.3A

you could shorten the command to this:

NCOPY F:MEMO.3A G:

When you use the shortened version, NCOPY assumes that you want the file name to be the same in drive G: as it was in drive F:.

Another shortcut you can use is to skip the drive letter if you are already in that drive. For our MEMO.3A example, if you're currently in drive F:, you could type this command:

NCOPY MEMO.3A G:

NCOPY assumes that you want it to find MEMO.3A in drive F:, since that is where you are currently working, and copy the file to drive G:, where it will give the file the same name it had in drive F:.

Using Wildcard Characters with NCOPY

To copy several or all the files from one drive to another at the same time, you can use *wildcard characters*. Wildcard characters are symbols that mean *substitute any character here*. Just as in DOS, the two wildcard characters are the question mark (?) and the asterisk (*). The question mark means *substitute one character in this place*. The asterisk means *substitute any number of characters here*.

For example, if you type this command:

NCOPY F:LETTER?.REQ G:

NCOPY copies all the files in drive F: that match that pattern of letters exactly. These files are copied:

LETTER1.REQ

LETTERA.REQ

LETTER6.REQ

These files are skipped:

LETTERPO.REQ

LETTER4.OLD

LETTER9

To copy all the files that begin with LET, regardless of how many other characters are in the file name or the extension, use asterisks. For example, if you type this command:

NCOPY F:LET*.* G:

these files are copied:

LETTER1.REQ

LETTERA.REQ

LETTER6.REQ

LETTERPO.REQ

LETTER4.OLD

LETTER9

and these files are skipped:

7LETTER.MY

ACCOUNT.LET

You can also combine wildcard characters in a command. If you type this command:

NCOPY F:LETTER?.* G:

these files are copied:

> LETTER1.REQ
>
> LETTERA.REQ
>
> LETTER6.REQ
>
> LETTER4.OLD
>
> LETTER9

and these files are skipped:

> LETTERPO.REQ
>
> 7LETTER.MY
>
> ACCOUNT.LET

COPYING FILES AND DIRECTORIES WITH FILER

When you use the FILER menu utility to copy a file, the file's attributes are also copied. Also, the owner of the copy of the file will be changed to the user who copied it.

To copy files or directories using the FILER utility, follow these steps:

1 · Start the FILER utility from your workstation by typing FILER and pressing the Enter key.

2 · From the Available Topics menu, use the arrow keys to move to the Directory Contents option and press the Enter key to select it.

3 · Move to the directory that contains the files you want to copy if you aren't already there.

The current directory is shown in the top bar of the utility screen. To move to a different directory, press the F2 key. In the window that appears, type the directory path and then press the Enter key. Alternatively, you can press Ins, choose the path from the directory list that appears, and press Esc to return to the destination directory window.

4 · Select the files or subdirectories you want to copy.

To select a single file or subdirectory, highlight it and press the Enter key. To copy several files or directories at a time, highlight each file or directory and press the F5 key to mark each selection. To unmark a selection, press F5 again.

5 · When you have marked all the files or directories you want, press the Enter key.

6 · In the window that appears, choose whether you want to copy or move your selection.

If you move a file instead of copying it, the original will be deleted from the original directory.

7 · In the next window, type the path of the *destination* directory (where you want to place the copies) and press the Enter key. Here, too, you can press the Ins key and choose the directory path from a list of directories instead of typing the path.

After you press the Enter key, the files and directories you selected are copied to the new directory you chose.

8 · To exit FILER, press the Esc key several times until you are asked if you want to exit, and then choose Yes.

Viewing Information about Files and Subdirectories

You can use either the NDIR or the FILER utility to view information about files and directories. For example, you can see who owns a file, the file's size, and the date it was created or changed.

GETTING FILE AND DIRECTORY INFORMATION WITH NDIR

NDIR is a NetWare command line utility that lists a directory's files, subdirectories, and related information. To see the information, type the command in the following format:

NDIR *path*

Substitute the directory path for *path*.

To also list any files contained within the directory's subdirectories, add the option /SUB:

NDIR *path* /SUB

If you are already working in the directory whose files and subdirectories you want to list, you can omit the *path* from the command.

The NDIR utility has a variety of options you can include to show different types of information about files and directories. NDIR also allows you to list files and subdirectories in various orders, to list only files and subdirectories that have certain characteristics, and so on. The following are some of the more common options:

▶ To list only the files in the directory, type

NDIR *path* /FilesOnly

▶ To list only the subdirectories in the directory, type

NDIR *path* /DirsOnly

▶ To list files and subdirectories in the order of their sizes, from smallest to largest, type

NDIR *path* /SORT SIZE

▶ To list files and subdirectories in the order of their sizes, from largest to smallest, type

NDIR *path* /REVERSE SORT SIZE

▶ To list only the files and subdirectories that are owned by user Ray, type

NDIR *path* /OWNER=RAY

▶ To list only Macintosh files and subdirectories (folders), type

NDIR *path* /MAC

To see the other options that are available with NDIR, use its online help. Type NDIR /HELP to display the Help information.

VIEWING FILE AND DIRECTORY INFORMATION WITH FILER

To see information about files or directories using the FILER menu utility, follow these steps:

1 · Start the FILER utility from your workstation by typing FILER and pressing the Enter key.

2 · From the Available Topics menu, use the arrow keys to move to the Directory Contents option and press the Enter key to select it.

3 · Move to the directory that contains the files you want to copy if you aren't already there.

The current directory is shown in the top bar of the utility screen. To move to a different directory, press the F2 key. In the window that appears, type the directory path and then press the Enter key. Alternatively, you can press Ins, choose the path from the directory list that appears, and press Esc to return to the destination directory window.

4 · Select the file or directory whose information you want to see, by highlighting it and pressing the Enter key.

5 · Select the View/Set File (or Directory) Information option. The information about the file or directory you selected appears on the screen.

6 · To exit FILER, press the Esc key several times until you are asked if you want to exit, and then choose Yes.

Review

In this chapter, you learned that files on a NetWare network are organized in a hierarchical filing system called the directory structure. This directory structure starts with the file server's hard disk, which is divided into one or more volumes. Each volume contains directories, which can contain both files and additional directories (called subdirectories).

The SYS: volume and four directories within the SYS: volume—SYSTEM, PUBLIC, MAIL, and LOGIN—are created automatically when the file server is installed. These directories contain the files necessary to run the NetWare network.

You create additional directories to contain workstation operating systems, applications, users' personal files, and users' daily work files. By carefully planning your directory structure, you can make it easier for your users to store and find their files and for you to manage network security.

You can create and work with directories by using your workstation's operating system commands or the NetWare utilities. FILER, the NetWare menu utility, allows you to create and delete directories, copy files and directories, and view information about directories and files. NCOPY is the NetWare command line utility for copying files and directories. NDIR is the command line utility for listing information about files and directories.

After you've planned and created your directory structure, your next step is to create user accounts and groups. The next chapter describes how to set up and manage your network users.

CHAPTER 4

Adding Network
Users and Groups

One of your responsibilities as network supervisor is to make sure that all your users have current accounts on the network. You will also need to make sure that users who have moved out of the company or department are removed from the network.

Beyond just adding and deleting users, you can also control some of your users' activities on the network by adding particular restrictions to their accounts. In addition, you can create groups of users to minimize some of the work you must do to maintain network security.

This chapter explains how to create and delete user accounts, restrict user accounts, and create user groups.

How Do Users and Groups Work Together?

Every person who wants to log in to the network must have a network user account. For example, suppose that Anne, in the Human Resources department, needs access to the personnel database and other network files. To set up a user account for her, you create a network user called ANNE and give her a password and certain rights to the network directories she needs to use.

In most cases, you will create a user account for each person you know will be using the network. In some cases, however, you may find it easier to create one user account that several people can use. For example, if you have several temporary workers who rotate doing the same job, you could create a user account called TEMP. Then any of those temporary employees could log in as TEMP and have the proper access to files. The problem with this approach is that it makes it more difficult to monitor who makes changes to network files. If network security is a concern, you should create a separate user account for each employee.

If several users need the same level of security in the same directories, you can simplify account setup by assigning those users to a group. For example, if all the employees in the Human Resources department need to access the personnel database, you could create a group called HR and assign the Human Resources employees to that group. Then, when you give trustee rights to the group HR, each user in that group will have the same level of access to the database. Users do not log in using the group name; they still log in with their own usernames. NetWare will then check the user's group assignments to determine whether the user is allowed to work in a particular directory.

Because a user can belong to several groups, using groups can give you a great deal of flexibility in managing your users.

Users and Groups Created Automatically

When you install NetWare, it automatically creates two user accounts and one group: the SUPERVISOR and GUEST users and the EVERYONE group.

SUPERVISOR is the user account you can use to set up and maintain the network. The SUPERVISOR user has all rights to every volume and directory on the network. Those rights cannot be taken away, and the SUPERVISOR account can never be deleted.

When you first install NetWare, SUPERVISOR doesn't have a password. Therefore, it is important to immediately assign SUPERVISOR a password and then keep that password safe. When you add users, you can create a user account for yourself using your own name, and then assign yourself a *security equivalence* to SUPERVISOR. Then you won't have to log in as SUPERVISOR every time you want to change something on the network—you can use your own user account. See Chapter 6 for more information about assigning security equivalence.

GUEST is a user account for "guests" to the network. Instead of setting up individual accounts for employees who use the network infrequently, you can have them use the GUEST account. For example, if people from other departments occasionally want to use your printer, they can log in as GUEST, print the file, and log out. You can limit GUEST's rights to certain directories, or you can delete the account altogether.

EVERYONE is a group that includes every user on the network. Whenever you create a new user, that user is automatically assigned to EVERYONE. This group is useful when all network users need access to the same directories, such as the SYS:PUBLIC directory and directories that contain applications. You can give rights to EVERYONE, limited to certain directories and files if necessary, instead of granting rights individually to every user. If you don't need this group, you can delete it, but it's generally recommended that you keep it.

How Do User Account Restrictions Work?

With NetWare, you can apply *account restrictions* to restrict users' work with the network in various ways. For example, you can limit the hours that a user can log in to the network, the workstations he or she can use, the amount of disk space that user can fill up, or the length of time he or she can use the same password. If a user exceeds one of these restrictions, that user's account will be disabled, and the user will be locked out of the network.

Before you apply any account restrictions, consider whether they are really necessary. In some cases, restrictions can create more work for you. For example, if you restrict a user from logging in on weekends, and then that user needs to work overtime to meet a deadline, you may get a phone call early Saturday morning asking you to come to the office to let that employee log in. On the other hand, if you have a strict company policy that forbids employees to work on weekends, restricting users' accounts is an effective way of enforcing that policy.

Passwords are also part of NetWare's account restrictions. You can specify the minimum number of characters a password can have, the length of time a password can be used, and whether the password must be one that the user hasn't used previously.

You can assign account restrictions on a systemwide basis or to individual users. When you specify systemwide restrictions, those restrictions apply to every user who is created from that point on. Any users who already exist will not be affected by the new restrictions. Therefore, you should apply your systemwide restrictions before you create any users. When you assign account restrictions to individual users, the individual assignments override any systemwide restrictions you may have also set.

Setting Systemwide Account Restrictions

You set systemwide account restrictions, which will apply to all users you create from this point on, with NetWare's SYSCON menu utility. To use SYSCON to set restrictions, log in to a workstation as SUPERVISOR or as a user who is supervisor-equivalent.

To start the SYSCON utility from your workstation, type

SYSCON

and press the Enter key.

Use the arrow keys to move to Supervisor Options and press the Enter key to select it. The Supervisor Options menu appears, as shown in Figure 4.1.

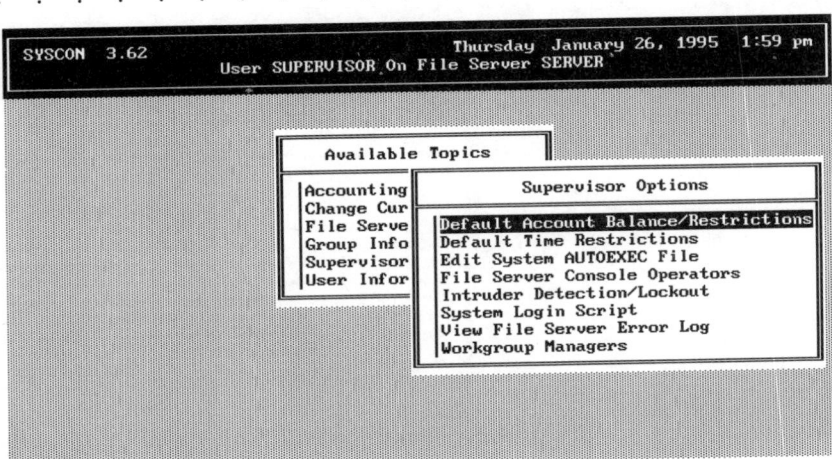

FIGURE 4.1

SYSCON's Supervisor Options menu

RESTRICTING LOG IN DAYS AND TIMES

If you want to restrict the days and times that users can log in, select Default Time Restrictions from the Supervisor Options menu. The Time Restrictions chart appears, as shown in Figure 4.2. This chart lists the days of the week down the left side, and the times of the day, beginning with midnight, across the top of the chart.

Each asterisk in the Time Restrictions chart means that users are allowed to log in at that time on that day. The first time the chart appears, it is completely filled with asterisks, because no time restrictions have been set yet.

To restrict users from logging in at certain times, delete the asterisks in those time slots. Move the cursor to the asterisk you want to delete and press the Del key. To remove a time restriction, move the cursor to that time slot and press the Ins key or type an asterisk. When you are finished, press the Esc key and then choose Yes to save the changes.

▶

FIGURE 4.2

The Time Restrictions chart

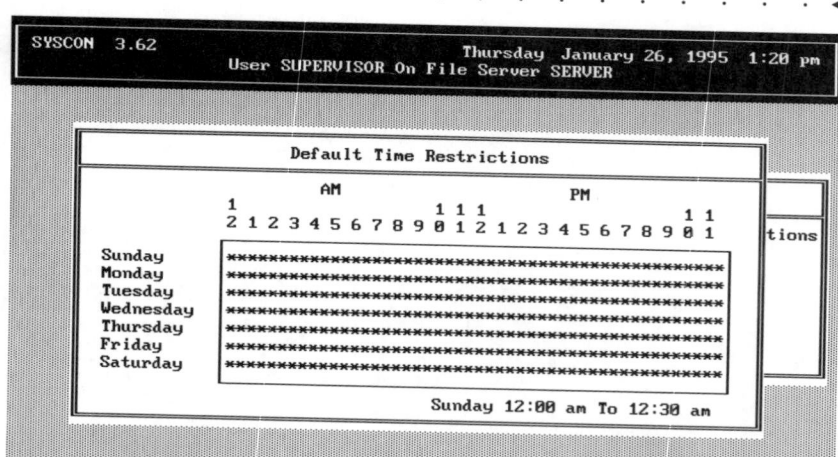

SETTING OTHER SYSTEMWIDE ACCOUNT RESTRICTIONS

To set other account restrictions, select Default Account Balance/Restrictions from the Supervisor Options menu. The next screen lists the restrictions you can set, as shown in Figure 4.3.

Change the settings for these restrictions as necessary. To change Yes/No options, type either Y or N and press the Enter key. To enter values for an option, highlight the field where the information belongs, type in the value, and then press the Enter key.

The options set restrictions as follows:

> ▶ **Account Has Expiration Date:** This option is useful only if you know most of your network users will be leaving at the same time. For example, if you are managing a network that is used primarily by students, and at the end of the semester the current users will leave and a new batch of students will become users instead, you could set this option to Yes. Otherwise, make sure this option is set to No.

FIGURE 4.3

SYSCON's other systemwide account restrictions

```
SYSCON  3.62                              Thursday  January 26, 1995  1:22 pm
                      User SUPERVISOR On File Server SERVER


                         Default Account Balance/Restrictions

        Account Has Expiration Date:                  No
           Date Account Expires:
        Limit Concurrent Connections:                 No
           Maximum Connections:
        Create Home Directory for User:               Yes
        Require Password:                             Yes
           Minimum Password Length:                   5
        Force Periodic Password Changes:             Yes
           Days Between Forced Changes:               40
           Limit Grace Logins:                       Yes
              Grace Logins Allowed:                    6
        Require Unique Passwords:                     Yes
        Account Balance:                               0
        Allow Unlimited Credit:                       No
           Low Balance Limit:                          0
```

▸ **Date Account Expires:** If you chose to make user accounts expire, you must fill in an expiration date.

▸ **Limit Concurrent Connections:** Set this option to Yes only if you need to restrict the number of times users can be logged in to the network simultaneously from different workstations. For example, if you have a ten-user version of NetWare, and you have eight employees, you may want to restrict the number of concurrent connections for each employee to one or two. Otherwise, if one employee decides to log in from four different workstations at the same time, two of your other users may not be able to log in at all because the first employee has used up all the available login connections.

▸ **Maximum Connections:** If you chose to limit concurrent connections, you need to enter the maximum number of connections.

▸ **Create Home Directory for User:** You will probably want to specify Yes for this option so that every time you add a new user, a home directory for that user is created automatically. Users can store their personal working files in their home directories. Only the user and the supervisor have access rights to the files in a user's home directory.

▸ **Require Password:** In most cases, you should specify Yes for this option so that passwords are required. If you require passwords, you will probably also want to specify values for the remaining password restrictions, which will help ensure that the passwords cannot be used by intruders.

▸ **Minimum Password Length:** Usually, requiring passwords to be at least five characters long is a safe practice.

▸ **Force Periodic Password Changes:** If you want users to change their passwords periodically, enter Yes. It is usually a good idea to require periodic changes; that way, if someone does guess a user's password, that person will be able to use it for only a few days before the user changes it.

▶ **Days Between Forced Changes**: If you chose to have users change their passwords periodically, enter the number of days the users can go between changes. If your network is in an area where security is more critical (for example, in a bank), you may want to set this time to be fairly frequent, such as every seven days. If security is less of an issue, making users change their passwords too frequently will become annoying to them and may increase the number of forgotten passwords you must deal with. Thirty days is usually adequate.

▶ **Limit Grace Logins**: When a user's password expires, the user is notified when he or she tries to log in. A message appears explaining that the password has expired and asking if the user would like to change the password. A *grace login* allows the user to finish logging in using the old password without changing it. Grace logins are useful if the user doesn't want to create a new password this time. If you want users to have an unlimited number of grace logins (effectively allowing the user to never change his or her password), enter No. If you want users to have a limited number of grace logins, enter Yes.

▶ **Grace Logins Allowed**: If you chose to limit the number of grace logins, enter the maximum number you want to allow.

▶ **Require Unique Passwords:** To prevent users from using the same passwords over and over, set this option to Yes. NetWare will then check to make sure that the new password a user just created is different from the last eight passwords that user had.

▶ **Account Balance, Allow Unlimited Credit, and Low Balance Limit:** These three options appear only if you install NetWare's accounting feature on your file server (by choosing the Accounting option from SYSCON's Available Topics menu). The accounting feature allows you to track the amount of time, disk space, and other network resources each person uses on your network. Accounting is useful if your network provides services to outside clients and you need to track their usage statistics so that you can charge them for using those resources. See the NetWare documentation for detailed instructions on setting up accounting, calculating charge rates, and so on.

▶ **Limit Server Disk Space:** (NetWare version 2.2 only) During the installation process for NetWare version 2.2, you can specify whether or not you want to limit the amount of the file server's disk space that each user can use. If you specified that you want to limit users' disk space, this account restriction appears on your screen, and you can set it to Yes. Otherwise, you will not see this option. (You can also use the DSPACE utility or SYSCON's User Information option to limit disk space, as explained later in this chapter.)

▶ **Maximum Server Disk Space (KB):** If this option is available to you and you selected Yes for the Limit Server Disk Space option, enter the maximum number of kilobytes each user can use.

When you are finished setting account restrictions, press the Esc key until you exit the SYSCON utility.

Adding Network Users

You can add individual network users with NetWare's SYSCON menu utility. If you need to create large numbers of users at the same time, you can use two other NetWare utilities: USERDEF and MAKEUSER. USERDEF allows you to create a user template (sort of a blueprint), and MAKEUSER creates the users based on that template. Refer to the NetWare documentation for details on using these utilities.

To create a user account with SYSCON, follow these steps:

1 · Log in to a workstation as SUPERVISOR or as a user who is supervisor-equivalent.

2 · Start SYSCON by typing

SYSCON

and press the Enter key.

3 · Use the arrow keys to move to the User Information option and press the Enter key to select it. A list of the current users appears.

4 · To add a new user, press the Ins key, type the login name of the new user (such as ANDY), and press the Enter key. If you set the system-wide account restrictions so that home directories are created automatically, you see a window showing a suggested home directory for the user, as shown in Figure 4.4.

5 · If you do not want the home directory to be created, press the Esc key from the home directory window. If you do want the home directory to be created, specify the correct directory path for it.

If this is the first user to be created, the suggested home directory is located under the SYS: volume, such as SALES\SYS:ANDY. However, you can change the suggested home directory path so that home directories will be created under another volume or under a parent directory. If the parent directory you specify doesn't exist, SYSCON will create it.

▶ · ◀

FIGURE 4.4

SYSCON's home directory window

```
SYSCON   3.62                          Thursday  January 26, 1995  1:19 pm
                      User SUPERVISOR On File Server SERVER

                    ┌─────────────────────────────────────────┐
                    │      Path to Create User's Home Directory │
                    └─────────────────────────────────────────┘
    SERVER/SYS:ANDY

        GUEST                    Current Server
        HEATHER                 erver Information
        LOREN                   Information
        NETMAN                  isor Options
        ROY                     nformation
        SUPERVISOR
        WILLIAM
        WJH
```

For example, to change Andy's home directory path to be in the HOME parent directory under VOL1 on server SALES, use the Backspace key to delete the existing directory path in the window, then type

SALES\VOL1:HOME\ANDY

Press the Enter key, then answer Yes to save the new home directory path.

The next time you create a user, the home directory path will be the same as the path you selected for the first user.

6 · To specify additional information about the new user account, highlight the new user's name in the list of users and press the Enter key. The User Information menu appears, as shown in Figure 4.5.

7 · From the User Information menu, choose various options (by highlighting the option and pressing the Enter key) to assign individual user account restrictions, create a login script, assign the user to groups, and so on. These options are explained in the next section.

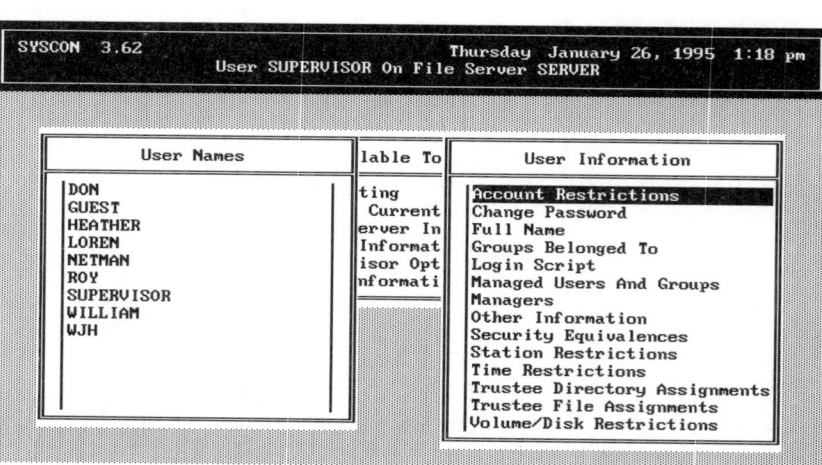

8 · When you are finished specifying information about the user, press the Esc key until you exit SYSCON.

Setting User Account Restrictions

The options on the User Information menu of the SYSCON utility allow you to set individual account restrictions for a user. Each of the options is explained below:

▶ **Account Balance:** The Account Balance option appears only if you installed NetWare's accounting feature on your file server, as mentioned earlier in this chapter (in the section about setting systemwide account restrictions).

▶ **Account Restrictions:** This option displays a screen for setting individual account restrictions for this user. The options are the same as those for systemwide account restrictions, which are described earlier in this chapter. You can also disable a user's account (lock the user out), or reenable the account (unlock a user's account). The restrictions you set here override any systemwide account restrictions.

▶ **Change Password:** This option lets you change the user's password. First, you are asked to type the new password and press the Enter key, and then you are prompted to type it again (to ensure you typed it correctly the first time).

▶ **Full Name:** This option allows you to indicate the user's full name. For example, if Louise's login name is LOUISE, you can indicate that her full name is Louise K. Snow.

▶ **Groups Belonged To:** This option shows the groups the user already belongs to, such as the group EVERYONE. You can also use this option to add the user to other groups. To add the user to a group, press the Ins key, select a group from the list that appears, and press the Enter key.

▶ **Login Script:** This option allows you to create an individual login script for this user. Enter the necessary login script commands in the window that appears, press the Esc key, and answer Yes to save the script. Chapter 7 describes how to create login scripts.

▶ **Managed Users and Groups:** This option displays a screen that lists the users and groups that this user has rights to control. In small networks, the network supervisor is usually the only user who has the right to add new users and control those users' access to network directories. On large networks, it may be beneficial to assign a few workgroup managers or user account managers, who can add and control some of the other network users. For more information about workgroup managers, see the NetWare documentation.

▶ **Managers:** This option lists the workgroup managers and user account managers that have control over this user.

▶ **Other Information:** This option lists other information about the user, such as his or her ID number. The user's ID number is also the number given to the user's LOGIN directory under the SYS: volume, which is where the user's login script is stored as a file. You cannot change the information in this option.

▶ **Security Equivalence:** Occasionally, you may discover that two users need identical rights. An easy way to give these users the same rights is to assign the rights to one user, and then make the other user "equivalent" to the first user. This option lists the users who this person has been made equal to. To make this user equal to another user, press the Ins key, select a user or group from the list that appears, and press the Enter key. To delete a security equivalence, select the user or group you no longer want this person to be equivalent to and press the Del key.

▶ **Station Restrictions:** This option lets you specify which workstations the user can log in from. Set this restriction if it is important that users use only certain workstations. The user can log in from any workstation shown in the list that appears. If the list is empty, the user can log in from any workstation. To restrict a user to workstations on a given network, press the Ins key, type in the workstation's network address, and then specify whether the user can log in from any workstation (node) that is on that network address. If you don't care which workstation the user logs in from, select Yes. To limit the user to a single workstation on that network address, answer No and type in the node address of the workstation. (You can see the workstation's network and node addresses by logging in to that workstation and typing USERLIST *yourname* /A.) To delete a workstation from the list, highlight the workstation and press the Del key.

▸ **Time Restrictions:** This option displays a screen for setting individual time restrictions for this user. The options are the same as those for systemwide time restrictions, which are described earlier in this chapter. The restrictions you set here override any systemwide time restrictions.

▸ **Trustee Directory Assignments:** This option lists the directories to which this user has trustee rights. To add a directory to the list, press the Ins key, type in the name of the directory, and press the Enter key. To see the rights that the user has in a directory in the list, highlight the name of the directory and press the Enter key. To add rights, press the Ins key and select rights from the new list that appears. To delete a right, highlight the right and press the Del key. For more information about assigning trustee rights, see Chapter 6.

▸ **Volume/Disk Restrictions:** This option is available in NetWare versions 3.*x* and 2.2, but it will appear in version 2.2 only if you specified that you want to limit the amount of the file server's disk space that each user can use when you installed NetWare. To limit a user's disk space, you can enter the amount of space, in kilobytes, that you want to allow this user. This option also shows how much disk space the user has already taken up. (You can also use the DSPACE utility to limit disk space, as described later in this chapter.)

Deleting Users

You can use the SYSCON utility to delete users. Follow these steps:

1 · Log in to a workstation as SUPERVISOR or as a user who is supervisor-equivalent.

2 · To start SYSCON, type

SYSCON

and press the Enter key.

3 · Use the arrow keys to move to the User Information option and press the Enter key.

4 · In the list of current users, highlight the user you want to delete and press the Enter key.

5 · From the User Information menu that appears, highlight the Other Information option. Write the user's ID number on a piece of paper. You will need this number to delete the user's mail directory. Press the Esc key to return to the list of users.

6 · To delete a user, highlight the user in the list and press the Del key.

7 · Answer Yes to confirm that you want to delete the user.

8 · When you are finished, press the Esc key repeatedly until you exit SYSCON.

To free some disk space, you can delete the former user's mail and home directories. The user's mail directory is located in SYS:MAIL and is named with the user's ID number. Delete any files in this user's directory, then delete the directory itself. Next, go to the former user's home directory and delete it and its files. (You may want to view the user's home files before you delete them to make sure you aren't deleting any important files that your company may need later.)

If you do not want to delete the user's mail directory, it's not necessary at this time. The NetWare BINDFIX utility removes mail directories and security assignments for users who no longer exist on the network. (See Chapter 8 for information about using BINDFIX to solve some problems that may occur with users and passwords.)

Using DSPACE to Control a User's Disk Space

As previously mentioned, if you want to limit a user's disk space on a NetWare version 2.2 file server, you must specify this when you install the file server. With NetWare version 3.x, you don't need to make this decision when you install the file server; you can limit a user's disk space at any time by using the SYSCON User Information option, as explained earlier in this chapter (in the section about setting user account restrictions). You can also use the DSPACE menu utility to control a user's disk space.

To use DSPACE, follow these steps:

1 · To start DSPACE from your workstation, type

    DSPACE

    and press the Enter key.

2 · Use the arrow keys to move to the User Restrictions option and press the Enter key to select it. A list of the current users appears.

3 · Highlight the user whose disk usage you want to see and press the Enter key. The screen that appears shows whether the user's space has been limited, how much space is still available to the user, and how much space the user is already using, similar to the display shown in Figure 4.6.

4 · When you are finished, press the Esc key repeatedly until you exit the DSPACE utility.

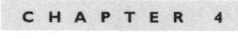

DSPACE's disk-usage display

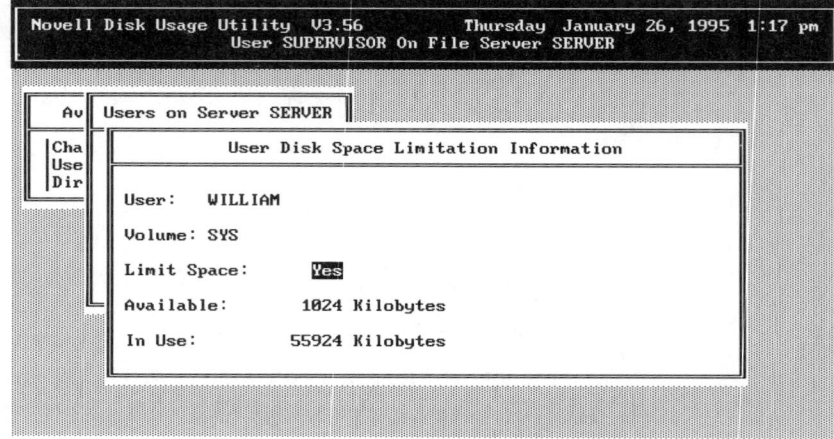

Creating Groups with SYSCON

You can create groups and add users to a group with NetWare's SYSCON menu utility. A group must exist before you can add users to it.

To create a group and add users to it, follow these steps:

1 · Log in to a workstation as SUPERVISOR or as a user who is supervisor-equivalent.

2 · To start SYSCON, type

SYSCON

and press the Enter key.

3 · Use the arrow keys to move to the Group Information option and press the Enter key to select it. A list of all the current groups appears.

4 · To create a new group, press the Ins key, type the name of the new group (such as ARTISTS), and press the Enter key. The new group now appears in the list of groups.

5 · Highlight the name of the new group in the list and press the Enter key.

6 · To add users to the group you just created, select Member List. The list that appears is empty, because you have not yet added any users to this group.

7 · Press the Ins key, and a list of all available users appears.

8 · Highlight the name of the user you want to add to the group and press the Enter key. To add several users at a time, highlight each user and press the F5 key to mark that name. When you have marked all the users, press the Enter key to add them to the group simultaneously.

9 · If you want to give the group you've created a full name, select Full Name, type in the full name of the group (for example, Landscape Artists), and then press the Enter key.

10 · If you want to assign this group trustee rights to directories, select Trustee Directory Assignments. A list of the directories to which this group has trustee rights appears (see Chapter 6 for more information about trustee rights). You can add or remove rights as follows:

  ‣ To add a directory to the list, press the Ins key, type in the name of the directory, and press the Enter key.

  ‣ To see the rights that the group has in a directory in the list, highlight the name of the directory and press the Enter key.

  ‣ To add rights to a directory, press the Ins key and select rights from the new list that appears.

  ‣ To delete a right to a directory, highlight the right and press the Del key.

11 · When you are finished, press the Esc key until you exit SYSCON.

To remove a user from the group, follow steps 1 through 6 above, and then highlight the name of the user you want to delete and press the Del key. When you are prompted to confirm the deletion, choose Yes.

Review

As a network supervisor, your responsibilities include creating user accounts for the people who need to access your network. You might also need to control how the users access the network, by assigning account restrictions. You use the SYSCON menu utility for most of these tasks.

Two users and one group are created automatically when a NetWare network is installed. SUPERVISOR is the account you use to set up and maintain the network, because SUPERVISOR has all rights to the entire network. GUEST is a convenient account name that infrequent users can use to log in with. GUEST usually has limited rights to public areas on the network. The group EVERYONE includes every user on the network. By assigning rights to EVERYONE in directories that all users need (such as the SYS:PUBLIC directory or your application directories), you can save yourself some time.

You can set systemwide account restrictions that apply to every user that is created from that point on. You can also set individual account restrictions for each user that will override any systemwide restrictions.

One account restriction you can use is to limit the amount of disk space that your users can access. You use either the SYSCON or DSPACE utility to set these restrictions.

You can create groups and add users to those groups to help simplify your task of assigning rights to commonly used directories.

Now that you have set up your users and groups, you can set up another important part of your network: printers. The next chapter describes how to plan and install network printing.

Setting Up Printers

Setting up your network printers can be the worst part of your job as a network supervisor. You must deal with many variables, such as which types of printers you're using, where you want to locate the printers on the network, what applications you will be printing from, and which types of paper forms you want to print on.

To set up your network printers, you need to understand how the three elements of NetWare printing fit together: printers, print servers, and print queues. You also should know which NetWare utilities to use to complete different steps of the installation process.

This chapter begins with a review of how network printing works and then provides some guidelines for planning your printing setup. The remainder of the chapter describes the procedures for installing network printers and setting up applications for network printing.

How Does NetWare Printing Work?

As explained in Chapter 1, NetWare printing provides all network users with access to the same printer. However, turning a department of 40 users loose on the same printer could quickly result in chaos or even outright battles. To prevent printing bottlenecks, NetWare includes regulating features, called the print server and the print queue.

A *print server* is a software program that can be installed in either the file server or a workstation. The print server controls how print queues and printers work together. When users send files, those files are placed in a special directory, called a *print queue*, in first-come-first-served order. The print jobs wait in the print queue until the printer is ready to print the next one; then the print server takes a job from the print queue and directs it to the printer.

Planning Your Network Printing

Because network printing can be very confusing and frustrating, it's important to make sure you've planned your setup before you jump in and start trying to hook everything up. The following sections describe some points you need to consider in preparing for network printing.

HOW MANY PRINT SERVERS AND PRINT QUEUES DO YOU NEED?

A print server can control up to 16 printers on a network. Generally, a small network requires only one print server.

Each print queue can feed print jobs to several printers. In addition, a single printer can service several print queues. However, for a small network, the simplest setup is to have one queue per printer. Figure 5.1 illustrates a possible network setup for a small network with three printers.

When you're setting up your network printers, NetWare asks you to name your printers and print queues. If you have more than one printer (or plan to add printers later), it's a good idea to choose printer and queue names that match each

FIGURE 5.1

A network using one print queue per printer

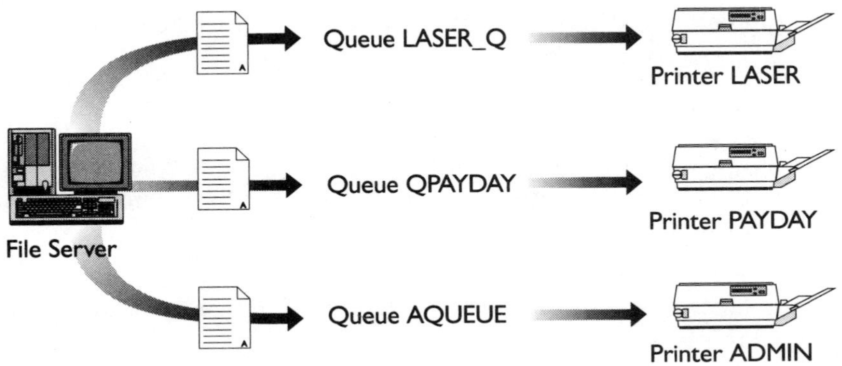

Queue LASER_Q → Printer LASER

Queue QPAYDAY → Printer PAYDAY

File Server

Queue AQUEUE → Printer ADMIN

other. For example, you could use names such as FRED and FRED_Q, ADMIN and AQUEUE, or FAST and QFAST. In Figure 5.1, the printer named LASER services the print queue named LASER_Q.

WHERE DO YOU WANT YOUR PRINT SERVER TO RUN?

With NetWare, you can run a print server in either a file server or a workstation. If you run the print server in a workstation, you must dedicate the workstation to being the print server; it cannot be used as a regular workstation.

The advantage of running the print server in a workstation is that it can improve the performance of both the print server and the file server. You can use any PC-compatible computer as a dedicated print server. For example, an older 8088 or 286 PC will work well as a print server. The advantage of running the print server in the file server is that you save the expense of an extra workstation.

If you are using NetWare version 3.x, you have two choices for the print server:

▶ Load PSERVER.NLM on the file server to run the print server in the file server.

▶ Run PSERVER.EXE on a DOS workstation to run the print server in the workstation.

If you are using NetWare version 2.2, you have three choices for the print server:

▶ Load PSERVER.VAP to run the print server in the file server.

▶ Run PSERVER.EXE on a DOS workstation to run the print server in the workstation.

▶ Use *core printing*. Core printing is a built-in print server that runs in the file server. With core printing, you can have a maximum of five printers on your network, and they all must be attached to the file server. If you need to use more than five printers, or if you want to attach any of your printers to a workstation instead of to the file server, don't use core printing.

Some printers are preconfigured with both a network board and print server software already installed in the printer itself. These printers function as their own print server, and they can be attached to the network cabling instead of to a file server or workstation. See your reseller for more information about these types of printers.

WHERE DO YOU WANT TO LOCATE YOUR PRINTERS?

The next step in planning your printing setup is to decide which computers you want your printers to be attached to. This will determine what software you need to run on the network.

Your printers do not necessarily need to be attached to the computer that is running the print server (either the file server or a dedicated workstation); they can be attached to any DOS workstation on the network. If a printer is attached directly to the print server, it is called a *local* printer. If the printer is attached to a workstation that is not running the print server (a workstation that is not dedicated to running the printer and can be used by an employee for regular work), it is called a *remote* printer. For remote printers, you need to run an extra software program, called RPRINTER.EXE, on the computer to which the remote printer is attached. RPRINTER allows the print server to find and communicate with the remote printer. Figure 5.2 illustrates remote and local printers.

To summarize, you can attach a printer to the network in three different places:

▶ To the file server that is running PSERVER.NLM or PSERVER.VAP. You don't need to run RPRINTER.EXE.

▶ To a dedicated print server (a workstation that is running PSERVER.EXE). You don't need to run RPRINTER.EXE.

▶ To a workstation that is *not* running the print server. You must run RPRINTER.EXE on this workstation. A print server must be running somewhere else on the network.

In addition, some types of printers can function as their own print server.

FIGURE 5.2

Remote and local printers

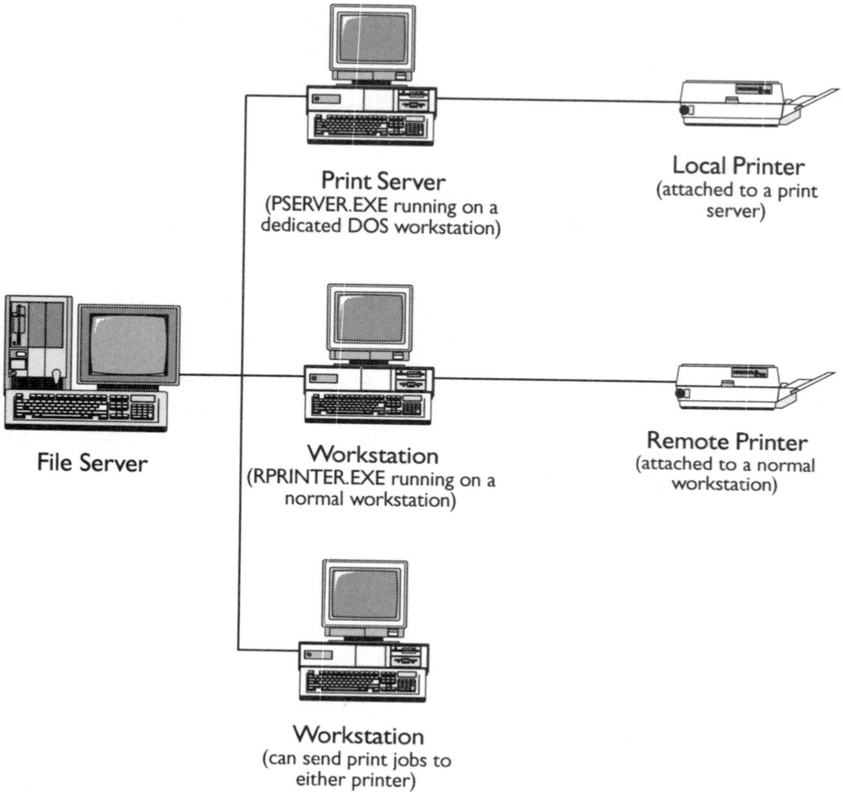

Print Server
(PSERVER.EXE running on a
dedicated DOS workstation)

Local Printer
(attached to a print
server)

File Server

Workstation
(RPRINTER.EXE running on a
normal workstation)

Remote Printer
(attached to a normal
workstation)

Workstation
(can send print jobs to
either printer)

WHO WILL BE THE PRINT QUEUE AND PRINT SERVER OPERATORS?

When you create print queues and print servers, you can specify which users you want to be the print queue and print server operators. The *print queue operator* can work with the print queue by deleting jobs from the queue, rearranging the order in which jobs are printed, and so on. By default, SUPERVISOR is the print queue operator. You may want to assign someone else (or your own user account) to be the print queue operator. Then you won't need to log in as SUPERVISOR every time you want to change something in the queue.

The *print server operator* is also, by default, SUPERVISOR. The print server operator can work with the print server setup. He or she can attach the print server to other file servers, change the queues that the print server services, change queue priorities, and so on. As with the print queue operator, you may want to assign someone else to be the print server operator, too.

You are also allowed to specify users for the print queue and print server you create. By default, the group EVERYONE is assigned as a print queue user and a print server user, so all the network users are allowed to use the queue and server. You probably will not need to change this assignment.

Installing Network Printing on a File Server or Workstation

After you've decided how many print servers and print queues you need, where your print server will run, and where your printers will be located, you can begin installing network printing. The following sections outline the basic procedure and provide guidelines for installing network printing when you will run the print server on a DOS workstation (with PSERVER.EXE), on a NetWare version 3.x file server (with PSERVER.NLM), or on a NetWare version 2.2 file server (with PSERVER.VAP). Refer to the *NetWare Print Server* manual for detailed instructions for running PSERVER.EXE, PSERVER.NLM, or PSERVER.VAP. Core printing with version 2.2 is discussed later in this chapter.

Setting up printing on your NetWare network involves the following basic steps:

1 • Connect the printer.

2 • Run the PCONSOLE utility.

3 • Load the print server software.

4 • If the printer will be a remote printer (attached to a workstation that is not running the print server), run RPRINTER.EXE.

5 · Set up your applications for network printing.

6 · If your users will be using the NPRINT and CAPTURE utilities, create a spooler assignment to specify a default queue for these utilities.

7 · If you have applications that aren't designed for network printing, or if your users need to print screens using the Shift-PrintScreen key combination, you may want to put a CAPTURE command in your login scripts or in a batch file.

8 · If your applications aren't designed for network printing, you may need to use NetWare's PRINTDEF and PRINTCON utilities to simplify your network printing.

Each of these steps is described in more detail in the following sections.

CONNECTING THE PRINTER

Often, network printing problems stem from a printer that wasn't configured correctly to begin with, not from its network connections. You should ensure that the printer is working correctly in stand-alone mode before you install that printer on the network.

Following the instructions in the printer documentation, connect the printer to a DOS workstation's port and try to print directly from the workstation. If the printer works in stand-alone mode (without being hooked up to the network), it should work on the network.

Record all configuration information about the printer and archive this information with the rest of your network information.

If the printer is not connected where you want it to reside permanently, disconnect the printer and attach it to its permanent home.

RUNNING THE PCONSOLE UTILITY

You use the PCONSOLE menu utility to set up print queues and printers. Remember to record the information about your printing setup, such as the names of print queues and printers, the users who are assigned to operate them, which queues are assigned to which printers, and so on.

To run PCONSOLE, you must be logged in to a workstation as SUPERVISOR or as a print server operator. Follow these steps to set up for printing:

1 · To start the utility, type

   PCONSOLE

   and press the Enter key.

2 · Select the Print Queue Information option from the Available Topics menu to create a print queue and assign users and an operator to that queue. (Press the Ins key to create a new queue.)

3 · Select the Print Server Information option from the Available Topics menu to create a print server account and assign a password, an operator, and users to the print server. (Press the Ins key to create a new print server.)

4 · From the Print Server Information menu, select the Print Server Configuration option to add a printer to the print server. Then define the printer by specifying if it will be local or remote and by specifying the port number.

If the printer is serial (connected to the COM1 or COM2 port of a file server or workstation), you must also specify its baud rate, data bits, stop bits, parity, and XON/XOFF protocol. See the printer documentation for this information.

5 · From the Print Server Configuration menu, select the Queues Serviced by Printer option to assign the print queue to its printer.

Optionally, you can also assign the queue a priority from the Print Server Configuration menu. If you have more than one queue assigned to the same printer, you can assign one queue priority 1 and another priority 2, for example. To assign a priority, press the Ins key at the File Server/Queue/Priority box. The default is priority 1.

LOADING THE PRINT SERVER SOFTWARE

Load the print server software onto the computer that will be running the print server:

▸ On a NetWare version 3.x file server, load PSERVER.NLM.

▸ On a NetWare version 2.2 file server, reboot the file server and answer Yes when it asks if you want to load the VAP.

▸ On a NetWare version 3.x or 2.2 workstation, modify the workstation's SHELL.CFG file or NET.CFG file to add the line

SPX=60

Then reboot the workstation, log in to the network, and run PSERVER.EXE.

RUNNING RPRINTER

If the printer will be a remote printer (attached to a workstation that is not running the print server), change the workstation's SHELL.CFG or NET.CFG file to add the line

SPX=60

and delete the line

LOCAL PRINTERS=0

Then reboot the workstation, log in to the network, and run RPRINTER.EXE.

If you will attach two remote printers to the same workstation, you must run RPRINTER twice. Each remote printer needs its own copy of RPRINTER.

SETTING UP APPLICATIONS FOR NETWORK PRINTING

Set up your applications for network printing by following the instructions in the application's documentation.

If your application asks for network printer numbers instead of print queues, you need to set up spooler assignments. *Spooler assignments* give a print queue name a corresponding printer number (0 through 4) so that the application and NetWare can communicate.

To create a spooler assignment, you type a SPOOL command at the file server console. You can also put spooler commands in the file server's AUTOEXEC.SYS (for NetWare version 2.2) or AUTOEXEC.NCF (for version 3.*x*) file so that they will automatically be in place whenever the file server is rebooted. The command format you use for creating spooler assignments is

SPOOL *n queuename*

Replace *n* with the printer number you want (0 to 4). Replace *queuename* with the name of the queue you want assigned to that printer number. Note that the printer numbers for spooler assignments are not the same as the printer numbers shown in the PCONSOLE utility.

CREATING A SPOOLER ASSIGNMENT FOR NPRINT AND CAPTURE

If your users will be using the NPRINT and CAPTURE utilities, create a spooler assignment to specify a default queue for these utilities to use. Set Spool 0 to the queue where you want NPRINT and CAPTURE to send print jobs. This allows users to execute NPRINT and CAPTURE commands without needing to specify a queue. For example, if you want CAPTURE and NPRINT to automatically send jobs to the queue named LASER_Q, type this command at the file server console:

SPOOL 0 LASER_Q

Then add this same command to the file server's AUTOEXEC.SYS (or AUTOEXEC.NCF) file.

ADDING CAPTURE TO LOGIN SCRIPTS OR BATCH FILES

If you will be using applications that aren't designed for network printing, or if your users need to print screens using the Shift-PrintScreen key combination, you may want to put a CAPTURE command in your login scripts or in a batch file. A stand-alone application expects a printer to be attached to a port on the workstation. Therefore, the application tries to send print jobs to that port. CAPTURE simply redirects the print jobs from the port to a network print queue.

You can include a CAPTURE command in login scripts if you want the command to be in effect all the time. Otherwise, you can place the CAPTURE command in a batch file in the user's home directory (or in the PUBLIC directory if all users need the same batch file) or in a menu as an option. (Creating menus for users is discussed in Chapter 7.)

For example, suppose you want a user to print from an application called Wild, which isn't designed for network printing. You want the user to execute the CAPTURE command to specify that jobs printed from this application should go to the LASER_Q queue. You also want the job to be printed without a banner page and to timeout after five seconds (which means the job will be sent to the printer after five seconds, whether or not you've exited the application). You can create a batch file called LASER.BAT that would execute the command for the user and run the Wild application automatically.

Use a text editor to create the batch file and save it as an ASCII file, or use DOS's COPY CON command to create the file directly from the command line. You can use the ENDCAP command to stop CAPTURE from redirecting print jobs when you exit the application if you need to release the workstation's port.

If you create the batch file with a text editor, type the following lines:

```
CAPTURE Q=LASER_Q NB TI=5
WILD
ENDCAP
```

To use the COPY CON command to create the same batch file, type these commands:

```
COPY CON LASER.BAT
CAPTURE Q=LASER_Q NB TI=5
```

```
WILD
ENDCAP
^Z
```

To create the ^Z at the end of the file, press the Ctrl and Z keys at the same time.

Now when the user types LASER at the command line, the CAPTURE command will be executed, and the Wild application will automatically open. Then when the user exits the Wild application, ENDCAP will execute and end the CAPTURE command.

For more information about using CAPTURE and ENDCAP, see the NetWare documentation.

USING THE PRINTDEF AND PRINTCON UTILITIES

If your applications aren't designed for network printing, you may need to use two additional NetWare utilities to simplify your network printing: PRINTDEF and PRINTCON.

Use PRINTDEF to specify the brand of printer you are using and the types of paper (called *forms*) you want to print on. This is helpful if you use applications that print on different types of paper, such as paychecks, invoices, and so on. Figure 5.3 shows the PRINTDEF screen for selecting paper forms.

Use PRINTCON to tell the printer how the print job should be printed on the form you set up in PRINTDEF. With PRINTCON, you set up print job configurations, which specify items such as whether or not a banner page will be printed and which queue the job should be sent to.

See the NetWare documentation for more information about using PRINTDEF and PRINTCON.

PRINTDEF's form
specification screen

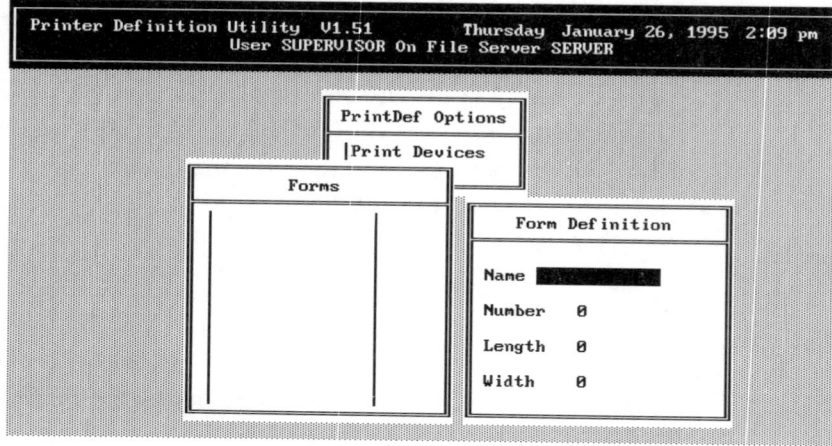

Installing NetWare Version 2.2 Core Printing

This section outlines the basic steps for setting up core printing with NetWare version 2.2. For more detailed instructions, refer to the NetWare version 2.2 *Using the Network* manual.

To set up core printing, you will execute several commands at the file server console. To make sure your printing is set up correctly every time the file server is rebooted, you should put several of these commands in your file server's AUTOEXEC.SYS file. As you follow the instructions, record the commands you execute so that you can put them in the AUTOEXEC.SYS file later.

1 · Using the printer manufacturer's documentation, connect the printer to a DOS workstation's port and try to print directly from the workstation.

2 · Record all configuration information about the printer and archive this information with the rest of your network information.

3 · If the printer works in stand-alone mode, disconnect it and attach it to the file server.

4 · Create a print queue by typing the following command at the file server console:

QUEUE *queuename* CREATE

You do not need to put this command in the server's AUTOEXEC.SYS file. The first time you execute this command, the queue is created permanently, so it's not necessary to reexecute the command every time the file server is booted.

5 · Define a printer by typing the following command at the file server console:

PRINTER *n* CREATE *port*

Replace *n* with a number from 0 to 4 (start with 0 for the first printer you define). Replace *port* with COM1, COM2, LPT1, LPT2, or LPT3, depending on the port to which you attached the printer.

The command shown above assumes the printer is using default configuration settings (baud rate, stop bits, and so on). If you are using a serial (COM1 or COM2) printer and you want to specify different configuration settings, add the options at the end of the PRINTER CREATE command. For example, to change the baud rate on printer 0 from the default 9600 to 19200, type

PRINTER 0 CREATE COM1 BAUD=19200

6 · Record the PRINTER CREATE command you used so that you can put it in the AUTOEXEC.SYS file later.

7 · Assign the queue to a printer by typing the following command at the file server console:

PRINTER *n* ADD *queuename*

Replace *n* with the number of the printer, and replace *queuename* with the name of the queue.

If you have more than one queue going to the same printer, you may want to assign the queues priorities. To assign a queue a priority, add the priority number at the end of the command:

PRINTER *n* ADD *queuename* PRIORITY *p*

Replace *p* with the priority you want the queue to have (such as 1 or 2). Assigning a priority is optional.

8 · Record the PRINTER ADD command you used so that you can put it in the AUTOEXEC.SYS file later.

9 · Set up your applications for network printing by following the application's documentation.

If your application asks for network printer numbers instead of print queues, you need to set up spooler assignments, as described earlier in the chapter (in the section about setting up applications for network printing). Record the SPOOL command you used so that you can put it in the AUTOEXEC.SYS file later.

10 · If your users will be using the NPRINT and CAPTURE utilities, create a spooler assignment to specify a default queue for these utilities to use, as described earlier in this chapter.

11 · Record the SPOOL command you used for CAPTURE so that you can put it in the AUTOEXEC.SYS file.

12 · Edit the AUTOEXEC.SYS file to add all the PRINTER and SPOOL commands to it.

13 · Use PCONSOLE from a workstation to assign queue operators and queue users if you need to change the defaults. As explained earlier in the chapter, SUPERVISOR is the default print queue operator, and the group EVERYONE is assigned to be users of the print queue.

14 · If you have applications that aren't designed for network printing, or if your users need to print screens using the Shift-PrintScreen keys, you may want to put a CAPTURE command in your login scripts or in a batch file, as explained earlier in this chapter.

15 · If your applications aren't designed for network printing, you may need to use NetWare's PRINTDEF utility to specify the brand of printer and the forms you will be using, and PRINTCON to tell the printer how the print job should be printed. See the section about these utilities earlier in this chapter and the NetWare documentation for more information about using PRINTDEF and PRINTCON.

Review

NetWare controls network printing by using print servers. A print server is a software program that can be installed in either the file server or a workstation. When users send jobs to be printed, the jobs are stored in a print queue, then the print server sends them one-by-one to the printer.

One print server can control up to 16 printers (unless you are using NetWare version 2.2 core printing, which supports up to 5 printers).

Print queues can feed print jobs to more than one printer, and printers can accept jobs from more than one queue. However, it usually makes life easier to have one queue per printer.

You can attach printers to any file server or DOS workstation on the network. If you attach a printer to a workstation that is not running the print server software (PSERVER.EXE), you must run RPRINTER.EXE on that workstation so that the printer will be recognized by the print server. Printers that are attached to print servers are called local printers. Printers that are attached to workstations that are not running print servers are called remote printers.

You can establish print queue and print server operators and users. SUPERVISOR is the default print queue and print server operator. You can assign additional users to be the operator, too. The group EVERYONE is assigned to be a user of the print server and print queues. This is acceptable when you want all your users to be able to see and use the print server and queues.

To install NetWare printing using PSERVER.EXE, PSERVER.NLM, or PSER-VER.VAP, use the PCONSOLE utility to set up your print queues and print servers. To install NetWare version 2.2 core printing, use the print server that is built into the file server. You also use several console commands to set up your print queues and print servers.

To set up your applications for printing on the network, follow the instructions in the application's documentation. If you have applications that were not designed for network printing, you may need to use some additional NetWare utilities. PRINTDEF lets you specify the type of printer and forms (paper) you will use. PRINTCON lets you set up print job configurations that specify how to print on the forms you specified with PRINTDEF. NPRINT and CAPTURE are utilities you can use to direct print jobs to the network instead of to a local printer.

To install NetWare version 2.2 core printing, you use the print server that is built into the file server. You also use several console commands to set up your print queues and print servers.

This and the previous chapters described how to install your network and set up your users and resources. The next chapter describes how to protect your network files. You will learn how to control users' access to network directories with trustee rights and other forms of network security.

CHAPTER 6

Securing Your Network

NetWare comes with a powerful set of security tools that help you protect the information on your network. With NetWare security, you can control who logs in, what files they can use, and what they can do with those files. In fact, NetWare security is so flexible, you can allow different users to do different things with your network files.

This chapter explains the features that make up NetWare network security and describes how to use those tools to your advantage. First you will learn how security rights affect users' access to network directories and files. Then you will learn how to view, grant, change, and remove rights, as well as assign and change file and directory attributes.

Why Is Network Security Important?

A network allows users to access and share files, applications, and other resources. On the surface, this type of open environment sounds great. But what if there are some files you don't want everyone to access, or files that you want users to be able to open but not change or delete? Without network security, everyone would have access to every network file. With network security, you can control who accesses network information and what they can do with it when they access it.

NetWare security allows you to protect the network in a variety of ways:

▸ Keep unauthorized users from logging in to your network and accessing your files.

▸ Prevent users from seeing confidential files, such as personnel records, budget files, personal memos, and so on.

▸ Protect applications from being copied, deleted, changed, or pirated.

▸ Prevent users from accidently deleting or overwriting important files.

What Makes Up NetWare Security?

NetWare provides several security tools that allow you to control access to your network:

- **Login security:** Passwords ensure that only authorized users can log in. You can use login and account restrictions to make sure that authorized users can log in only during allowed times, that they don't use more than their allotted disk space or time, and that they change their password when they are supposed to.

- **Trustee rights:** You can assign various trustee rights to each user and group. Trustee rights determine what a user can do to a particular directory or file. For example, trustee rights control whether a user can read a file, change it, change its name, delete it, or manage other users' rights to it.

- **Rights Masks:** Every directory in NetWare version 2.2 has a Maximum Rights Mask, which can block out rights that a trustee may have been given to that directory. In NetWare version 3.x, every directory and file has an Inherited Rights Mask, which can filter out trustee rights that a user may be inheriting from a parent directory.

- **Directory and file attributes:** Attributes are assigned to files and directories. These attributes affect all users and override trustee rights. Attributes control whether the file or directory can be shared by several users, whether it can be deleted, and so on.

Each of these NetWare security tools is explained in this chapter.

Login Security: Controlling Who Logs In

When you create a user account on your network, you authorize that user to log in to the network. You can also assign that user a *password*. Without the correct password, the user can't log in, even if the user has an account. Passwords help ensure that an intruder can't log in as another user. Assigning passwords is described in Chapter 4.

When you add a network user, you also have the option of setting various *account restrictions* and *login restrictions* for that user. Generally, restrictions help you control your network by regulating when users can log in, how much disk space they can use, and so on. Account and login restrictions are also described in Chapter 4.

Passwords and login restrictions help you control who can get into your network. To control what users can do with the network files and directories after they've logged in, you use trustee rights and directory and file attributes.

How Do Trustee Rights Work?

Trustee rights give users or groups permission to perform various tasks with a file or directory. For example, trustee rights control whether a user can see the files in a directory, read the files, delete them, change them, change their names, or change other users' rights to those files.

You can assign a user any combination of trustee rights to a directory or file. This allows you greater flexibility to control exactly how a user can work with a directory or file. For example, you can assign a user the rights to see and read the files in a directory called REPORTS, but restrict the user from changing or deleting any files in that directory. You can protect personnel files by granting certain users the rights they need to work with the files and restricting everyone else from even seeing those files.

Once you have given a user trustee rights to a directory, the user can inherit those trustee rights in all of that directory's subdirectories. You need to keep this in mind as you create subdirectories. When you first create a subdirectory, any user that has rights to the parent directory will get identical rights to the new subdirectory.

You can change users' rights to a subdirectory in two ways. One method is to give the users new rights to the subdirectory, which will override the rights the users would have otherwise inherited from the parent directory. Note that if you change a user's rights in a subdirectory, then create a new subdirectory beneath the first subdirectory, the user will inherit those new rights in the second subdirectory.

The other way to change users' rights to a subdirectory is to block the users' rights with a Rights Mask, which belongs to the directory. Working with Rights Masks is described later in this chapter.

Shortcuts: Assigning Trustee Rights to Several Users

You can use two shortcuts to assign identical trustee rights to several users. One shortcut is to assign trustee rights to a group. The other is to use security equivalence. These methods are described in the following sections.

USING GROUPS

Suppose several users need identical trustee rights to work in a word processing directory. By using the SYSCON utility, you can create a group and assign several users to that group. Then you can grant the group the necessary trustee rights to the word processing directory. All users in the group get the same level of access to the directory, and you saved time by not needing to grant rights to each individual user. Using the SYSCON utility to create groups and assigning users to groups are described in Chapter 4.

USING SECURITY EQUIVALENCES

Another shortcut for assigning rights is to use a NetWare feature called *security equivalence*. NetWare lets you specify that one user is "equivalent" to another user. This gives the second user the same trustee rights that are explicitly given to the first user.

The key phrase here is "explicitly given." A security equivalence does not transfer one user's group rights or other security equivalences to the second user. Security equivalence gives the second user only those trustee rights that were specifically assigned to the first user.

For example, if user Ian is security equivalent to user Jonathan, Ian will be able to exercise all the trustee rights that Jonathan has been given through individual trustee assignments. Ian will not get any trustee rights that Jonathan received by belonging to a group. Also, if Jonathan is security equivalent to user Pascale, Ian will *not* be security equivalent to Pascale as well. Figure 6.1 illustrates which rights Ian will get because of his security equivalence to Jonathan.

One valuable way to use security equivalence is to create a user account and make it security equivalent to the user SUPERVISOR. The user SUPERVISOR is the most powerful user on the network. SUPERVISOR has all rights to all files

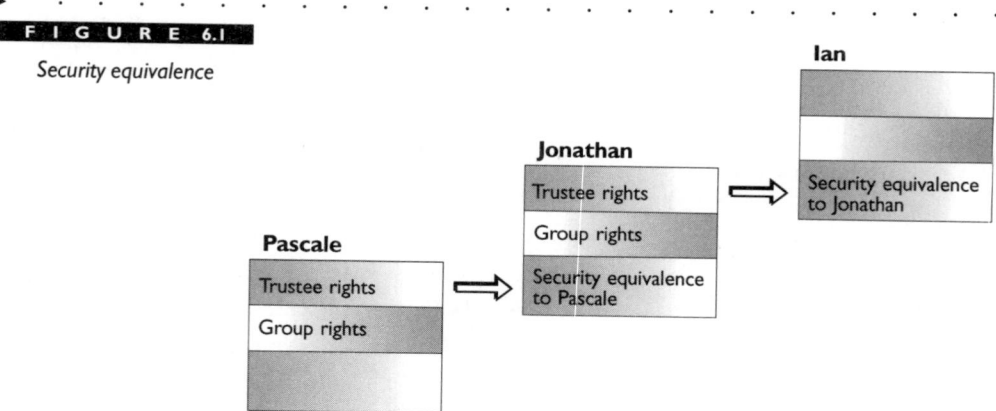

FIGURE 6.1

Security equivalence

and directories and is the only user authorized to perform many important network tasks. Because this user is so important, it is critical that you don't forget the SUPERVISOR's password. If you do lose this password, you'll need to call NetWare technical support for help.

Therefore, a good safety practice is to create another user and give that user security equivalence to the SUPERVISOR. This is sometimes called "the backdoor." You can be your own backdoor by giving your own account a security equivalence to SUPERVISOR. Then your user account, which is probably your own name, will have the equivalent rights of SUPERVISOR. This also means if you are already logged in under your own name and you need to perform a supervisory task on the network, you don't have to log out of your own account and log in as SUPERVISOR. You already have all of SUPERVISOR's rights.

You can also use security equivalences to give ordinary users identical rights to other users. For example, suppose user John goes on vacation and user Anne needs to access some of John's files, which are located in several directories to which Anne doesn't have rights. You can give Anne security equivalence to John so that Anne can access the same directories John could. But Anne also gets rights to John's home directory, so you probably will want to delete the equivalence as soon as Anne no longer needs access to John's files.

You might also use security equivalences if you employ several temporary workers who don't have their own personal directories and who all need access to the same directories. You could create one user account that is permanent and give it rights to all the necessary directories. Then every time another temporary worker is hired, you can create an account for the new employee and assign that person a security equivalence to the permanent user account. This way, you won't need to remember all the directories that person needs to access and the various combinations of rights required.

You can assign security equivalences with the NetWare SYSCON utility, as described later in this chapter.

Using Trustee Rights

Both NetWare versions 2.2 and 3.*x* use trustee rights to control file and directory access, but there are two differences:

▸ NetWare version 2.2 includes seven trustee rights that can be assigned to users. NetWare version 3.*x* has the same seven trustee rights as version 2.2, plus an eighth one, Supervisory, which gives the user complete control over the file or directory.

▸ In NetWare version 2.2, trustee rights apply to directories only. In NetWare 3.*x*, trustee rights can be applied to directories and to individual files.

NetWare versions 2.2 and 3.*x* also both use Rights Masks to further control access to files. Version 2.2's directories have Maximum Rights Masks; version 3.*x* directories and files have Inherited Rights Masks.

The following sections describe trustee rights in NetWare versions 2.2 and 3.*x*. You grant and manage trustee rights by using NetWare utilities, as explained later in this chapter.

TRUSTEE RIGHTS AND RIGHTS MASKS IN NETWARE VERSION 2.2

In NetWare version 2.2, the combination of trustee rights you assign to a user regulates how that user can work in a particular directory, as well as in its files and subdirectories. The seven trustee rights that you can assign to users with version 2.2 are described in Table 6.1. The abbreviations that NetWare uses for trustee rights are also shown in the table.

TABLE 6.1	RIGHT	ABBREVIATION	EXPLANATION
NetWare Version 2.2 Trustee Rights	Read	R	Allows you to open and read files in the directory.
	Write	W	Allows you to open and write to (change) files in the directory.
	Create	C	Allows you to create subdirectories and files and write to files in the directory.
	Erase	E	Allows you to delete the directory and its files and subdirectories.
	Modify	M	Allows you to change the name, directory attributes, or file attributes of the files and subdirectories in the directory.
	File Scan	F	Allows you to see the names of all files and subdirectories in the directory.
	Access Control	A	Allows you to change the directory's Maximum Rights Mask and trustee assignments.

The Maximum Rights Mask: Blocking Users' Trustee Rights

Just because you've been given rights to a directory doesn't necessarily mean you will be able to exercise those rights. Every directory created in NetWare version 2.2 has a *Maximum Rights Mask* assigned to it automatically. A directory's Maximum Rights Mask controls what rights a user can exercise in that directory. By default, this mask contains all the available trustee rights, so that a user can exercise any right he or she has been granted in that directory.

For example, if a user is given the Read and File Scan rights to a directory and that directory's Maximum Rights Mask contains all the rights, the user will be able to exercise the Read and File Scan rights. But if you remove the Read right from the directory's mask, the user will be able to exercise only the File Scan right in that directory. Figure 6.2 illustrates how removing a right from the Maximum Rights Mask prevents the user from exercising that right.

The point to keep in mind is that if a right does not appear in the Maximum Rights Mask, no user can exercise that right. On the other hand, if a right *does* appear in the mask, that doesn't mean all users can exercise that right. Only those users who are specifically granted that right through a trustee assignment will be able to exercise it.

Effective Rights in NetWare Version 2.2: What Rights Does a User Really Have?

You should understand that several different factors affect the rights that a user can really exercise in a directory. The user can get rights by either inheriting rights from a parent directory or by being given specific trustee assignments in the directory through individual assignments, group assignments, security equivalences, or any combination of these.

You can take rights away from a user by blocking rights with the Maximum Rights Mask or by overriding inherited rights by giving the user a new trustee assignment in that directory. Any new trustee assignment, whether it is through an

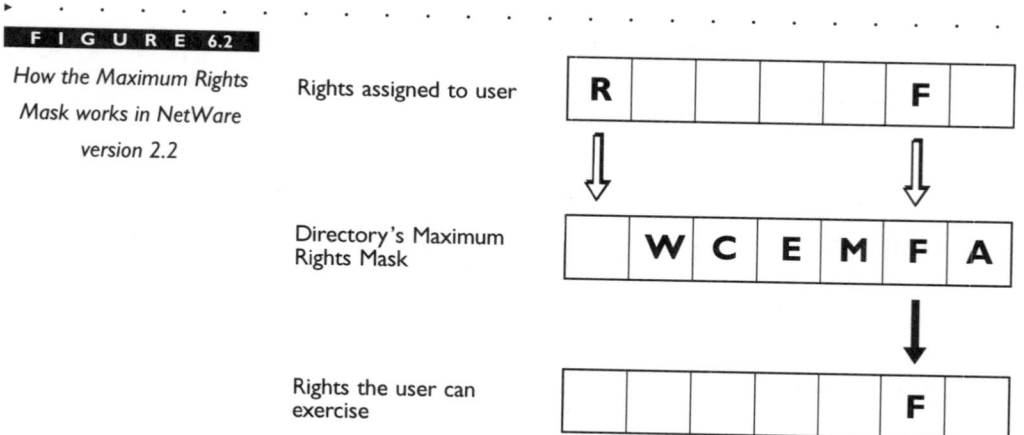

FIGURE 6.2

How the Maximum Rights Mask works in NetWare version 2.2

Rights assigned to user

| R | | | | F | |

Directory's Maximum Rights Mask

| | W | C | E | M | F | A |

Rights the user can exercise

| | | | | F | |

individual assignment, a group assignment, or a combination of the two, will replace a user's inherited rights.

The rights that a user can ultimately exercise in a directory are called the user's *effective rights*. Effective rights are all the rights that the user has been granted, minus those that are blocked by the Maximum Rights Mask.

All directories, by default, allow all rights in their Maximum Rights Mask. If you don't change a directory's mask, a user's effective rights in the directory are the sum of all of his or her rights from the following sources:

- Rights inherited from a parent directory

- Individual trustee assignments

- Trustee assignments given to groups the user belongs to

- Security equivalences

For example, if the Maximum Rights Mask for the directory RESEARCH.NEW allows all rights to be exercised, Ted's effective rights in that directory are the sum of all of his assignments. Figure 6.3 shows how these assignments form his effective rights.

Now suppose you modify the Maximum Rights Mask for the directory RESEARCH.NEW to block all but the Read and File Scan rights. Regardless of whether Ted has been granted other trustee rights to the directory, the only rights he will be able to exercise are Read and File Scan. Figure 6.4 shows Ted's effective rights in the directory with a modified mask.

Trustee Rights and Rights Masks in NetWare Version 3.x

In NetWare version 3.x, the combination of trustee rights you assign a user regulates how that user can work in a particular directory, as well as in its files and subdirectories. Table 6.2 describes the eight trustee rights that you can assign to users. It also lists the abbreviation NetWare uses for each trustee right.

R					**F**	

Rights Ted inherits from a parent directory

	W	**C**				

Ted's trustee assignment for this directory

			E			

Group trustee assignment for this directory

				M		

Security equivalence to another user

R	**W**	**C**	**E**	**M**	**F**	

Ted's total possible rights

R	**W**	**C**	**E**	**M**	**F**	**A**

This directory's Maximum Rights Mask

R	**W**	**C**	**E**	**M**	**F**	

Ted's effective rights in this directory

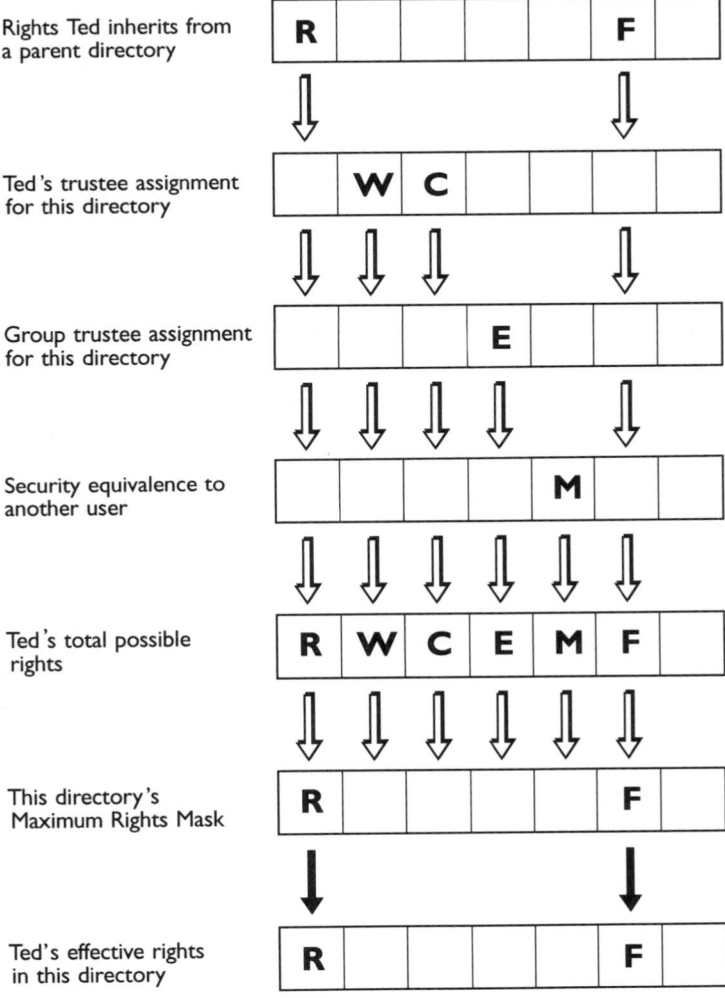

FIGURE 6.4

A user's effective rights after the Maximum Rights Mask is changed

Rights Ted inherits from a parent directory

Ted's trustee assignment for this directory

Group trustee assignment for this directory

Security equivalence to another user

Ted's total possible rights

This directory's Maximum Rights Mask

Ted's effective rights in this directory

RIGHT	ABBREVIATION	EXPLANATION
Read	R	In a directory, allows you to open and read files in the directory. In a file, allows you to open and read the file.
Write	W	In a directory, allows you to open and write to (change) files in the directory. In a file, allows you to open and write to the file.
Create	C	In a directory, allows you to create subdirectories and files and write to files in the directory. In a file, allows you to salvage the file if it is deleted.
Erase	E	In a directory, allows you to delete the directory and its files and subdirectories. In a file, allows you to delete the file.
Modify	M	In a directory, allows you to change the name, directory attributes, and file attributes of the files and subdirectories in the directory. In a file, allows you to change the name or file attributes of the file.
File Scan	F	In a directory, allows you to see the names of all files and subdirectories in the directory. In a file, allows you to see the name of the file.
Access Control	A	In a directory, allows you to change the directory's Inherited Rights Mask and trustee assignments. In a file, allows you to change the file's Inherited Rights Mask and trustee assignments.

TABLE 6.2
NetWare Version 3.11
Trustee Rights (continued)

RIGHT	ABBREVIATION	EXPLANATION
Supervisory	S	In a directory, gives you all rights to files and subdirectories in the directory. In a file, gives you all rights to the file. The Supervisory right cannot be taken away.

The Inherited Rights Mask: Blocking Users' Inherited Rights

Just because you've inherited rights to a directory or file from a parent directory doesn't necessarily mean you will be able to exercise those rights. Every directory and file that is created in NetWare version 3.*x* has an *Inherited Rights Mask* assigned to it automatically. An Inherited Rights Mask controls what rights a user can inherit from a parent directory and use in the subdirectory or file.

By default, the Inherited Rights Mask permits all available trustee rights to be inherited. This means that it will allow a user to inherit and exercise any right that the user had in the parent directory.

For example, if a user has the Read and File Scan rights in the parent directory, and the subdirectory's mask contains all the rights, the user will be able to exercise the Read and File Scan rights in the subdirectory. On the other hand, if you remove the Read right from the subdirectory's mask, the user will be able to exercise only the File Scan right in the subdirectory. Figure 6.5 illustrates how removing a right from the Inherited Rights Mask prevents the user from inheriting and exercising that right.

The Inherited Rights Mask affects only the rights the user is inheriting from a parent directory. If a user is given a specific trustee assignment in a subdirectory, that assignment cancels any inherited rights, so restrictions in the Inherited Rights Mask are not considered.

Remember that if a right does not appear in the Inherited Rights Mask, no user can inherit that right. On the other hand, if a right *does* appear in the mask, that doesn't mean all users can inherit that right. Only those users who had that right in the parent directory will be able to inherit it.

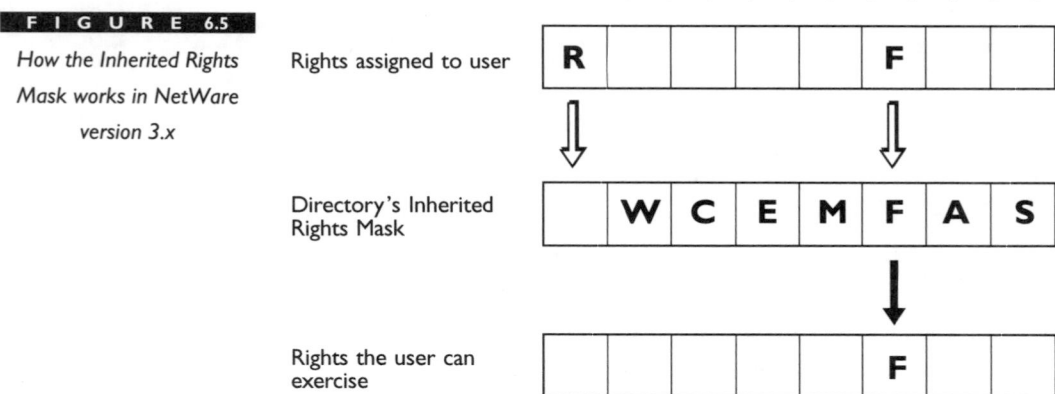

FIGURE 6.5

How the Inherited Rights Mask works in NetWare version 3.x

Effective Rights in NetWare Version 3.*x*: What Rights Does a User Really Have?

Several different factors affect the rights that a user can really exercise in a directory. The user can get rights either by inheriting rights from a parent directory or by being given specific trustee assignments in the directory through individual assignments, group assignments, security equivalences, or any combination of these.

You can take rights away from a user either by blocking inherited rights with the Inherited Rights Mask, or by overriding inherited rights by giving the user a new trustee assignment in that directory. Any new trustee assignment, whether it is through an individual assignment, a group assignment, or a combination of the two, will replace a user's inherited rights.

The rights that a user can ultimately exercise in a directory are called the user's *effective rights*. Effective rights are calculated in one of two ways:

▸ The rights the user is inheriting from the parent directory, minus the rights blocked by the Inherited Rights Mask

▸ The sum of all individual and group trustee assignments and security equivalences (these assignments are not affected by the Inherited Rights Mask)

When a new directory or file is created, that directory's or file's Inherited Rights Mask permits all rights to be inherited. Therefore, if a user has trustee rights in a parent directory, the user will inherit those rights and be able to exercise them in the subdirectory, as long as the subdirectory's default Inherited Rights Mask has not been changed.

For example, suppose that user Shari has the Read and File Scan rights in the directory ALPHA. Then a new subdirectory, called BETA, is created beneath the ALPHA directory. BETA's Inherited Rights Mask permits all rights to be inherited. Therefore, Shari will inherit and be able to exercise the Read and File Scan rights in the subdirectory BETA. Figure 6.6 illustrates this situation.

Now suppose that in another directory, called GREECE, Shari has all but the Supervisory right. A subdirectory of GREECE, called ATHENS, has had its Inherited Rights Mask modified so that it contains only the Read and File Scan rights. In the ATHENS subdirectory, Shari will be able to inherit and exercise only the Read and File Scan rights, even though she has almost all trustee rights in the parent directory. Figure 6.7 shows how the Inherited Rights Mask of the ATHENS subdirectory blocked Shari's inherited rights.

FIGURE 6.6

A user's effective inherited rights in NetWare version 3.x

Rights Shari has in the directory ALPHA

| R | | | | | F | | |

The subdirectory BETA's Inherited Rights Mask

| R | W | C | E | M | F | A | S |

Rights Shari can exercise in BETA

| R | | | | | F | | |

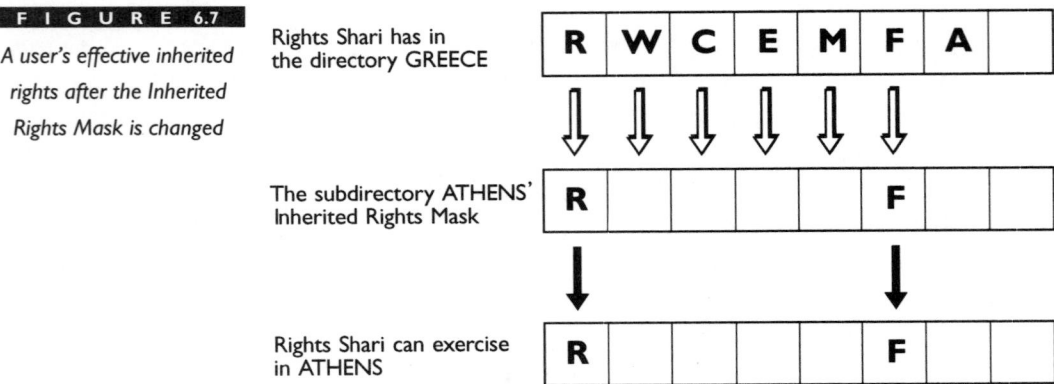

A user's effective inherited rights after the Inherited Rights Mask is changed

Rights Shari has in the directory GREECE

| R | W | C | E | M | F | A | |

The subdirectory ATHENS' Inherited Rights Mask

| R | | | | | F | | |

Rights Shari can exercise in ATHENS

| R | | | | | F | | |

When a user is granted a trustee assignment to a directory, that new trustee assignment is *not* added to the user's inherited rights; the new trustee assignment completely *replaces* any inherited rights the user had. This explains why the Inherited Rights Mask affects only the rights a user is inheriting from a parent directory. The mask has no effect on any trustee rights that the user may be granted specifically in that directory. For example, if Shari were granted individual trustee rights or group trustee rights to the ATHENS subdirectory, or if she had a security equivalence to someone who has trustee rights to ATHENS, the Inherited Rights Mask would be ignored. Figure 6.8 shows Shari's new trustee rights to ATHENS.

FIGURE 6.8

The Inherited Rights Mask doesn't affect individual trustee rights

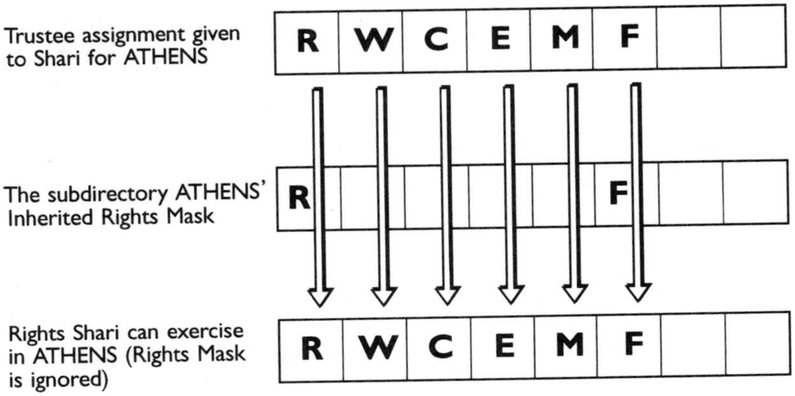

Trustee assignment given to Shari for ATHENS

| R | W | C | E | M | F | | |

The subdirectory ATHENS' Inherited Rights Mask

| R | | | | | F | | |

Rights Shari can exercise in ATHENS (Rights Mask is ignored)

| R | W | C | E | M | F | | |

Using NetWare Utilities to Assign and Manage Rights

You can use several NetWare utilities to work with rights:

▸ **RIGHTS:** This command line utility allows you see your own effective rights in a directory (or file in NetWare version 3.x).

▸ **TLIST:** This command line utility allows you to see the list of users who are trustees of a directory (or file in NetWare version 3.x).

▸ **GRANT:** This command line utility allows you to assign trustee rights to other users.

▸ **FILER:** This menu utility allows you to see all the trustee rights to a directory (or file in version 3.x) and change those rights. It also lets you modify the directory's (or file's in version 3.x) Rights Mask.

▶ **SYSCON:** This menu utility allows you to see all the trustee assignments a user or group has and change those rights. It also lets you assign security equivalences.

▶ **REMOVE:** This command line utility allows you to delete all of another user's trustee rights and remove the trustee from the directory's (or file's in version 3.x) trustee list.

▶ **REVOKE:** This command line utility allows you to remove some or all of another user's trustee rights but still leave that user in the directory's (or file's in version 3.x) trustee list.

▶ **SECURITY:** This command line utility allows you to check for security holes in your network setup.

SEEING YOUR EFFECTIVE RIGHTS WITH RIGHTS

To see your effective rights in a directory, use the RIGHTS command line utility. For example, to see your effective rights in the directory that is mapped to drive G:, type

RIGHTS G:

In NetWare version 3.x, you can use RIGHTS to see your effective rights in a file. For example, to see your rights in the REPORT.3 file, which is located in drive G:, type

RIGHTS G:REPORT.3

LISTING THE TRUSTEES OF A DIRECTORY OR FILE WITH TLIST

To list all the users and groups who have trustee rights to a directory (or a file in NetWare version 3.x), use the TLIST command line utility. For example, to see the users and groups who have rights to the SYS:PUBLIC directory, which is mapped to drive Y:, type

TLIST Y:

GRANTING TRUSTEE RIGHTS TO A USER WITH GRANT

To give a user trustee rights to a directory (or file, in NetWare version 3.*x*), you must have the Access Control right to the directory (or file).

To assign trustee rights to your network users, use the GRANT command line utility. The command format for GRANT is

GRANT *rights* FOR *path* TO *trustees*

Use the abbreviation for each right, and separate each right with a space. For example, to grant user Scott the Read, Write, and File Scan rights to the directory that is mapped to drive P:, type

GRANT R W F FOR P: TO SCOTT

If you have a group name that is the same as a username, use either the word USER or GROUP in front of the name to specify which one you want. For example, if Scott is the name of a group as well as a user, and you want to assign Read, Write, and File Scan rights to the *group* Scott, type

GRANT R W F FOR P: TO GROUP SCOTT

GRANTING AND REVOKING TRUSTEE RIGHTS WITH FILER

If you have the Access Control right in a directory or file, you can use the FILER menu utility to add or delete trustees and change their rights to a directory or file. Follow these steps:

1 · Start the FILER utility from your workstation by typing FILER and pressing the Enter key. The Available Topics menu appears.

2 · If you are in the directory whose trustees you want to see, use the arrow keys to move to the Current Directory Information option and press the Enter key to select it. If you want to see the trustees for a sub-directory or file, choose the Directory Contents option and select the subdirectory or file from the list that appears. Then select View/Set Directory (or File) Information.

3 · Move the cursor to the Trustees option and press the Enter key. A list of all the trustees and their rights appears, as shown in the example in Figure 6.9.

4 · Take one of the following actions, depending on the task you wish to accomplish:

> ▸ To add a trustee to the directory or file, press the Ins key and highlight the user or group you want to add. Then press the Enter key.

> ▸ To delete a trustee from the directory or file, highlight the user or group and press the Del key. Then confirm that you want to delete it by choosing Yes. If you delete the user from the trustee list, that user will no longer have an explicit trustee assignment to the directory or file. This means that the user may be able to exercise inherited rights from a parent directory. If you want a user to have no rights to the directory or file, you can leave him or her listed as a trustee but delete all the rights, as described below.

FIGURE 6.9

*FILER's list of a directory's
trustees and rights*

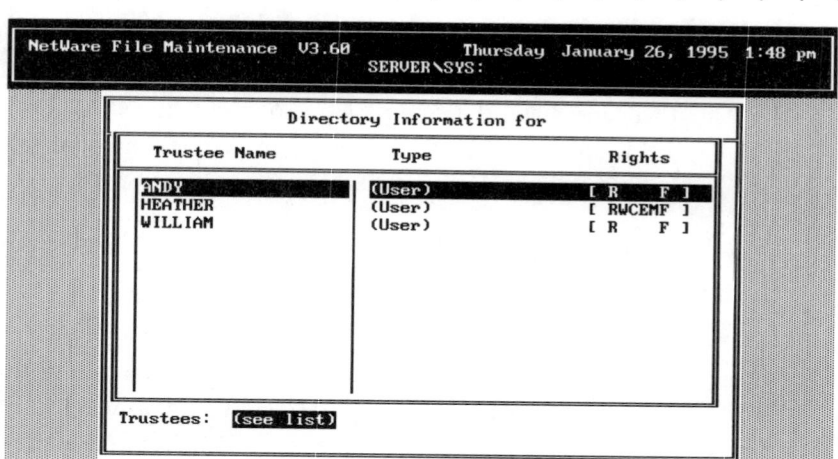

‣ To change a trustee's rights, highlight the trustee's name and press the Enter key. A list of the trustee's current rights appears. To add a right, press the Ins key, highlight the right you want to grant from the list that appears, and press the Enter key. To revoke a right, highlight the right and press the Del key. Then confirm that you want to delete it by answering Yes.

5 · To exit FILER, press the Esc key several times until you are asked if you want to exit FILER, then choose Yes.

CHANGING THE RIGHTS MASK WITH FILER

If you have the Access Control right in a directory or file, you can use the FILER menu utility to modify the directory's or file's Rights Mask (a directory's Maximum Rights Mask in NetWare version 2.2 or a directory's or file's Inherited Rights Mask in version 3.x). Follow these steps:

1 · Start the FILER utility from your workstation by typing FILER and pressing the Enter key. The Available Topics menu appears.

2 · If you are in the directory whose trustees you want to see, use the arrow keys to move to the option Current Directory Information and press the Enter key to select it. If you want to see the trustees for a subdirectory or file, choose Directory Contents and select the subdirectory or file from the list that appears. Then select View/Set Directory (or File) Information.

3 · Move the cursor to the Maximum Rights Mask or Inherited Rights Mask option and press the Enter key. A list of all the rights that are currently allowed in the Rights Mask appears, as shown in the example in Figure 6.10.

4 · Add or delete a right as follows:

‣ To add a right to the mask, press the Ins key and highlight the right you want to add. Press the Enter key to add it to the list.

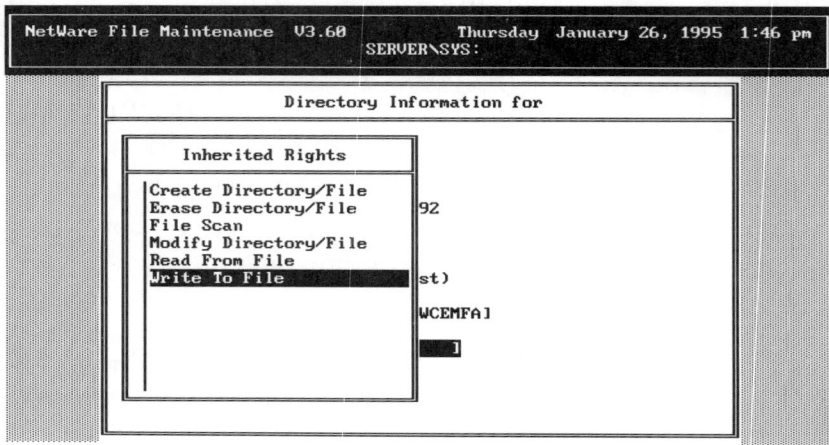

FIGURE 6.10

FILER's list of rights allowed in a Rights Mask

> ▸ To delete a right from the mask, highlight the right and press the Del key. Then confirm that you want to delete it by choosing Yes.

5 · To exit FILER, press the Esc key several times until you are asked if you want to exit FILER, then choose Yes.

LISTING AND CHANGING A USER'S TRUSTEE ASSIGNMENTS WITH SYSCON

If you have supervisor equivalence, you can use the SYSCON menu utility to see all of the trustee assignments that a user or group has. This can be handy if you want to see, for example, all the directories where user Andy has rights. You can also add or remove trustee assignments to directories or files.

Following these steps to view or change trustee assignments:

I · Start the SYSCON utility from your workstation by typing SYSCON and pressing the Enter key. The Available Topics menu appears.

2 · Move the cursor to either the Group Information or User Information option, depending on whether the trustee is a group or a user, and press the Enter key. A list of all the users or groups appears.

3 · From the list, highlight the user or group and press the Enter key.
A menu of information about that user or group appears.

4 · Highlight the Trustee Directory Assignments option and press the
Enter key. You see a list of all the directories where the user or group
has rights, as shown in the example in Figure 6.11.

5 · Add, delete, or change rights as follows:

▸ To add another directory or file to the list of assignments, press the
Ins key. A box appears asking you for the directory that the trustee
will have rights to. Type the directory path in the box, or press the
Ins key to select the path from a list of servers, then volumes, then
directories, and so on. When the directory path appears in the
box, press the Esc key, then the Enter key.

▸ To delete a directory or file from the list of assignments, highlight
the directory and press the Del key. Then confirm that you want to
delete it by choosing Yes. Realize that this user or group may be

FIGURE 6.11

SYSCON's list of directories

in which a user has rights

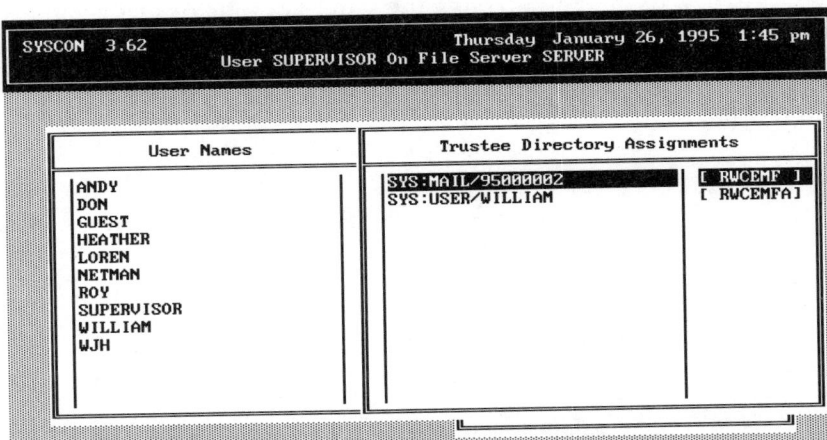

able to exercise inherited rights in the directory you just removed. If you truly want the user or group to have no rights at all to the directory, do not delete the directory from this list. Instead, just delete all rights from the assignment by changing the rights.

‣ To change trustee rights in a directory or file, highlight the directory and press the Enter key. In the list of rights that appears, use either the Del key or the Ins key to delete or add trustee rights as necessary.

6 · To exit SYSCON, press the Esc key several times until you are asked if you want to exit SYSCON, and then choose Yes.

GRANTING AND REMOVING SECURITY EQUIVALENCE WITH SYSCON

If you have supervisor equivalence, you can use the SYSCON menu utility to make one user security equivalent to another or remove a security equivalence. Follow these steps:

1 · Start the SYSCON utility from your workstation by typing SYSCON and pressing the Enter key. The Available Topics menu appears.

2 · Move the cursor to the User Information option and press the Enter key. A list of all the available users appears.

3 · From the list of users, highlight the one you want to make equivalent to another user or group (or whose security equivalence you want to remove) and press the Enter key. A menu of information about that user appears.

4 · Highlight the Security Equivalence option and press the Enter key. You see a list of all the users or groups to which the user has been given a security equivalence, as shown in the example in Figure 6.12.

5 · Grant or remove a security equivalence as follows:

‣ To make the user equivalent to another user or group, press the Ins key. From the list of users and groups that appears, highlight the name of the user or group you want and press the Enter key.

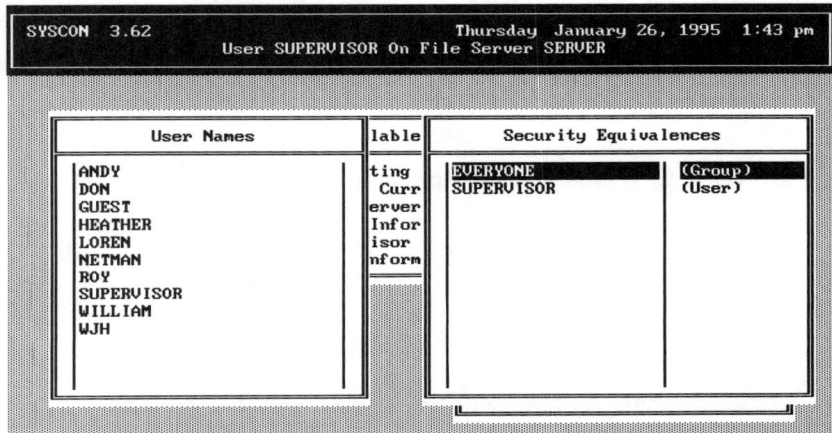

► To delete a security equivalence, highlight the user or group you want to delete and press the Del key. Then confirm that you want to delete it by choosing Yes. The user is now no longer equivalent to that user or group.

6 · To exit SYSCON, press the Esc key several times until you are asked if you want to exit SYSCON, and then choose Yes.

REMOVING A TRUSTEE WITH REMOVE

You use the REMOVE command line utility to remove all of a user's trustee rights to a directory and then remove the user from the directory's trustee list. To remove a trustee from a directory (or file in NetWare version 3.*x*), you must have the Access Control right to the directory (or file).

The REMOVE utility takes all the user's rights away and completely removes the user from the directory's (or file's) trustee list. If you don't want to take away all of the user's trustee rights, or if you want the user to have an empty trustee assignment (which prevents the user from inheriting trustee rights from a parent directory), use the REVOKE utility instead of REMOVE.

The command format for REMOVE is

REMOVE *trustee* FROM *path*

For example, to remove user Scott from the directory that is mapped to drive P:, type

REMOVE SCOTT FROM P:

If you want to remove Scott from all the subdirectories beneath drive P:, add the option /SUB at the end of the command:

REMOVE SCOTT FROM P: /SUB

If you have a group name that is the same as a username, use either the word USER or GROUP in front of the name to specify which one you want removed. For example, if Scott is the name of a group as well as a user, and you want to remove the *group* Scott, type

REMOVE GROUP SCOTT FROM P:

REVOKING TRUSTEE RIGHTS FROM A TRUSTEE WITH REVOKE

If you have the Access Control right in a directory or file, you can use the REVOKE command line utility to remove some or all of another user's trustee rights but still leave that user in the directory's (or file's in NetWare version 3.*x*) trustee list.

REVOKE is slightly different from REMOVE, in that REVOKE allows you to take away some of a user's trustee rights while leaving others intact. It also allows you to remove all of a user's trustee rights without removing the user from the trustee list. This ensures that the user does not inherit any trustee rights from a parent directory. (You can also use the Rights Mask to block inheritance, but that will block *all* users' rights.) Use REMOVE if you need to remove all of a user's trustee rights.

The command format for REVOKE is

REVOKE *rights* FOR *path* FROM *trustee*

For example, if user John has all trustee rights to the directory that is mapped to drive P: and you want to take away his Access Control right but leave all of his other rights, type

REVOKE A FOR P: FROM JOHN

If you want to remove John from all the subdirectories beneath drive P:, add the option /SUB at the end of the command:

REVOKE A FOR P: FROM JOHN /SUB

If you have a group name that is the same as a username, use either the word USER or GROUP in front of the name to specify which one you want. For example, if John is the name of a group as well as a user, and you want to remove the *user* John, type

REVOKE A FOR P: FROM USER JOHN /SUB

CHECKING FOR SECURITY HOLES WITH SECURITY

NetWare provides a utility that allows you to see how secure your network is. The SECURITY command line utility checks your entire network setup for possible security violations in the following areas:

▸ **Passwords:** Which users don't have passwords, which have passwords that are the same as their usernames, and which do not have adequate password restrictions (such as minimum length and grace logins).

▸ **Supervisor equivalence:** Which users have a security equivalence to the SUPERVISOR.

▸ **Rights to the root directory:** Which users have trustee rights in the root directory of any volume. Any user who has rights at the root of a volume inherits those rights throughout the entire directory structure unless you block those rights with Rights Masks or new trustee assignments. It's a good idea to avoid granting users any more than Read and File Scan rights at the root directory.

▸ **Login scripts:** Which users don't have user login scripts. If a user doesn't have a login script, an intruder could create one and place it into that user's MAIL directory, thus gaining illegal access to the network. For this reason, it is strongly recommended that every user have a login script. Even if you don't want to include any commands in a user login script, you can create one that contains a single space. Open the script, type a space by pressing the spacebar, and save the script.

▸ **Rights in NetWare directories:** Which rights users have in the four NetWare directories. All users should have only Read and File Scan rights in SYS:PUBLIC and SYS:LOGIN, the Create right to SYS:MAIL, and the Write and Create rights to their own MAIL subdirectories. Only the SUPERVISOR should have any rights at all in SYS:SYSTEM.

You must have supervisor equivalency to run the SECURITY utility. When you use the SECURITY utility, you can display the information it finds on the workstation screen, or you can send the information to a file so that you can print it. To see the information on the screen, type

SECURITY

To stop the information from scrolling, press the Ctrl-S key combination. Then press Ctrl-S again to resume scrolling. Figure 6.13 shows an example of the information found by SECURITY.

You may want to send the SECURITY information to a file so that you can print it and keep it in your network records. Sending this information to be saved in a file is called *redirecting*, or *piping*, to a file. To redirect SECURITY's display to a file, type

SECURITY > *filename*

FIGURE 6.13

SECURITY's information
about possible network
security violations

```
File Server Security Evaluation Utility

Checking for network security holes, please wait.

User ANDY
    Has unlimited grace logins
    Is not required to change passwords periodically
    Can have passwords that are too short
    Does not require a password
    Has no password assigned

User LOUISE
    Is security equivalent to user SUPERVISOR
    Has unlimited grace logins
    Is not required to change passwords periodically
    Can have passwords that are too short
    Does not require a password
    Has no password assigned

Group EVERYONE
    Has [RW C  ] rights in SYS:MAIL (maximum should be [ W C   ])
```

Replace *filename* with the name of the file you want to create. For example, if you want to name the file APRIL.95, type

SECURITY > APRIL.95

Using Attributes to Secure Files and Directories for All Users

Attributes are another major tool that NetWare provides for protecting your network directories and files. Attributes, which are sometimes called *flags*, control whether users can share a file or directory, delete it, rename it, change it, and so on.

Attributes differ from rights in the following ways:

▶ Attributes are assigned directly to files and directories; rights are assigned to users.

▶ Attributes control the actions of all users, including the SUPERVISOR; rights affect only the user to whom the rights are assigned.

▸ Attributes override rights. For example, if you have the Write right to a file, but that file has the Read Only attribute, you won't be able to change the file. Your Write right is ineffective because the Read Only attribute is dominant.

▸ Attributes do not grant rights. Regardless of the attributes that a file or directory may have, you still must have appropriate rights to be able to exercise those rights. For example, if a file has the Read Write attribute, which permits users to change the file, only users that have the Write right will actually be able to change the file.

▸ Attributes control some features that rights do not, such as whether a file (such as a utility or an application's executable file) can be used by more than one user at the same time.

▸ To change a file's or directory's attributes, you must have the Modify right to that file or directory. To change a user's rights to a file or directory, you must have the Access Control right to that file or directory.

When a directory or file is assigned an attribute, it is referred to as having been *flagged* with that attribute. For example, "Flag the file Read Only and Shareable" means to assign the Read Only and Shareable attributes to that file.

Some attributes can be assigned to directories, some can be assigned to files, and some can be assigned to either. Tables 6.3 and 6.4 list the file and directory attributes available in NetWare version 2.2. Tables 6.5 and 6.6 show the file and directory attributes available in NetWare version 3.x.

WHEN DO YOU NEED TO CHANGE ATTRIBUTES?

In most cases, the default attributes are adequate. The default attribute that is assigned to new files you create is Read Write. This means any user with the Read and Write rights can work with that file. You can usually safely leave your files set with the Read Write attribute, and control users' access to those files through trustee rights.

TABLE 6.3	FILE ATTRIBUTE	ABBREVIATION	EXPLANATION
NetWare Version 2.2 File *Attributes*	Archive Needed	A	Automatically assigned to files that have been changed since the last time they were backed up.
	Execute Only	X	Use with caution. Must be assigned by a supervisor-equivalent user. Prevents executable files (those with .EXE or .COM extensions) from being copied, changed, or deleted. Once assigned, this attribute cannot be removed, so assign it only if you have a backup copy of the file. It is recommended that you assign the Read Only attribute to executable files instead.
	Hidden	H	Hides files and prevents them from being copied and deleted. They do not appear when you use DOS's DIR command to list files, but they do appear when you use NetWare's NDIR utility. You must remove the Hidden attribute before you can delete the file.
	Indexed	I	Allows extremely large (256 kilobytes and larger) database files to be accessed more quickly.
	Read Audit	Ra	Not used. (It appears in the list of available attributes but is not supported.)

TABLE 6.3

NetWare Version 2.2 File

Attributes (continued)

FILE ATTRIBUTE	ABBREVIATION	EXPLANATION
Read Only	Ro	Allows users to read the file but not change it. It can be changed to the Read Write attribute. All NetWare files in SYS:SYSTEM, SYS:PUBLIC, and SYS:LOGIN are Read Only.
Read Write	Rw	Allows users to read and change the file. It can be changed to the Read Only attribute. Most files are set to Read Write automatically.
Shareable	S	Allows several users to open the file at the same time. It is useful for utilities, commands, application files, and some database files. All NetWare files in SYS:SYSTEM, SYS:PUBLIC, and SYS:LOGIN are Shareable. Most data files (documents, memos, and so on) should not be Shareable, so users do not conflict with each other's work.
System	Sy	Indicates system files (such as DOS files). Protects files by hiding them and preventing them from being copied or deleted. They do not appear when you use DOS's DIR command to list files, but they do appear when you use NetWare's NDIR utility. You must remove the System attribute before you can delete the file.

	FILE ATTRIBUTE	ABBREVIATION	EXPLANATION
TABLE 6.3 *NetWare Version 2.2 File* *Attributes (continued)*	Transactional	T	Use on database files to allow NetWare's Transactional Tracking System (TTS) to protect the files from being corrupted if the power goes out during a transaction. See the NetWare documentation for more information about TTS.
	Write Audit	Wa	Not used. (It appears in the list of available attributes but is not supported.)

	DIRECTORY ATTRIBUTE	ABBREVIATION	EXPLANATION
TABLE 6.4 *NetWare Version 2.2* *Directory Attributes*	Hidden	H	Hides directories and prevents them from being copied and deleted. They do not appear when you use DOS's DIR command to list files, but they do appear when you use NetWare's NDIR utility. You must remove the Hidden attribute before you can delete the directory.
	Private	P	Allows users to see the directory but not its subdirectories. Used only by Macintosh workstations—all Macintosh folders are automatically set to Private.

TABLE 6.4
NetWare Version 2.2
Directory Attributes
(continued)

DIRECTORY ATTRIBUTE	ABBREVIATION	EXPLANATION
System	Sy	Indicates system directories (such as DOS directories). Protects directories by hiding them and preventing them from being copied or deleted. They do not appear when you use DOS's DIR command to list files, but they do appear when you use NetWare's NDIR utility. You must remove the System attribute before you can delete the directory.

TABLE 6.5
NetWare Version 3.x File
Attributes

FILE ATTRIBUTE	ABBREVIATION	EXPLANATION
Archive Needed	A	Automatically assigned to files that have been changed since the last time they were backed up.
Copy Inhibit	C	Prevents Macintosh files from being copied. It does not apply to DOS files.
Delete Inhibit	D	Prevents users from deleting the file.
Hidden	H	Hides files and prevents them from being copied and deleted. They do not appear when you use DOS's DIR command to list files, but they do appear when you use NetWare's NDIR utility. You must remove the Hidden attribute before you can delete the file.

TABLE 6.5

NetWare Version 3.x File
Attributes (continued)

FILE ATTRIBUTE	ABBREVIATION	EXPLANATION
Purge	P	Purges the file as soon as the file is deleted. Purged files cannot be restored with the SALVAGE utility.
Read Audit	Ra	Not used. (It appears in the list of available attributes but is not supported.)
Read Only	Ro	Allows users to read the file but not change it. It can be changed to the Read Write attribute. All NetWare files in SYS:SYSTEM, SYS:PUBLIC, and SYS:LOGIN are Read Only. Assigning the Read Only attribute also automatically assigns the Delete Inhibit and Rename Inhibit attributes.
Read Write	Rw	Allows users to read and change the file. It can be changed to the Read Only attribute. Most files are set to Read Write automatically.
Rename Inhibit	R	Prevents users from renaming the file.

TABLE 6.5

NetWare Version 3.x File

Attributes (continued)

FILE ATTRIBUTE	ABBREVIATION	EXPLANATION
Shareable	S	Allows several users to open the file at the same time. It is useful for utilities, commands, application files, and some database files. All NetWare files in SYS:SYSTEM, SYS:PUBLIC, and SYS:LOGIN are Shareable. Most data files (documents, memos, and so on) should not be Shareable, so users do not conflict with each other's work.
System	Sy	Indicates system files (such as DOS files). Protects files by hiding them and preventing them from being copied or deleted. They do not appear when you use DOS's DIR command to list files, but they do appear when you use NetWare's NDIR utility. You must remove the System attribute before you can delete the file.
Transactional	T	Use on database files to allow NetWare's Transactional Tracking System (TTS) to protect the files from being corrupted if the power goes out during a transaction. See the NetWare documentation for information about TTS.
Write Audit	Wa	Not used. (It appears in the list of available attributes but is not supported.)

	DIRECTORY ATTRIBUTE	ABBREVIATION	EXPLANATION
TABLE 6.6 *NetWare Version 3.x Directory Attributes*	Delete Inhibit	D	Prevents users from deleting the directory.
	Hidden	H	Hides directories and prevents them from being copied and deleted. They do not appear when you use DOS's DIR command to list files, but they do appear when you use NetWare's NDIR utility. You must remove the Hidden attribute before you can delete the directory.
	Purge	P	Purges all files in the directory as soon as they are deleted. Purged files cannot be restored with the SALVAGE utility.
	Rename Inhibit	R	Prevents users from renaming the directory.
	System	Sy	Indicates system directories (such as DOS directories). Protects directories by hiding them and preventing them from being copied or deleted. They do not appear when you use DOS's DIR command to list files, but they do appear when you use NetWare's NDIR utility. You must remove the System attribute before you can delete the directory.

All NetWare files in SYS:SYSTEM, SYS:PUBLIC, and SYS:LOGIN are automatically flagged Shareable and Read Only, which allows more than one user at a time to use the files but prevents users from changing or deleting those files. There is usually no reason for you to change these files' attributes.

Some operating system files, such as DOS files, are automatically flagged Hidden and System to prevent users from accidentally erasing them. Leave these system files flagged this way for security.

In a few situations, you may want to change attributes:

▶ When you install an application, you may want to flag the application's executable files (usually those files that have .EXE or .COM extensions) with the Shareable and Read Only attributes. This allows users to share executable files but prevents users from deleting or changing those files.

▶ If you are using NetWare's Transactional Tracking System (TTS) to protect your database files, flag those database files with the Transactional attribute. TTS prevents your database files from being corrupted if the power goes out in the middle of a transaction. The whole transaction is *backed out* (discarded) so that the database is restored to its original state. This prevents partially updated transactions from being saved in your database file. See the NetWare documentation for more information about TTS.

▶ If you are using NetWare version 2.2, you can set a file to be Execute Only, which means no one can delete it, copy it, or change it. However, you cannot change the Execute Only attribute once it is set. Therefore, it is recommended that you not use this attribute. Instead, flag executable files with the Read Only attribute.

To assign attributes to a file or directory, you can use the FILER menu utility, the FLAG command line utility (for file attributes), or the FLAGDIR command line utility (for directory attributes).

ASSIGNING ATTRIBUTES TO A DIRECTORY OR FILE WITH FILER

To see and change your current directory's attributes, you can use the FILER menu utility. Follow these steps:

1 · Start the FILER utility from your workstation by typing FILER and pressing the Enter key.

2 · If you are in the directory whose attributes you want to see, use the arrow keys to move to the Current Directory Information option and press the Enter key to select it. If you want to see the attributes for a subdirectory or file, choose Directory Contents and select the subdirectory or file from the list that appears. Then select View/Set Directory (or File) Information. The screen that appears lists various information, such as the owner, the creation date, and the attributes.

3 · Move the cursor to the Directory Attributes option and press the Enter key. You see a list of the attributes that are currently assigned to the directory, as shown in the example in Figure 6.14.

F I G U R E   6.14

FILER's list of a directory's current attributes

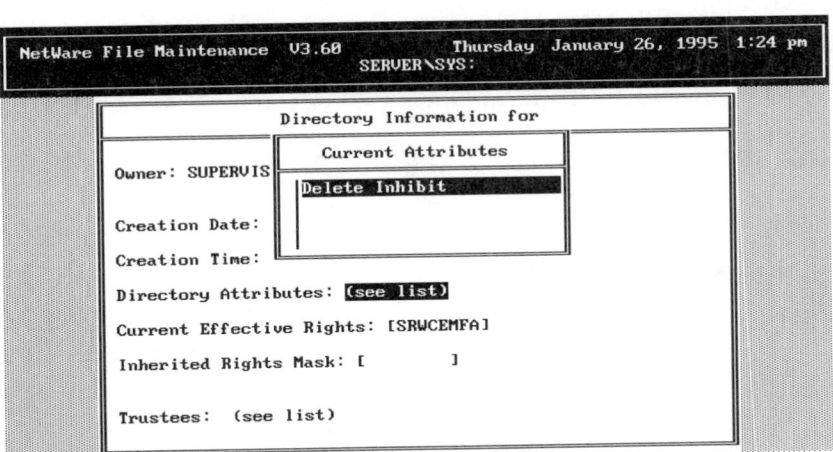

4 · Add or delete an attribute as follows:

> ‣ To add an attribute to the directory, press the Ins key and highlight the attribute you want to add. Press the Enter key to add it to the list.

> ‣ To delete an attribute from the directory, highlight the attribute and press the Del key. Then confirm that you want to delete it by choosing Yes.

5 · To exit FILER, press the Esc key several times until you are asked if you want to exit FILER, then choose Yes.

ASSIGNING ATTRIBUTES TO A DIRECTORY WITH FLAGDIR

To see and change the attributes for directories, you can use the FLAGDIR command line utility. The basic format for using the FLAGDIR utility is

FLAGDIR *path attributes*

To see what attributes are currently assigned to the directory you're working in, type

FLAGDIR

To see the attributes assigned to any other directory, add the directory path or a drive letter to the command:

FLAGDIR VOL1:APPS\WP

or

FLAGDIR F:

To change the attributes of a directory, specify the path, then add the list of attributes you want the directory to have. Use the attribute abbreviations in the command and separate the attributes with a space. If you want to change the attributes of your current directory, you must specify the current directory by typing a period (.).

Notice that if you just want to see the existing attributes of your current directory, you don't need to specify a path. However, to change the attributes for the current directory, you must use a period to indicate the current directory's path. This is because the FLAGDIR utility assumes that the first set of letters after the word FLAGDIR will be a directory name. If you skip the name and enter a list of attributes, FLAGDIR will consider the first attribute as the name of a directory, and it won't work correctly.

You can change a directory's attributes in one of two ways:

- ▸ Assign a new list of attributes, which will erase any previous attributes that had been assigned.

- ▸ Specify that the new attributes be either added to or subtracted from the existing attributes.

To replace the existing attribute assignment completely with the new attributes, just list the attribute abbreviations. For example, this command flags the directory that is mapped to drive J: with the Delete Inhibit and Rename Inhibit attributes, and any other attributes the directory had will be removed:

FLAGDIR J: D R

If drive J: is your current directory, you could type the following command instead:

FLAGDIR . D R

Now suppose you want to add the Hidden attribute to the same directory in drive J:. You can either list all three attributes in the FLAGDIR command:

FLAGDIR J: D R H

or you can use the plus sign (+) to indicate that you want to add the H attribute to the existing D and R attributes:

FLAGDIR J: +H

Both commands achieve the same result.

To subtract an attribute from the directory's existing list, use the minus sign (–). You can have both subtractions and additions in the same command. For example, this command removes the Delete Inhibit from the directory and adds the System attribute at the same time:

FLAGDIR J: –D +Sy

By default, new directories are created without attributes, which means there are no restrictions on what users can do. The simplest way to reset a directory to have no attributes is to flag the directory Normal (the abbreviation is N). For example, this command resets the directory mapped to drive J: to the Normal state:

FLAGDIR J: N

ASSIGNING ATTRIBUTES TO A FILE WITH FLAG

To see and change the attributes for files, you can use the FLAG command line utility. FLAG uses the same command format as FLAGDIR, except that you must include the file's name in your command. The basic format for using the FLAG utility is

FLAG *path file attributes*

For example, to see what attributes are currently assigned to the file REPORTS, which is in your current directory, type

FLAG REPORTS

If the file is not in your current directory, you must include the directory path (or drive letter) in the command:

FLAG VOL1:RESEARCH\PROJECTS\REPORTS

or

FLAG G:REPORTS

To change the attributes of a file, you specify the path and file name, then add the list of attributes you want the file to have. Use the attribute abbreviations in the command and separate the attributes with a space.

As with FLAGDIR, you can change a file's attributes either by assigning a new list of attributes, which will erase any previous attributes that had been assigned, or by specifying that the new attributes be added to or subtracted from the existing attributes.

To replace the existing attribute assignment completely with the new attributes, just list the attribute abbreviations. For example, this command flags the REPORTS file with the Read Only and Shareable attributes, and any other attributes the file may have had will be removed:

FLAG REPORTS Ro S

Now suppose you want to add the Transactional attribute to the same file. You can either list all three attributes in the FLAG command:

FLAG REPORTS Ro S T

or you can use the plus sign (+) to indicate that you want to add the T attribute to the existing Ro and S attributes:

FLAG REPORTS +T

Both commands get the same result.

To subtract an attribute from the file's existing list, use the minus sign (−). You can have both subtractions and additions in the same command. For example, to remove the Transactional attribute from the file and add the Hidden attribute at the same time, type

FLAG REPORTS −T +H

By default, new files are created with the Read Write attribute, which means any user with Read or Write rights can work with those files. The simplest way to reset a file to the default state of just the Read Write attribute is to flag the file Normal (the abbreviation is N). To reset the REPORTS file to its Normal state, type

FLAG REPORTS N

You can assign all available attributes to a file by using the word ALL instead of listing the individual attributes. For example, to assign all available attributes to the REPORTS file, type

FLAG REPORTS ALL

Review

NetWare provides several tools to help you secure your network:

- ▶ Login security

- ▶ Trustee rights

- ▶ Rights Masks (Maximum Rights Mask in NetWare version 2.2; Inherited Rights Mask in version 3.x)

- ▶ Directory and file attributes

Login security controls who can log in to your network by verifying that each user logs in using a legal username and a valid password.

Trustee rights are assigned to users and control what types of tasks a user can do within a directory or file, such as deleting, changing, reading, or renaming it. NetWare version 2.2 has seven trustee rights, all of which can only be assigned to directories. NetWare version 3.x includes eight rights, and they can be assigned to either directories or files. You can grant trustee rights to both users and groups. You can also make one user security equivalent to another user. This allows the first user to have the same trustee rights as the second user. To see your effective rights in a directory, use the RIGHTS command line utility. To assign trustee rights, use either the SYSCON menu utility or the GRANT command line utility.

In NetWare version 2.2, the Maximum Rights Mask allows you to restrict the trustee rights of any user. Each directory has its own Maximum Rights Mask, which by default allows all users to exercise any rights that have been granted to them. To restrict any user from exercising a particular trustee right, use the FILER menu utility to remove that right from the directory's Maximum Rights Mask.

In NetWare version 3.x, directories and files have Inherited Rights Masks. The Inherited Rights Mask restricts the rights that a user may inherit from a parent directory, but has no effect on any trustee assignments the user is specifically assigned for that directory or file. To restrict any user from inheriting a trustee right, use the FILER menu utility to remove that right from the directory's or file's Inherited Rights Mask.

Attributes are assigned directly to directories and files. Attributes affect all users and override any trustee rights that users may be given. Attributes can control whether several users can share a file at the same time and whether users can delete files, change them, and so on. You can assign attributes using either the FILER menu utility or the FLAG and FLAGDIR command line utilities.

Setting up the proper protection for your network files will make your job as network supervisor easier. The next chapter describes some steps you can take to reduce the amount of work your users need to do to use the network.

CHAPTER 7

Making Life Easy
for Your Users

NetWare networks are designed to increase productivity by allowing users to share files, applications, printers, and other resources. However, if those users need to spend a large portion of their time learning how to use the network, their productivity goes down. Therefore, the best way to maximize your users' productivity is to automate their workstations so that they never even need to know they're on the network. As icing on the cake, the less your users need to deal with the network, the fewer chances they'll have of making mistakes and creating problems for you to solve.

You can use two NetWare tools to automate workstations for your users: login scripts and menus. This chapter explains how to use these tools and provides examples that may help you plan your own login scripts and menus.

Using Login Scripts to Set Up the Work Environment

A *login script* runs automatically when a user logs in to the network. Login scripts save users time by executing commands that those users would otherwise need to repeat every time they log in. The commands in a login script can map drives to network directories, display messages on the user's screen, and even launch an application.

WHAT IS THE DEFAULT LOGIN SCRIPT?

The first time you log in as SUPERVISOR, the LOGIN utility executes the *default login script*. This simple login script, which is built into the LOGIN utility, gives you access to the utilities you need to set up directories, create users, establish security, and so on. The default login script also executes for any other users who log in to the file server so that they, too, have access to the utilities they need.

The default login script contains a few basic commands that will perform the following tasks:

- Display a greeting to the user.

▶ Map a drive to the user's home directory (as long as the home directory is located in the SYS: volume).

▶ Map a drive to the SYS:PUBLIC directory so that the user can access the NetWare utilities.

▶ Map a drive to the SYS:SYSTEM directory if the user who logged in is SUPERVISOR. If the user is not SUPERVISOR, the default script will not map a drive to SYS:SYSTEM.

This login script will work adequately in many cases, but it is rather limited. Although you can't delete the default login script, you should replace it by creating other login scripts customized to your needs.

THE TWO TYPES OF LOGIN SCRIPTS YOU CAN CREATE

You can replace the default login script by creating two types of login scripts that work together to customize each user's workstation environment: The system login script and user login scripts.

The *system login script* executes for every user who logs in to the file server. By creating a system login script, you can make sure everyone on the network has identical drive mappings, messages, and so on. This is a good place to put drive mappings to application directories that are available to all of your users. The system login script is actually a text file called NET$LOG.DAT, and it is located in the SYS:PUBLIC directory.

In addition, each user can have his or her own *user login script*. A user login script contains commands that apply only to a single user, such as specific drive mappings to his or her personal work directories. The user login script executes after the system login script and adds to any drive mappings that the system login script already set up. Each user's login script is a text file called LOGIN, located in that user's ID directory under SYS:MAIL.

The user login script replaces the default script. This means that if user Jennifer has a user login script, that login script will execute instead of the default login script when she logs in. However, if Jennifer doesn't have her own user login script, the default login script will run.

Figure 7.1 illustrates how the system login script, the user login script, and the default login script execute. In Figure 7.1, Mel and Louise have user login scripts, but Jennifer does not. Therefore, when Mel and Louise log in, the system login script and their own user login scripts both execute. When Jennifer logs in, the system login script and the default login script run.

Although you do not have to create either of these types of login scripts, it's highly recommended that you create both. By creating your own system login script and user login scripts, you can automate some of the tasks your users perform to begin using their workstations every day, which often means fewer cries for help.

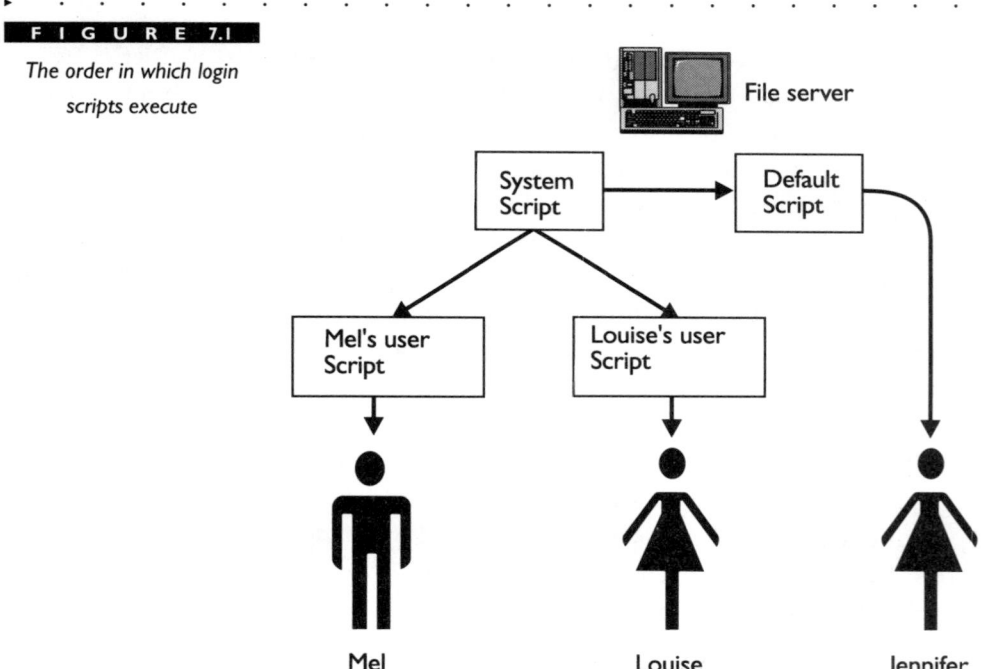

FIGURE 7.1

The order in which login scripts execute

PLANNING YOUR LOGIN SCRIPTS

You should create the system login script first, before you create user login scripts. Put any commands that all your users need, such as drive mappings to commonly used application directories, in the system login script. Having the common commands in the system login script makes it easier to maintain your login scripts. For example, if you put an application drive mapping into the system login script and then need to change that mapping later, you can make one change to the system login script instead of making the same change to every user login script.

After you create the system login script, create a user login script for each user. A user login script should include commands that are particular to that user, such as a drive mapping to that user's personal project directory or to an application that only that person uses.

Since the user login script executes after the system login script, it is possible for the user login script to overwrite some of the commands executed by the system login script. Be careful to plan your drive mappings so that you don't inadvertently map a drive letter to one directory in the system login script, then to another directory in the user login script.

If you don't create user login scripts, the default login script will execute after the system login script. If you've created drive mappings in your system login script, the default login script might overwrite some of those drive mappings. This is one of the reasons it's a good idea to create user login scripts. If you don't need to put any commands in the user login script, but you want to prevent the default login script from running, you can create a blank user login script. To do this, just type a space in each user's login script, and then save it.

To create login scripts, you use the SYSCON menu utility. As the network supervisor, you can create both the system login script and the user login scripts for every user. Individual users can use the SYSCON utility to create or modify their own user login scripts, although they cannot see anyone else's login script or the system login script.

Before you begin creating login scripts, you should plan which commands you will include. The following sections describe the most common login script commands.

Common Login Script Commands

There are numerous commands you can put in login scripts, all of which can be used in both system and user login scripts. However, for a small network, you will probably need to use only a few of these commands. The other login script commands are more specialized, and they are seldom needed in a small network environment.

The following are the nine most common login script commands:

```
MAP
WRITE
IF...THEN
REMARK
FIRE PHASERS
#
COMSPEC
EXIT
PCCOMPATIBLE
```

By using some combination of these commands (even as few as four or five), you can create useful system and user login scripts. The following sections describe how to use these commands in your login scripts. For a complete list of login script commands, refer to the NetWare documentation.

MAPPING DRIVES WITH THE MAP LOGIN SCRIPT COMMAND

The MAP command allows you to map drives to network directories. By putting MAP commands in a login script, you ensure that those drive mappings will automatically be set up for your users every time they log in. This way, users don't waste time mapping drives to the same directories day after day.

Use the MAP login script command to map drives to network directories just as you use the MAP utility at the DOS prompt. For more information about mapping drives, refer to Chapter 3.

Handling MAP's Display

If you don't turn off MAP's display, each MAP command will appear on the screen as it is executed in the login script. Although it is not really a problem for these mappings to appear on the screen, they can be distracting to the user (they scroll off the screen as other commands are executed). You can keep the screen from being cluttered during the login process by placing this command at the beginning of your login scripts:

MAP DISPLAY OFF

This command prevents each subsequent MAP command you put in the login script from displaying on the screen when it is executed.

After all your drive mappings are complete, you can turn the display back on. Toward the end of the login script, add the following two commands:

MAP DISPLAY ON
MAP

The first command turns on the display of drive mappings. The second command, MAP, displays a list of all the current drive mappings. When the login script is finished executing, the complete list of the user's drive mappings remains on the screen. This way, the user can see at a glance which drive mappings are available.

Mapping Search Drives

As explained in Chapter 3, *search drives* are special drive mappings to directories that contain applications, utilities, or other program files. By using search drives, you can allow users to execute an application regardless of the directory they are currently in.

In your login scripts, it is important to map some search drives in a particular order. In your system login script, map the following two search drives before you create additional search drives:

▶ Map S1: (the first search drive) to the SYS:PUBLIC directory. SYS:PUBLIC contains the NetWare utilities and other files that users need.

▶ Map S2: (the second search drive) to the DOS directory you created if your users will be running DOS from the network instead of from their local drives.

After you map these two search drives, you can map additional search drives in any order you want. For example, you can map a third search drive to the directory that contains your database application, a fourth one to the directory that contains your word processing application, and so on.

For example, the search drive mappings in your system login script might appear similar to the following:

```
MAP S1:=SYS:PUBLIC
MAP S2:=SYS:PUBLIC\%MACHINE\%OS\%OS_VERSION
MAP S3:=VOL1:APPS\DB
MAP S4:=VOL1:APPS\WORD
```

Instead of mapping search drives in sequential order (S3, S4, S5, and so on), you can use the last available search drive number (S16) for each mapping. By mapping S16, you insert the drive mapping at the end of the list of search drives. This way, if you delete a search drive later, NetWare adjusts the order of the remaining search drives automatically. For example, instead of mapping S3 and S4 to your application directories, you could have the following commands in your login script:

```
MAP S1:=SYS:PUBLIC
MAP S2:=SYS:PUBLIC\%MACHINE\%OS\%OS_VERSION
MAP S16:=VOL1:APPS\DB
MAP S16:=VOL1:APPS\WORD
```

Mapping Users' Home Directories

A common practice is to map the first network drive (not search drive) to the user's home directory. For example, suppose your users' home directories are located in the VOL1 volume, under the parent directory HOME. Since the first network drive is usually drive F:, you could add the following command to your system login script so that every user's first network drive is mapped to his or her home directory:

MAP F:=VOL1:HOME\%LOGIN_NAME

%LOGIN_NAME is an identifier variable that automatically substitutes the user's login name. For example, if user Ray logged in, his name would be substituted for the %LOGIN_NAME, and his first network drive would be mapped to VOL1:HOME\RAY. You can use this variable in your system login script instead of entering an individual drive mapping in every user's personal login script. Using identifier variables in login scripts is described in more detail later in this chapter.

Mapping to Available Drives

Instead of using the exact drive letters in login script drive mappings, you can map each available drive in order. This allows drive mappings to be more dynamic; if you delete a drive mapping, the other mappings adjust automatically.

To assign available network drives to directories, use an asterisk, followed by a number. For example, instead of typing

MAP F:=VOL1:HOME\%LOGIN_NAME

you could type

MAP *1:=VOL1:HOME\%LOGIN_NAME

The *1 indicates that you want the first available network drive to be assigned to this directory. Use *2 to indicate the second available drive, and so on.

Mapping a Fake Root

Some applications require that they be installed at the root of the volume. If you would rather install the application in a subdirectory, you can use MAP to map a *fake root* to the subdirectory that contains the application.

For example, suppose you have an application called JobMaker that needs to be installed at the root. However, you would rather install it in a directory called JOBMAKER under the parent directory APPS, which is on volume VOL1. To map a fake root to this directory and map a search drive to it at the same time, you could add the following MAP command to your login script:

```
MAP ROOT S16:=VOL1:APPS\JOBMAKER
```

Then the application will think it is located at the root of the volume instead of in a subdirectory, and your users will have a search drive to that directory, too.

DISPLAYING MESSAGES WITH THE WRITE LOGIN SCRIPT COMMAND

The WRITE command allows you to display brief messages on the users' workstation screen when they log in. For example, you could add a WRITE command to a login script so that users see the message "It's a great day to make widgets!" every time they log in.

To use the WRITE command, you type the word WRITE, followed by the text you want to appear on the user's screen. The text must be enclosed in quotation marks.

For example, to display the message about making widgets on your users' screens every time they log in, put the following command in your system login script:

```
WRITE "It's a great day to make widgets!"
```

Displaying Multiline Messages

To display a message that takes up several lines, it generally works best to start each line with the command WRITE. For example, suppose you added the following lines to your login script:

```
WRITE "Don't forget to turn in your budget report by"
WRITE "the first Friday of the month, or you will need to"
WRITE "file an amendment and serve on the committee!"
```

The message that appears on the users' screens will appear on three lines, similar to the following:

```
Don't forget to turn in your budget report by
the first Friday of the month, or you will need to
file an amendment and serve on the committee!
```

Using Identifier Variables for User-Specific Messages

If you want to display specific messages for each user, you can use identifier variables with the WRITE command. Identifier variables allow you to put a generic variable, such as DAY_OF_WEEK or LOGIN_NAME, in a login script command. Then when the user logs in, the login script substitutes real values for the variable.

To use an identifier variable to display only the value of the variable, without an additional message, put just the identifier variable after the command WRITE. For example, the following command will display only the name of the user:

```
WRITE LOGIN_NAME
```

You can display the value of the variable and a message in either of two ways:

- ▸ Include the variable with the text of the message inside the quotation marks

- ▸ Use a semicolon to join the variable to the text

Generally, the easiest method is to put the variable inside the quotation marks with the rest of the message.

To put a variable inside the quotation marks, you must add a percent sign to the beginning of the variable and be sure to type the variable in uppercase letters.

For example, to display the message "Hello Ian!" when user IAN logs in, use the command

WRITE "Hello, %LOGIN_NAME!"

You can display the same message by joining the variable to the text using a semicolon:

WRITE "Hello, "; LOGIN_NAME; "!"

But with this method, you must be careful to type the elements in the correct order to make the spaces and punctuation appear where you want them. Notice how the WRITE command has three elements that must be joined with semicolons. The first element is the text "Hello, ". The comma and a space are enclosed in the quotation marks so that the words are spaced correctly when displayed. The second element is the variable LOGIN_NAME, which is joined to the first text by a semicolon. Finally, to get the exclamation point to display after the name, you need to add another semicolon, then the text "!".

Using identifier variables in login scripts is discussed in more detail later in this chapter.

CONTROLLING COMMAND EXECUTION WITH THE IF…THEN LOGIN SCRIPT COMMAND

IF…THEN is a powerful command that lets you specify when to execute another command. For example, you could use the IF…THEN command in combination with the WRITE command to have the message "Status meeting is today at 3:00" display only on Tuesdays.

By using the IF…THEN command, you can control when an action is taken. For example, you can make commands in a login script execute only on certain days, during specific times of day, when a particular user logs in, or only when a user belongs to a certain group.

The command uses the following basic format:

IF *something is true* THEN
execute this command

ELSE *execute a different command*
END

The ELSE part of the command is optional. You use ELSE only when you have two or more different commands you want to execute, based on different circumstances. For example, if you want "Status report is due today" to appear on Fridays, and "Have a nice day" to appear on all other days, use the ELSE command like this:

```
IF DAY_OF_WEEK="Friday" THEN
WRITE "Status report is due today."
ELSE
WRITE "Have a nice day!"
END
```

If you don't want any message to appear on the other days of the week, just include the following lines instead:

```
IF DAY_OF_WEEK="Friday" THEN
WRITE "Status report is due today."
END
```

The "IF *something is true*" part of the command can be a little confusing. This part of the command is called a *conditional statement* because this is the condition that causes the rest of the command to execute. To use a conditional statement, you specify the variable you need, such as the day of week, and the value you want that variable to have, such as "Tuesday." Then, whenever the value of the variable matches the one you specified in the command (in other words, on every Tuesday), the command executes.

Using Identifier Variables with IF...Then

You can use many different variables (called identifier variables) in an IF...THEN command, and you can specify how the identifier variable matches the value in six ways:

=	Equals (Example: IF DAY_OF_WEEK = "Tuesday" means *If it's Tuesday*)
<>	Doesn't equal (Example: IF AM_PM <> "AM" means *If it isn't morning*)
>	Is greater than (Example: IF HOUR > "8" means *If the hour is 9:00 or later*)
>=	Is greater than or equal to (Example: IF HOUR >= "8" means *If the hour is 8:00 or later*)
<	Is less than (Example: IF HOUR < "8" means *If the hour is 7:00 or earlier*)
<=	Is less than or equal to (Example: IF HOUR <= "8" means *If the hour is 8:00 or earlier*)

In a conditional statement, you must enclose the value in quotation marks. For a list of the most common identifier variables and more rules on using them, see the discussion on using identifier variables in login scripts, later in this chapter.

Examples of Using IF...THEN

The following are examples of ways you can use the IF...THEN command in login scripts.

```
IF DAY_OF_WEEK = "Monday" THEN
WRITE "Welcome back!"
END
```

In this example, the message "Welcome back!" appears on the user's screen whenever he or she logs in on Monday. On other days of the week, no message is displayed.

```
IF MEMBER OF "ADMIN" THEN
MAP *5:=VOL1:APPS\RECORDS
END
```

In this example, if the user who logs in happens to belong to the group called ADMIN, the user's fifth available network drive is mapped to the RECORDS sub-directory under the APPS directory, which is located on the VOL1 volume. If the user who logs in does not belong to the group ADMIN, that user will not get this drive mapping. The login script will simply skip to the next command in the script.

```
IF DAY <= "5" THEN
FIRE PHASERS 2 TIMES
WRITE "Is your monthly sales report completed yet?"
MAP *6:=VOL1:APPS\ACCT\REPORTS
ELSE
WRITE "Find a new client today!"
END
```

This example has an ELSE command in it. This means that one of two different series of commands will execute, depending on whether or not the condition in the first line is true. The conditional in the first line

```
IF DAY <= "5"
```

means *If the day of the month is less than or equal to 5*, or in other words, *If today is the first, second, third, fourth, or fifth day of the month*. Therefore, the commands that execute in this example depend on the day of the month.

Whenever a user logs in on the first five days of the month, three things happen: a phaser sound occurs twice, the message "Is your monthly sales report completed yet?" appears on the screen, and the user's sixth available network drive is mapped to VOL1:APPS\ACCT\REPORTS.

When the user logs in on any day after the fifth of the month, a different message appears: "Find a new client today!" There will not be any phaser sounds or drive mapping on those days.

ADDING NOTES WITH THE REMARK LOGIN SCRIPT COMMAND

The REMARK command lets you add notes to yourself (or to anyone else who might be editing your login scripts) in a login script. These remarks do not display on the users' screens, nor do they execute any tasks. You use remarks merely to remind yourself why you put certain commands in the login script or to explain what the command is doing.

You can indicate that a line in a login script is simply a remark rather than a command in four ways: use the whole word REMARK, the shortened word REM, an asterisk (*), or a semicolon (;). You must put one of these words or symbols at the beginning of any line you want included as a note to yourself.

It's a safe practice to use remarks liberally in your login scripts. You can use remarks to remind yourself why you mapped a drive to a particular directory, list the users for whom this login script will run, indicate why a given command was included, and so on.

For example, the remark in this login script provides information about a drive mapping:

```
REM The next mapping is to the students' tutorial program.
IF MEMBER OF "Students" THEN
MAP S16:=VOL1:APPS\TRAINING
END
```

In this example, if the user who logs in belongs to the group STUDENTS, a search drive is mapped to the TRAINING directory. The remark indicates that this directory contains a tutorial program that students may need to access.

The remark in the following example helps the network supervisor to remember a maintenance task:

```
* Delete this mapping when we transfer files to Jane's department.
MAP *3:=VOL2:ACCTS\ACTIVE\NEW
```

A drive is mapped to the NEW directory. However, the remark reminds the supervisor to delete the drive mapping to this directory when the files in this directory are sent to another person's department.

SOUNDING PHASERS WITH THE FIRE PHASERS LOGIN SCRIPT COMMAND

The FIRE PHASERS command may not be the most important login script command you could use, but it does have its appeal. This command makes a phaser sound emit from the workstation, and you can specify how many times (up to nine) the phaser sound occurs.

While the command may sound frivolous, it can actually be useful when you want to draw attention to a message displayed with the WRITE command. For example, to make the phaser sound happen three times when you display a message reminding your users about an important sales meeting, add the following two lines to your system login script:

```
FIRE PHASERS 3 TIMES
WRITE "Come to the sales meeting today at 3:00!"
```

EXECUTING OTHER NETWARE COMMANDS WITH THE # LOGIN SCRIPT COMMAND

Occasionally, you may want to execute a command, such as a NetWare utility, from a login script. To execute this type of command from within a login script, you must precede the command with the # symbol. When the command is finished executing, the login script takes over again and continues running.

One of the most common uses of the # command is to execute the CAPTURE command, which sets up a workstation's printing capabilities. For example, the following line executes a CAPTURE command that will send the user's print jobs to a queue named LASERJET:

```
#CAPTURE Q=LASERJET TI=10 NB
```

For more information about using the CAPTURE command and printing on the network, see Chapter 5.

RUNNING DOS FROM A NETWORK DIRECTORY WITH THE COMSPEC LOGIN SCRIPT COMMAND

If your workstations are running DOS from the network, you must use the COMSPEC command to tell the workstation where the DOS *command processor* is located. The DOS command processor is the COMMAND.COM file, and the workstation needs to find this file in order to successfully run DOS.

If your users are running DOS from their local drives instead of from a network directory, you do not need the COMSPEC command in the login script. By default, the workstation will look for the COMMAND.COM file in the root directory on the boot disk.

To put a COMSPEC command in the login script, use the following format:

COMSPEC=*path* COMMAND.COM

For *path*, type the path of the directory that contains DOS (or the drive that is mapped to the DOS directory).

For example, suppose you map the second search drive to the directory that contains DOS by using the following MAP command in your login script:

MAP S2:=SYS:PUBLIC\%MACHINE\%OS\%OS_VERSION

Since the DOS COMMAND.COM file is located in this directory, you need to tell the workstation where to find it. Use the COMSPEC command like this:

COMSPEC=S2:COMMAND.COM

You use S2 for the path because that is the second search drive, which has already been mapped to the DOS directory.

EXECUTING A MENU OR AN APPLICATION WITH THE EXIT LOGIN SCRIPT COMMAND

Normally, when the user login script finishes executing, it returns the user to the DOS prompt. From there, the user can start up an application and begin working in it. However, you can automate this step so that instead of the DOS prompt, the application or menu appears on the workstation screen, and the user can begin working immediately.

To automatically send the user into an application or a menu when the login script is finished running, put the EXIT command, followed by the name of the application or menu in quotation marks, at the end of the login script.

For example, to send the user into a menu program you created called DP, add the following lines to your login script:

```
EXIT "MENU DP"
```

If you want members of the group ADMIN to enter the DP menu, and members of the group ARTISTS to enter the application CAD, put the following lines at the end of the login script:

```
IF MEMBER OF "ADMIN" THEN
EXIT "MENU DP"
END
IF MEMBER OF "ARTISTS" THEN
EXIT "CAD"
END
```

Users who are not members of ADMIN nor of ARTISTS would return to the DOS prompt when the login script finished running.

Note that if you put the EXIT command at the end of the system login script, the user login scripts will *not* execute.

Creating menu programs and using NetWare's MENU utility to run them are described later in this chapter.

USING THE PCCOMPATIBLE LOGIN SCRIPT COMMAND WITH NON-IBM PCS

You need to use the PCCOMPATIBLE login script command only if you are using the EXIT command *and* if you have changed the workstation's long machine name in the SHELL.CFG or NET.CFG file to something other than IBM_PC. For example, if your Hewlett-Packard workstations have the machine name HE_PAC in their SHELL.CFG files, and you want those users to go directly to an application, add the PCCOMPATIBLE command to the login script before the EXIT command.

If you use the EXIT command without the PCCOMPATIBLE command and the workstations are not compatible with IBM PCs, the EXECUTE command won't execute.

Using Identifier Variables in Login Script Commands

You can use special variables, called *identifier variables*, in some login script commands to make those commands more flexible. Identifier variables can be a user's login name, the day of the week, the time of day, the current month, and so on.

Identifier variables let you put a generic command into the login script. Then, when a user logs in, the login script inserts the specific values into the generic command and executes the command using those values.

For example, if you put the identifier variable DAY_OF_WEEK in a command, the login script would substitute the real value (Monday, Tuesday, and so on) for the variable, depending on what day it is when the login script is executed.

Although there are many identifier variables, usually only some of them are needed in login scripts for small networks. Table 7.1 lists 14 of the most commonly used identifier variables, along with their possible values and examples. You must type the variable exactly as shown in Table 7.1, including underscore characters (_).

For more information about using identifier variables with the WRITE command and the IF...THEN command, see the discussions of those commands earlier in this chapter. For a complete list of identifier variables, refer to the NetWare documentation.

TABLE 7.1	IDENTIFIER VARIABLE	EXPLANATION
Identifier Variables for Login Script Commands	DAY	Represents: Day's date Values: 01 through 31 Example: IF DAY="15"
	DAY_OF_WEEK	Represents: Day's name Values: Monday, Tuesday, etc. Example: WRITE "Today is %DAY_OF_WEEK."
	MONTH	Represents: Month's number Values: 01 through 12 Example: IF MONTH>"11"
	MONTH_NAME	Represents: Month's name Values: January, February, etc. Example: IF MONTH_NAME="October"
	SHORT_YEAR	Represents: Last two numbers in the year Values: 93, 94, 95, etc. Example: WRITE "Today is %MONTH-%DAY-%SHORT_YEAR."
	YEAR	Represents: All four numbers of the year Values: 1993, 1994, 1995, etc. Example: IF YEAR>="2000"
	AM_PM	Represents: Before noon or after noon Values: AM or PM Example: WRITE "%HOUR:%MINUTE %AM_PM"

TABLE 7.1	IDENTIFIER VARIABLE	EXPLANATION
Identifier Variables for Login Script Commands (continued)	GREETING_TIME	Represents: General time of day
		Values: Morning, Afternoon, or Evening
		Example: WRITE "Good %GREETING_TIME, %LOGIN_NAME."
	HOUR	Represents: Hour on a 12-hour clock
		Values: 1 through 12
		Example: IF HOUR<"7"
	HOUR24	Represents: Hour on a 24-hour clock
		Values: 00 through 24 (00=midnight)
		Example: IF HOUR24>="20"
	MINUTE	Represents: Minute
		Values: 00 through 59
		Example: WRITE "The time is currently %HOUR:%MINUTE %AM_PM"
	FULL_NAME	Represents: The user's full name
		Values: The user's full name as listed in SYSCON
		Example: WRITE "This is user %FULL_NAME."
	LOGIN_NAME	Represents: The user's login name
		Values: The name the user uses to log in to the network.
		Example: WRITE "Hello, %LOGIN_NAME!"

IDENTIFIER VARIABLE	EXPLANATION
MEMBER OF "*group*"	Represents: Group that the user belongs to
	Values: A group name
	Example: IF MEMBER OF "Photo"
	You can also use the word NOT with this variable.
	Example: IF NOT MEMBER OF "Photo"

Creating Login Scripts

To create and edit login scripts, you can use NetWare's SYSCON menu utility. Since the login scripts are text files, you can also use any text editor to edit them.

To create the system login script or user login scripts for users other than yourself, you must be logged in as the user SUPERVISOR or have supervisor rights. (See Chapter 6 for more information about rights and network security.) Other network users can create and modify their own user login scripts. If you want users to be able to modify their own login scripts, you will need to give them information about using login script commands, as well as instructions on how to use the SYSCON utility.

Any drive mappings or commands you put into a login script will not take effect until the next time users log in.

The following section explains how to create a system login script. Creating a user login script is described later in this chapter.

CREATING THE SYSTEM LOGIN SCRIPT

To create a system login script for your file server, follow these steps:

1 · Log in to a workstation as SUPERVISOR or as a user who is supervisor-equivalent.

2 · To start the SYSCON menu utility from your workstation, type

SYSCON

and press the Enter key.

3 · Use the arrow keys to move to Supervisor Options and press the Enter key to select it. The Supervisor Options menu appears.

4 · Select the System Login Script option.

The next window shows the commands that are currently in the system login script. If this is a new server and you haven't yet created a login script, the window will be empty.

5 · In this window, type the commands you want to put into the system login script. SYSCON uses a very basic text editor to allow you to create or edit the login script from this window. Use the following techniques to work in this window:

- To move the cursor around in the login script box, use the arrow keys.

- To erase characters, use the Backspace and Del keys.

- To cut or copy a block of text, position the cursor at the beginning of the text you want and press the F5 key. Then move the cursor to the end of the text you want; the text you're copying is highlighted. Press the Del key. The text disappears, but it is stored temporarily in memory. Move the cursor to the place you want to paste the text, and press the Ins key. The deleted text reappears.

6 · When you're finished creating or editing your system login script, press the Esc key. A message appears, asking if you want to save the login script.

7 · To save the login script you just created, answer Yes.

8 · Press the Esc key repeatedly until you exit the SYSCON utility.

Now the next time any user logs in, this system login script will execute and establish the workstation environment you specified. Then either the user login script or the default login script will execute and add drive mappings, messages, and so on.

EXAMPLES OF SYSTEM LOGIN SCRIPTS

The following sections show examples of system login scripts and explain what each of the commands do. Your login scripts may be similar to those shown or they may be quite different; the contents of your system login scripts vary depending on your particular situation.

A Simple System Login Script

Figure 7.2 shows a basic system login script, which contains only the most necessary commands and drive mappings.

The first line in the script

MAP DISPLAY OFF

turns off the MAP command's display so that drive mappings don't appear on the screen as they are created.

────────

FIGURE 7.2

A basic system login script

```
MAP DISPLAY OFF
MAP *1:=VOL1:HOME\%LOGIN_NAME
IF "%1"="SUPERVISOR" THEN MAP *1:=SYS:SYSTEM
MAP S1:=SYS:PUBLIC
MAP S2:=SYS:PUBLIC\%MACHINE\%OS\%OS_VERSION
COMSPEC=S2:COMMAND.COM
MAP DISPLAY ON
MAP
```

The next command

MAP *1:=VOL1:HOME\%LOGIN_NAME

maps the first network drive to the user's home directory, which is located under HOME on volume VOL1:.

An IF...THEN command follows:

IF "%1"="SUPERVISOR" THEN MAP *1:=SYS:SYSTEM

If the user who logs in is SUPERVISOR, this command maps the first network drive to the SYS:SYSTEM directory instead of to a home directory. Because this command fits on one line, the END command can be omitted.

The next two lines map search drives:

MAP S1:=SYS:PUBLIC

maps the first search drive to the SYS:PUBLIC directory, which contains NetWare utilities, and

MAP S2:=SYS:PUBLIC\%MACHINE\%OS\%OS_VERSION

maps the second search drive to the DOS directory. When you use identifier variables with percent signs instead of the name of the DOS directory, workstations can find the particular type of DOS they need if there is more than one version of DOS on the network.

The following command

COMSPEC=S2:COMMAND.COM

tells the workstation where to find the COMMAND.COM file for DOS. In this case, COMMAND.COM is located in the DOS directory, which is mapped to the second search drive, S2.

Then the command

MAP DISPLAY ON

allows drive mappings to be displayed.

The final command is

MAP

which lists all the drive mappings that are now in effect.

A More Complex System Login Script

Figure 7.3 shows a more complex system login script. It starts out with the necessary commands and drive mappings, as in the previous example, but it includes additional drive mappings to application directories. It also shows how to use the MEMBER OF "*group*" identifier variable to specify different drive mappings for users who belong to different groups.

The first six commands are the same as those in the simple system login script (Figure 7.2). Then the script continues with two search drive mappings:

```
MAP S16:=VOL1:APPS\WP
MAP S16:=VOL1:APPS\DB
```

which map the next two available search drives to a word processing directory and to a database directory, both under the APPS parent directory on volume VOL1.

The next five lines

```
IF MEMBER OF "ACCTS" THEN
MAP ROOT S16:=VOL1:APPS\COUNTER
MAP *2:=VOL1:WORK\PROJECTS\NEW
MAP *3:=VOL1:WORK\PROJECTS\STATUS
END
```

execute only if the user who logs in is a member of the group ACCTS. If the user is a member of that group, then the user's next available search drive is mapped

F I G U R E 7.3

A complex system login
script

```
MAP DISPLAY OFF
MAP *1:=VOL1:HOME\%LOGIN_NAME
IF "%1"="SUPERVISOR" THEN MAP *1:=SYS:SYSTEM
MAP S1:=SYS:PUBLIC
MAP S2:=SYS:PUBLIC\%MACHINE\%OS\%OS_VERSION
COMSPEC=S2:COMMAND.COM
MAP S16:=VOL1:APPS\WP
MAP S16:=VOL1:APPS\DB
IF MEMBER OF "ACCTS" THEN
MAP ROOT S16:=VOL1:APPS\COUNTER
MAP *2:=VOL1:WORK\PROJECTS\NEW
MAP *3:=VOL1:WORK\PROJECTS\STATUS
END
IF MEMBER OF "ARTISTS" THEN
MAP S16:=VOL1:APPS\DRAW2
MAP *4:=VOL1:GRAPHICS
END
#CAPTURE Q=LASER_Q NB TI=10
MAP DISPLAY ON
MAP
WRITE "Good %GREETING_TIME, %LOGIN_NAME."
IF DAY_OF_WEEK = "Friday" THEN
WRITE "Hang in there! The weekend's coming!"
FIRE PHASERS 2 TIMES
END
```

as a fake root to the COUNTER directory. In this case, the application in the COUNTER directory requires that it be installed in the root of the volume. Then the next two available network drives are mapped to the NEW directory and the STATUS directory, where the user can store work files. END signals that this is the end of the IF...THEN command.

The next four commands

```
IF MEMBER OF "ARTISTS" THEN
MAP S16:=VOL1:APPS\DRAW2
```

```
MAP *4:=VOL1:GRAPHICS
END
```

execute only if the user who logs in is a member of the group ARTISTS. If the user is a member of that group, then the user's next available search drive is mapped to the DRAW2 directory. Then the next available network drive is mapped to the GRAPHICS directory, where the user can store work files. END signals that this is the end of the IF...THEN command.

The following command

```
#CAPTURE Q=LASER_Q NB TI=10
```

executes the NetWare utility CAPTURE, which directs the user's print jobs to the print queue called LASER_Q, specifies that no banner be printed, and assigns a timeout of 10 seconds. (For more information about using the CAPTURE utility, see Chapter 5.)

The next two MAP commands

```
MAP DISPLAY ON
MAP
```

turn back on the display of drive mappings and list all the drive mappings that are now in effect.

The WRITE command

```
WRITE "Good %GREETING_TIME, %LOGIN_NAME."
```

displays a greeting to the user, with the appropriate time of day and username inserted. For example, when Andy logs in at 8:00 a.m., the message on his screen will be "Good morning, ANDY."

The last four lines in the script

```
IF DAY_OF_WEEK = "Friday" THEN
WRITE "Hang in there! The weekend is coming!"
FIRE PHASERS 2 TIMES
END
```

display the message "Hang in there! The weekend's coming!" and fire two phaser blasts, but only on Fridays.

CREATING A USER LOGIN SCRIPT

To create a user login script, follow these steps:

1 · To start the SYSCON menu utility from your workstation, type SYSCON and press the Enter key.

2 · Use the arrow keys to move to User Information and press the Enter key to select it. A list of all the users on the network appears.

3 · From the list of users, select the user whose login script you want to create or edit. If you logged in as a supervisor-equivalent user, you can see the login script for any user on the network. Otherwise, you can only see your own.

4 · Select Login Script from the list of options that appears.

The next window shows the login script commands that are currently in the user's login script. If this user does not yet have a login script, the window will be empty.

5 · In this window, type the commands you want to put into the user's login script.

Use SYSCON's text editor to create or edit the login script as described in step 4 of the previous section. You can also copy text from one user's login script to another one. In the first user's login script, position the cursor at the beginning of the text you want to copy and press the F5 key. Move the cursor to the end of the text and press the Del key to cut the highlighted block of text. Press the Ins key to paste the text back into the first login script. The text is still in memory. Now press Esc twice to exit the first login script and return to the list of users. Select a different user from the list and select Login Script to display the login script for the second user. Position the cursor where you want to paste the text and press the Ins key to insert it.

6 · When you're finished creating or editing the user's login script, press the Esc key. A message appears, asking if you want to save the login script.

7 · To save the login script you just created, answer Yes.

8 · Press the Esc key repeatedly until you exit the SYSCON utility.

Now the next time this user logs in, the system login script will run, and then this new user login script will execute and add the new drive mappings, messages, and so on.

EXAMPLES OF USER LOGIN SCRIPTS

The following sections show examples of user login scripts and explain the commands. You can refer to these examples to get ideas for login scripts for your network users. When you create user login scripts, remember that the system login script will have already created some drive mappings by the time the user login script begins running, so be careful not to remap any of the same drive letters to different directories.

A Simple User Login Script

Figure 7.4 shows a basic user login script for the user Louise. This user login script shows how you can direct the login script to execute a menu called CHOOSE1 for Louise. When the login script finishes executing, the menu automatically appears on the screen. Louise doesn't enter any commands at the DOS

FIGURE 7.4

A basic user login script

```
MAP DISPLAY OFF
MAP *5:=VOL1:HOME\LOUISE\LOGS
MAP *6:=VOL1:SITES\EXOTIC
PCCOMPATIBLE
EXIT "MENU CHOOSE1"
```

prompt; she can select options from the menu instead. Creating menus for users is described later in this chapter.

As in the examples of system login scripts, the first command in the simple user login script is

MAP DISPLAY OFF

which prevents drive mappings from displaying as they are created.

The second and third commands map network drives:

MAP *5:=VOL1:HOME\LOUISE\LOGS
MAP *6:=VOL1:SITES\EXOTIC

Louise's next two available network drives are mapped to her personal directory called LOGS and a directory called EXOTIC.

The next command

PCCOMPATIBLE

allows computers that aren't IBM PC compatible to run the EXIT command, which follows.

The final command

EXIT "MENU CHOOSE1"

stops the login script and executes a menu program called CHOOSE1. Louise never sees the DOS prompt; the menu automatically appears on her screen.

A More Complex User Login Script

Figure 7.5 shows a more complex user login script for the user Ray. In this example, the login script does not execute a menu program. Instead, Ray will be at the DOS prompt when the login script finishes running, and Ray will see drive mappings and some messages displayed on his screen.

FIGURE 7.5

A complex user login script

```
MAP DISPLAY OFF
MAP *5:=VOL1:HOME\RAY\SCHEDULE
MAP *6:=VOL1:SITES\PLANNING
MAP *7:=VOL1:SITES\EXOTIC
#CAPTURE Q=PRIORITY NB TI=5
MAP DISPLAY ON
MAP
WRITE "Beam me up, Scotty!"
FIRE PHASERS 3 TIMES
IF DAY_OF_WEEK = "Monday" THEN
WRITE "Status report is due by noon today."
FIRE PHASERS 5 TIMES
END
```

After turning off the MAP command display, the user login script maps Ray's three next available network drives:

```
MAP *5:=VOL1:HOME\RAY\SCHEDULE
MAP *6:=VOL1:SITES\PLANNING
MAP *7:=VOL1:SITES\EXOTIC
```

first to his personal directory called SCHEDULE, then to a directory called PLANNING, and then to a directory called EXOTIC.

The next command

```
#CAPTURE Q=PRIORITY NB TI=5
```

executes the NetWare utility CAPTURE. A CAPTURE command was executed by the system login script, but Ray needs to send his print jobs to a different print queue. The CAPTURE command in Ray's user login script will override the CAPTURE command that the system login script already executed.

Then the following two commands

```
MAP DISPLAY ON
MAP
```

allow drive mappings to be displayed and list all the drive mappings that are now in effect.

Next comes a message and phaser sounds:

```
WRITE "Beam me up, Scotty!"
FIRE PHASERS 3 TIMES
```

These two lines display the message "Beam me up, Scotty!" while blasting three phaser sounds.

The last four lines

```
IF DAY_OF_WEEK = "Monday" THEN
WRITE "Status report is due by noon today."
FIRE PHASERS 5 TIMES
END
```

execute only on Mondays, to remind Ray that his status report is due by noon.

Creating Menus for Your Users

NetWare includes a utility that allows you to set up a menu program for your users. You can create a menu that lists the users' choices of applications to use. Then when they select an application from that menu, it will run automatically.

For example, if you have several users who need to use a spreadsheet program and a word processing program on a regular basis, you could create a menu for those users. The menu would contain an option for accessing the spreadsheet program and another option for accessing the word processing program. The users could then select the program they want from your menu, rather than typing in commands.

Menus are optional; you are not required to use them. However, many network supervisors create menus to let users avoid drive mappings, the DOS prompt, and commands and utilities. Menus also help prevent users from "trying things out" on their own. You can create a single menu for all your users, or you can set up several menus to be used by different groups or individuals.

To create a menu program in NetWare 3.12, see Chapter 11. To create a menu in NetWare 2.2, 3.1, or 3.11, first create a menu program with any text editor that will save files in ASCII format. The file you create with a text editor will contain various commands that specify the options on the menu and where the menu appears on the screen. You can name this file anything you want, but you must give it an extension of .MNU (for example, BASIC.MNU, MYMENU.MNU, or TEAM.MNU). Then store the file in a directory that has a search drive mapping, such as SYS:PUBLIC, or in the directory that will be the user's current directory when the menu is executed.

Then, after you've created the menu program file, you use the NetWare MENU utility to execute your menu. You can also include the MENU utility in login scripts to make your menu execute automatically so that the users don't need to do anything except wait for the menu to appear on their screens.

There are also several good third-party programs you can use to create menus for your NetWare workstations. If you have another menu program, see its documentation for instructions on programming menus for NetWare.

PLANNING YOUR MENU PROGRAM

Before you create a menu program, you need to plan how you want the menu to work. Menus can be as simple or as complex as you want them to be. You can use a single menu with a few options or have layers of menus, so that selecting an option from the first menu displays a submenu with additional options. Obviously, the simpler your menu the better, as far as your users are concerned.

You should consider the following elements:

▸ The tasks you want users to perform from the menu

▸ Whether you want a single menu or layers of submenus

▸ The commands necessary to execute the tasks in the menu

▸ The location of the menu (and submenus) on the screen

Each of these considerations is discussed in the following sections.

What Tasks Do You Want Users to Perform?

Plan the tasks you want your users to be able to execute from the menu. Here are some of the tasks you may consider:

▶ Executing applications (spreadsheets, word processors, and so on)

▶ Entering an electronic mail program

▶ Executing NetWare utilities or DOS commands

▶ Exiting the menu to get to the DOS prompt

▶ Logging out of the network (it's a good idea to include this option)

Do You Want to Use Submenus?

After you've identified the tasks, plan whether you want all the tasks to be executed from a single menu, or if you want some tasks to be included in a submenu, beneath an option on the first menu. For example, you could put the option DOS Commands in the initial menu and have that option display a submenu with the options COPY, FORMAT, and XCOPY. However, you should try to keep the layers of menus to a minimum.

Figure 7.6 illustrates a sample menu that a network supervisor has planned for user Mel. This example displays a single menu with five options: Budget Spreadsheet, Inventory Spreadsheet, Word Processing, Mail, and Logout.

Another way to organize these options would be to create submenus. The first menu could contain four options: Spreadsheet, Word Processing, Mail, and Logout. When the user selects the Spreadsheet option, a submenu with the options Budget and Inventory appears. Figure 7.7 illustrates the menus for this example. However, you would use a submenu here only if you needed to list more options beneath Spreadsheet. It makes more sense to stick with a single menu unless your network situation requires many options.

What Commands are Needed to Execute the Tasks?

Next, identify the commands that are necessary to execute the tasks you want to put into your menu. For example, to start up the WordPerfect word processing

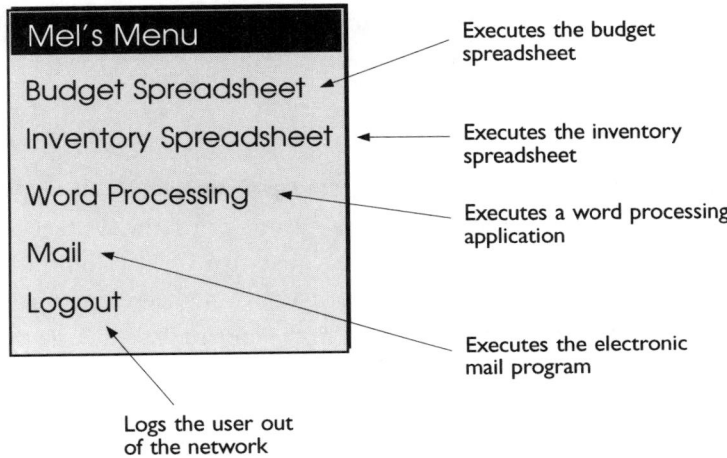

FIGURE 7.6

Planning a single menu

Executes the budget spreadsheet

Executes the inventory spreadsheet

Executes a word processing application

Executes the electronic mail program

Logs the user out of the network

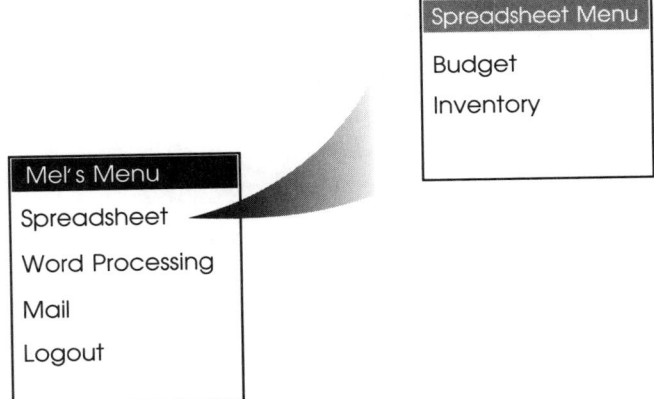

FIGURE 7.7

Planning a menu with submenus

program, you type the command WP. Also plan any other prompts or messages that need to appear on the user's screen. For example, if you include an option to change the password, you may want to display messages similar to "Enter your old password" and "Enter the new password." You will need to specify the commands and messages in the menu program.

Where Do You Want the Menu to Appear?

Finally, plan where you want the menu to appear on the workstation screen. It's easy to center a menu on the screen, because that is the default location. For a single menu, the center of the screen is usually an acceptable location. However, if you are including submenus, you may want the submenus to display to the right or left of the initial menu so that the user can see both the submenu and the previous menu at the same time.

In your menu program, you specify the menu's location by indicating the number of lines from the top and side edges of the screen to the center of the menu. The center of the screen is 12 lines from the top and 40 spaces from the left edge. To place a menu in the center of the screen, however, you can specify 0 (zero) instead of the number of lines (0 is the default, which automatically centers the menu).

Figure 7.8 shows how to determine the vertical and horizontal placements of your menus. In the illustration, the center of Menu 1 is 12 lines from the top of the screen and 40 spaces from the left edge (the center of the screen). The center of Menu 2 is 18 lines from the top of the screen and 60 spaces from the left edge of the screen. Therefore, when Menu 2 appears on the screen, it will be in the lower-right section of the screen.

EXAMPLE OF A SIMPLE MENU PROGRAM

When you create a menu, you are actually writing a simple computer program. The computer will read the program you created and execute the commands in it to draw the menu on the workstation screen. Therefore, the commands that you put in this file must be in a particular order for the menu to work correctly.

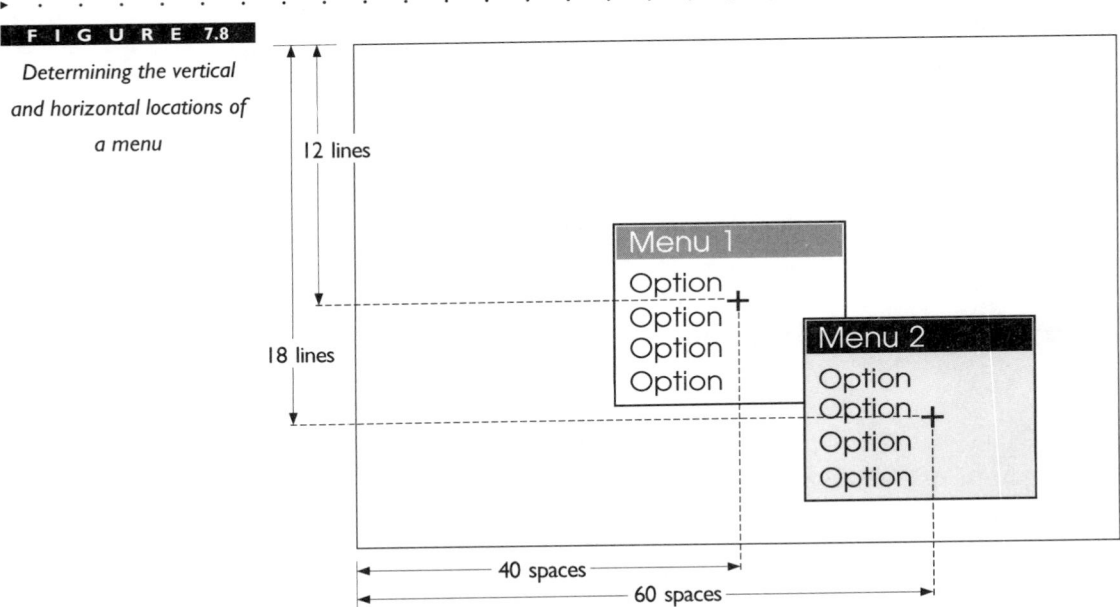

FIGURE 7.8

*Determining the vertical
and horizontal locations of
a menu*

An example of a simple menu was shown earlier in Figure 7.6. To create this menu, the network supervisor put specific commands into an ASCII file. Figure 7.9 shows the ASCII file that contains the menu program, which the supervisor has named MEL.MNU.

In the menu program file, the first line shows the heading of the menu. This heading will appear at the top of the menu when the menu is displayed on the user's screen. In the menu file, the heading must be flush with the left margin and preceded by a percent sign.

Every menu and submenu that will appear in your menu program must have a heading. You can use any phrase or word as the heading of your menu, such as Main Menu, Available Options, Select a Task, Choose an Option, and so on. Use a heading that makes sense in your situation.

On the same line as the heading in this example, two numbers indicate the placement of the menu on the screen. The first number shows the number of

FIGURE 7.9

A simple menu program

(MEL.MNU)

```
%Mel's Menu,0,0
Budget Spreadsheet
     COUNT BUDGET
Inventory Spreadsheet
     COUNT INV
Word Processing
     WP
Mail
     M:
     EMAIL
     F:
Logout
     !LOGOUT
```

lines from the top of the screen to the center of the menu. The second number shows the number of spaces from the left edge of the screen to the center of the menu. In this example, the numbers 0,0 indicate that the supervisor wants to use the default settings for vertical and horizontal positioning, which means the menu will be centered on the screen.

This menu will show five options. Options must be typed on separate lines, flush with the left margin. Do not put a percent sign in front of options. When the menu is displayed on the screen, NetWare will automatically alphabetize the options. If you want the options alphabetized, the order you list them in this file doesn't matter. If you want the options to appear in a different order, you can number them, such as

```
1. Budget Spreadsheet
     COUNT BUDGET
2. Inventory Spreadsheet
     COUNT INV
```

Following each option in the file are the commands necessary to execute the option. All commands must be indented two to five spaces or they will not be interpreted correctly. In the example, to execute the company's spreadsheet program, the command is COUNT. This fictional spreadsheet program allows a user to enter a particular spreadsheet file by including the name of the file with the COUNT command: COUNT BUDGET for the spreadsheet file called BUDGET and COUNT INV for the file called INV. Therefore, these commands are indented under the two spreadsheet options to send user Mel directly into the correct spreadsheet files.

In some cases, a single command may not be adequate to execute the option. In the example, the electronic mail system used by this company must be executed from the directory that is mapped to drive M:. However, most of the rest of the work that user Mel performs requires him to be in drive F:. The commands to switch drives are included in the menu program, under the Mail option:

M:
EMAIL
F:

The first of these commands, M:, changes Mel's current directory to drive M:, where the electronic mail program is stored. The next command, EMAIL, executes the electronic mail program. The last command, F:, changes Mel's current directory back to drive F: when he exits the mail program.

The last option, Logout, is the option that Mel should use when he wants to log out of the network and turn off his workstation. The command to execute this option is !LOGOUT.

A simple menu like this one may work well for your situation. Substitute the correct names for your own options and include the commands necessary to execute those options, and your menu will be complete. You can now use NetWare's MENU utility to run your menu, as described later in this chapter.

For a look at a more complex menu and some of the more advanced features of menus, read the following section.

EXAMPLE OF A COMPLEX MENU PROGRAM

In some cases, a simple menu program with a single menu may not be adequate. You may need to use submenus or provide more sophisticated options, such as letting the user get to the DOS prompt and back.

Figure 7.10 shows an example of a more complex menu program. A network supervisor created this menu program, named MANAGERS.MNU, to be used by managers in the company who need access to several applications and to the DOS prompt. The supervisor planned the menus to appear as shown in Figure 7.11.

F I G U R E 7.10

*A more complex
menu program
(MANAGERS.MNU)*

```
%Select a Task,0,0
1. Spreadsheet
        %Choose a Spreadsheet File
2. Word Processing
        CLS
        ECHO Please wait while WordPerfect is loading
        WP
3. Mail
        M:
        EMAIL
        F:
4. Copy a file
        CLS
        NCOPY @1"Enter source drive and file" @2"Enter destination
drive"
        DIR /P @2
        PAUSE
5. Exit to DOS
        ECHO OFF
        CLS
        PROMPT=$P (Type 'Exit' when you're finished) $G
        COMMAND
6. Logout
        !LOGOUT
%Choose a Spreadsheet File, 15, 60
1. Budget
        COUNT BUDGET
2. Inventory
        COUNT INV
```

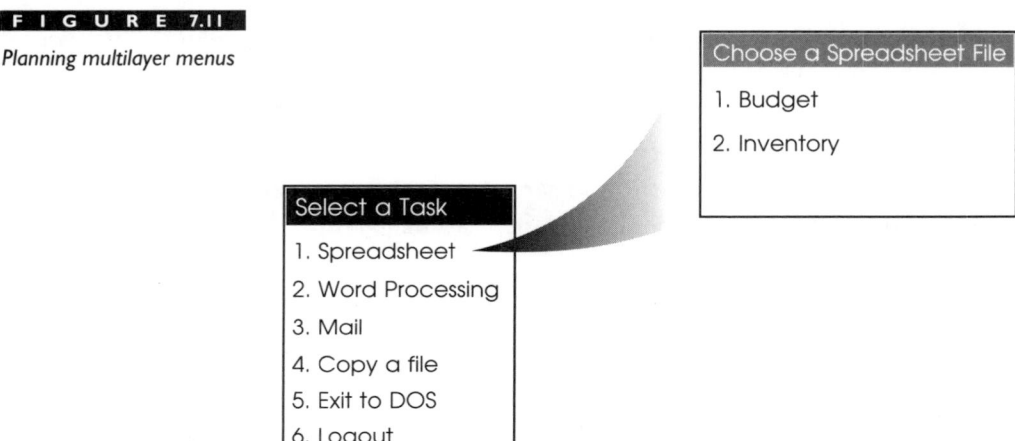

FIGURE 7.11

Planning multilayer menus

This menu program uses the same basic format as the simple menu program shown in the previous section:

▶ The heading of the initial menu, Select a Task, is preceded by a percent sign and is followed by the two numbers that designate the vertical and horizontal positions (in this case, 0,0 again designates the default placement, which is in the center of the screen).

▶ Each option that appears on the initial menu is flush with the left margin.

▶ Indented on the lines below each option are the commands that execute that option.

However, this menu program also includes submenus, messages, variables, and an exit to DOS. Programming each of these elements is described in the following sections.

Including Submenus in the Menu Program File

Toward the end of the program in Figure 7.11 is a second menu heading that begins with a percent sign and is flush with the left margin. This is the heading of a submenu. The submenu, Choose a Spreadsheet File, contains two options: Budget and Inventory. The numbers next to the submenu's heading name indicate that this submenu will appear a little to the right and down from the center of the screen. (You may need to try different settings to position the menu just where you want it on the screen.)

This submenu should appear when the user selects the Spreadsheet option from the initial menu. Therefore, underneath the Spreadsheet option earlier in the file, the line that would normally contain a command to execute the option contains the submenu's heading instead. When the menu program sees the submenu's heading, it knows to search through the rest of the file until it finds the lines that describe that submenu's options and commands.

Displaying Messages to the User

In some cases, you may want an informational message to appear on the screen while a particular task is being performed by the menu program. To display a message, you can use the ECHO command. Any words you include after ECHO will be displayed on the workstation screen. For example, under the Word Processing option, the line

ECHO Please wait while WordPerfect is loading

displays the message "Please wait while WordPerfect is loading" while the WP command is being executed.

The CLS command clears the screen of any previous messages so that the following messages don't clutter the screen.

Using Variables in the Menu Program File

Another advanced feature in the sample menu program is the variables (preceded by @) used in the Copy a File option:

NCOPY @1"Enter source drive and file" @2"Enter destination drive"

When you need the user to supply a piece of information to complete a task, you can assign that piece of information a variable in the menu. When the menu program tries to complete the task and encounters a variable, it waits for input from the user, then substitutes that information for the variable and proceeds with the task.

In this example, the user needs to supply information to complete the NCOPY command. The command syntax for the NCOPY command is

NCOPY *sourcefile destinationfile*

The user must supply the drive and file name of the original file and the destination drive to which the file will be copied. To tell the menu program that this information is to be supplied by the user, the supervisor who created the menu used the variable @. Because there are two different pieces of information that the user needs to supply, the supervisor numbered the variables @1 and @2.

When the user selects the Copy a File option, the NCOPY command begins to execute, encounters the first variable, and waits for user input. While it is waiting, it displays the message "Enter source drive and file" on the user's screen. In order for these words to be displayed, they must be enclosed in quotation marks. When the user types in the source file's name, the NCOPY command proceeds until it encounters the second variable, @2. While it waits for input here, it displays the message "Enter destination drive." When the user types in the destination drive, the NCOPY commands finishes its operation.

Once the user has supplied information for a variable, that same information will be used automatically anywhere else that variable appears within the commands for that option. For example, after the NCOPY command, the supervisor added the command

DIR /P @2

This command will display a directory listing of all the files contained in variable @2, which is the destination directory specified for variable @2 in the previous command.

The other two commands under the Copy a File option are provided for the convenience of the user. CLS clears the screen before the following commands are executed so that the workstation screen isn't cluttered. PAUSE makes the menu program wait until the user presses any key before it continues with any additional commands. The PAUSE command is useful after the DIR command, because it allows the user to read the list of files before the menu program begins executing other commands.

Exiting to DOS from a Menu

You can include an option in your menu that will allow users to leave the menu and go to the DOS prompt. From the DOS prompt, users can execute various DOS and NetWare commands. When the users are finished working at the DOS prompt, they can return to the menu by typing Exit.

The command for sending the users to the DOS prompt is COMMAND. You can also include a PROMPT command to display a message telling users how to get back to the menu from the DOS prompt. In the example, the user's DOS prompt has been changed so that it shows the message "Type 'Exit' when you're finished."

The four commands under the Exit to DOS option in the menu program file prevent the commands from appearing on the screen, clear the screen, change the DOS prompt, and exit to DOS:

```
ECHO OFF
CLS
PROMPT=$P (Type 'Exit' when you're finished) $G
COMMAND
```

RUNNING A MENU PROGRAM

After you've created a menu program, you use the NetWare MENU utility to execute it. For example, to execute the menu called MANAGERS.MNU, type

```
MENU MANAGERS
```

To run Mel's menu, which is named MEL.MNU, type

```
MENU MEL
```

RUNNING MENUS FROM LOGIN SCRIPTS

An efficient way to run menus is through login scripts. You can make your login script execute your menu automatically. To do this, combine the MENU command with the EXIT login script command. Then the EXIT command will stop the login script and go directly into the menu. For example, to make Mel's user login script go directly into his menu, add the following line at the very end of Mel's login script:

EXIT "MENU MEL"

If you want to send only the users who belong to the group MANAGERS into the MANAGERS.MNU menu program, you could include the following commands in the system login script:

IF MEMBER OF "MANAGERS" THEN
EXIT "MENU MANAGERS"

Only the managers would be sent directly to the menu. The user login scripts would execute for the other users.

Review

NetWare provides two tools you can use to automate workstations for your users: login scripts and menus.

You can use login scripts to map drives to network directories, display messages on the screen, and execute other commands for the users. You should replace the default login script with a system login script and user login scripts. A system login script executes for everyone who logs in. User login scripts belong to individual users.

NetWare also includes a utility called MENU, which allows you to set up a menu program for your users. You can create a menu screen that lists the applications you want your users to choose from. Then when they select an application from that menu, it will automatically be executed for them. To create a menu program, you use a text editor to specify the menu options and formatting instructions in a file. Then you use the MENU utility to run the file you created.

You can include a command in a login script to execute a menu program. Then, when the login script finishes running, it sends the user into the menu program instead of leaving the user at the DOS prompt.

CHAPTER 8

Routine Network Maintenance and Troubleshooting

If you own a car, you know that periodically you need to do some routine maintenance to keep the car running smoothly and efficiently. Occasionally, you check the car's fluids, such as the oil, transmission fluid, and radiator water, to make sure that they are at the correct level. You may need to add antifreeze, buy a new battery, or change the oil. And periodically you give the car a tune up, replacing worn parts, adjusting other parts, and so on.

Every once in a while, however, something that you couldn't prevent goes wrong with your car. A tire goes flat, a belt breaks, or a funny knocking noise develops in the engine. When this happens, you *troubleshoot*—you search for and isolate the problem, then fix it.

Just as a car runs more smoothly and efficiently if it receives routine maintenance, so will your network. But problems will still occur, and you'll need to troubleshoot to get everyone back on the job. This chapter will describe some of the routine maintenance you can do to make sure your network continues to run in the fast lane, as well as some hints for troubleshooting network problems if they do occur.

What Does Routine Maintenance Include?

Routine maintenance of your network does not need to eat up a large portion of your time. And, as with most things in life, a little preventative maintenance can save you time in the long run.

Network maintenance may be different for every network, depending on the types of applications that users are running, the type of equipment on the network, and the particular network features that are being used. However, there are some common, routine tasks you can do that will add to the stability and longevity of your network:

- Documenting your network
- Backing up and restoring network files

▶ Deleting and purging unnecessary files

▶ Monitoring your file server's statistics, to see if it is running out of memory, cache buffers, and so on

▶ Updating NetWare software

▶ Monitoring security

▶ Monitoring the error log files for the file server, the volumes, and the Transaction Tracking System

Making backups of your network files is an extremely important task. *Backing up* files means making copies of them in case the original files on the network accidently get deleted or corrupted. Without good backups, your users might lose hours, days, or even weeks of work in the event of an accidental deletion. Backing up your network files is covered in a chapter of its own (Chapter 9).

The other routine maintenance tasks listed above are described in this chapter. But bear in mind that this list is not exhaustive. Analyze your network and needs, and then establish your own list of maintenance tasks.

Documenting Your Network

Paperwork: The word alone can strike fear into the heart of any network supervisor. However, it's a necessary evil, and you'll be glad you did it the next time you need to add new hardware to the network, resolve an interrupt conflict, balance your equipment budget, get a workstation repaired under warranty, justify a new purchase to management, or train your backup network supervisor (or your replacement when you move on to bigger and better things).

How you keep track of your network information is your decision. You can store records in folders, in a three-ring binder labeled *Network Maintenance*, in a database, or in any other system that fits your style.

So what records do you need to keep?

- ▸ Existing inventory and new purchases of hardware and software

- ▸ Hardware configuration of network boards, workstations, file servers, printers, and so on

- ▸ Maintenance records: when equipment was repaired, how much it cost, and so on

- ▸ Your network layout

- ▸ Login scripts, menus, batch files, and so on

- ▸ Your backup schedule and the location of backup tapes or disks

RECORDING EXISTING INVENTORY AND NEW PURCHASES

To begin with, you need to inventory all your existing hardware and software. Then make sure you keep records of every new hardware and software purchase. Record the name of the product, the version number, the serial number, the vendor you bought it from, the price, the purchase date, the length of the warranty, and so on.

An inventory can be useful for many reasons, most of which are financial. By keeping your inventory records up to date, you can supply management with information about current capital assets, track your expenditures against your budget, and plan for the coming year's budget. By tracking purchases, you can tell at a glance whether a workstation is under warranty, which vendor you used, and which products you have that may need to be upgraded soon.

Also, make sure you fill out and return all registration cards or forms. Some companies will not honor a warranty unless you have registered your purchase with them. In addition, many companies offer incentives for registering, such as free technical support, notification of upgrades or bug fixes, reduced prices for upgrades, newsletters, special offers, and sometimes even free gifts.

Figure 8.1 shows a worksheet format you can use to record your hardware and software purchases. You can copy this worksheet and use it for your record keeping,

FIGURE 8.1

Document your hardware
and software purchases

WORKSHEET A:
RECORD OF HARDWARE AND SOFTWARE PURCHASES

Name of product: _____

Version number: _____

Serial number\Part number: _____

Manufacturer name, address, phone: _____

_____

_____

_____

_____

Vendor name, address, phone: _____

_____

_____

_____

_____

Purchase price: _____

Purchase date: _____

Purchase order number: _____

Length of the warranty: _____

Current location of hardware or software: _____

_____

Warranty or Registration Card mailed in?   Yes _____   No _____

Comments: _____

_____

_____

or you can design your own form. Many people find it more convenient to use a
database to track their inventories. Use whichever method you prefer.

RECORDING HARDWARE CONFIGURATIONS

One of the more common problems that network supervisors encounter is a configuration conflict between two pieces of hardware. For example, every workstation on the network must have a different node address. If two workstations have the same address, they will conflict with each other. Another common problem is when the interrupt setting on a network board is identical to the interrupt of another circuit board in the same workstation.

It can be time-consuming to track down the conflicting pieces of hardware when problems occur. Therefore, recording the configuration settings of each piece of hardware can help you plan addresses and interrupts that won't interfere with each other in the first place, as well as help you identify the potential culprit when a problem does occur.

You also may need to supply this configuration information in various software programs. For example, if you use settings that are different than the default configuration on a network board, you may need to specify those settings in the workstation's NET.CFG file before the workstation will be able to access the network.

Figure 8.2 shows a worksheet format for recording configuration information for your file server and workstations. Figure 8.3 shows a similar worksheet for recording configuration information about your printers. Again, you can copy and use these worksheets, or you can design your own for recording your hardware information.

RECORDING MAINTENANCE HISTORIES

It's a good idea to keep a history of all repairs made to your network hardware, both for warranty and budgeting reasons. You may want to file all paperwork associated with repairs along with the worksheet that documents your original purchase of the item (Figure 8.1).

FIGURE 8.2

Document your hardware settings

WORKSHEET B:
RECORD OF HARDWARE CONFIGURATION SETTINGS

File server or Workstation: _____

Current location: _____

Make and model: _____

Serial number\Part number: _____

Size of floppy disk drives: A: _____   B: _____

Size of hard disk drives: C: _____ D: _____

Memory: _____

Network boards:

Name:_____   Settings: _____

Node address: _____

LAN driver: _____

Name: _____   Settings: _____

Node address: _____

LAN driver: _____

Name: _____   Settings: _____

Node address: _____

LAN driver: _____

Name: _____   Settings: _____

Node address: _____

LAN driver: _____

Other boards (graphics, modem, etc.):

Name: _____   Settings: _____

Name: _____   Settings: _____

Name: _____   Settings: _____

Name: _____   Settings: _____

Comments: _____

_____

_____

FIGURE 8.3

Document your printer

settings

WORKSHEET C:
RECORD OF PRINTER CONFIGURATION SETTINGS

Current location: _____

Make and model: _____

Serial number\Part number: _____

Local (attached to print server) or remote?: _____

Printer number: _____

Serial printer configuration:

    Port (COM1 or COM2?): _____

    Baud rate: _____

    Word size: _____

    Stop bits: _____

    Parity: _____

    XON/XOFF: _____

    Poll: _____

    Interrupt (COM1=4, COM2=3): _____

Parallel printer configuration:

    Port (LPT1, LPT2, or LPT3?): _____

    Poll: _____

    Interrupt (LPT1=7, LPT2=8): _____

Print queues: _____

_____

_____

Print queue operators: _____

Print server operators: _____

Comments: _____

_____

_____

RECORDING YOUR NETWORK LAYOUT

Some network supervisors find it useful to have a drawing of their network on file, showing how all the workstations, file servers, printers, and peripheral equipment are connected. A drawing of your network can be a useful visual aid when you try to explain to a new employee or to upper management how your network operates.

To draw your network, sketch out the general layout of equipment (it doesn't necessarily have to be to scale). You may want to label each workstation with its make and model (such as *PS/2 Model 50*), its location (*Marketing office*), and its user (*Barb*). Show the cable that connects each piece of hardware to the network, and show what type of cable it is (such as *Ethernet*). Figure 8.4 shows a sample network layout drawing.

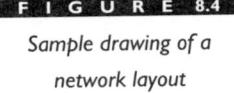

FIGURE 8.4

Sample drawing of a network layout

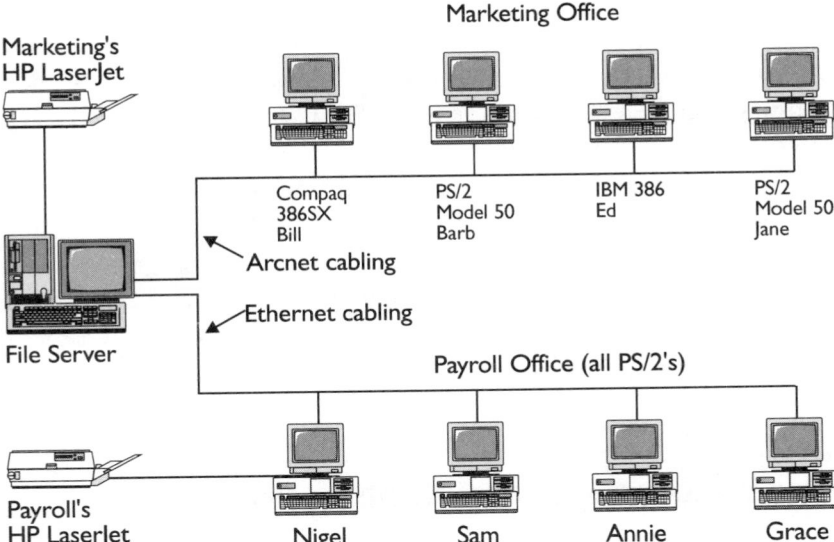

RECORDING YOUR LOGIN SCRIPTS, MENUS, AND BATCH FILES

Creating useful login scripts, menus, and batch files for your users takes some careful planning on your part, and probably some trial and error to get them working correctly. After going to that much effort, you might be quite discouraged if something accidently happened to those files and they were deleted or corrupted. The thought of starting over again is never appealing, and you know that problems like this occur only when you can least afford the time to correct them.

Therefore, keeping both a printed copy and a diskette copy of those files can be a real time-saver. Login scripts, menus, and batch files are all ASCII text files, so you can print them from any word processing application that allows you to print text files.

The system login script is a text file called NET$LOG.DAT, and it is located in the SYS:PUBLIC directory. Each user's script is a text file called LOGIN, located in that user's ID directory under SYS:MAIL.

To determine a user's ID directory, use the SYSCON menu utility. Run the utility and select User Information, then the user's name from the list of users that appears, and then Other Information. The user's ID number is listed in the window that appears. Write down this number, then exit SYSCON. The user's ID directory is located under SYS:MAIL, and it is named with the user's ID number.

Menus and batch files may be in SYS:PUBLIC or in users' home directories. Batch files, such as AUTOEXEC.BAT, may also be on the user's boot disk.

Print all of these and any other types of files you want to keep a printed copy of, and store them with the rest of your network information. Be sure you mark each printout with the name of the file, its purpose, the user to which it belongs, and so on.

RECORDING BACKUP INFORMATION

It is important to keep a written record of your backup schedule. Because most backup systems allow a great deal of flexibility in how and when network files and data can be backed up (*archived*), many network supervisors do different types of backups at different times.

Whatever scheme you're using, you should document it clearly so that if you're gone, someone else can restore necessary files. Record not only your schedule, but also the type of backup system you use, the labeling system you use to identify your tapes or disks, the location of the tapes or disks, and any other information you think someone may need in order to restore files if you're gone.

Chapter 9 explains how to select a backup system, establish a backup schedule, and store your backup tapes or disks.

Deleting and Purging Unnecessary Files

As users create more and more files on the network, the file server's disk space begins to fill up. If your disk space is limited, you may want to pay attention to the amount of space available on the file server's disks.

One way to regain disk space is to delete unnecessary files. You may want to make a once-a-month practice of going through the network directories and deleting unnecessary or outdated files. You may also want to ask your users to do the same thing.

In NetWare version 3.x, files that are deleted are not really deleted; they appear to be gone, but they are actually saved in a special directory. This allows users to salvage deleted files if they make a mistake, by using the SALVAGE utility. These deleted files can use up a lot of disk space. If the disk begins to get full, the oldest deleted files are *purged* from the special directory to make more disk space available. Only when a file is purged is it actually erased from the network. If you do not want deleted files to take up disk space, you can purge these files yourself.

To purge files, use the PURGE utility from a workstation. (Just make sure you really want to purge the files—once they're purged, they can't be recovered.) You can use PURGE to purge a single file, several files, all the files in a directory, or all the files in a directory and its subdirectories.

For example, to purge a single file named SMOOTH that you deleted from your current directory, type

PURGE SMOOTH

To purge all files whose names begin with an S, type

PURGE S*.*

To purge all files in a directory, add the directory path to the PURGE command:

PURGE F:*.*

or

PURGE VOL1:HOME\ANDY

NetWare version 2.2 does not keep deleted files around as long as version 3.*x*. In version 2.2, a deleted file is kept in a salvageable condition only until the user who deleted the file deletes a second file, creates a new file, or logs out of the network. Therefore, purging files on a NetWare version 2.2 network is not as helpful as it is on a version 3.*x* network.

Monitoring Your File Server's Statistics

Another type of routine task you, as a network supervisor, should do is monitor various file server statistics to see how your server is performing. You can see how the server's memory is being used, how many cache buffers it is using, and so on. These statistics can help you determine if you need to add enhancements to your file server, such as more memory or more disk space.

The following sections described some of the more meaningful statistics. If you want to know more about optimizing your server's performance, turn to the NetWare documentation. If you're using NetWare version 2.2, refer to the "Fine-tune Your File Server's Performance" and "FCONSOLE" sections in the *Using the Network* manual. If you're using version 3.*x*, refer to the *System Administration* manual for descriptions of the SET and MONITOR server utilities, as well as to the chapter entitled "Troubleshooting Guide" in the same manual.

MONITORING YOUR FILE SERVER'S MEMORY

It is important to install enough memory, also called *RAM* (random-access memory), in your file server. This memory allows the file server to run several processes at once. If your file server is low on memory, its performance can slow down, and you may start receiving error messages.

With NetWare version 3.x, you can use the MONITOR server utility to see the number of cache buffers that your server is using. This information can help you determine if you need to give your server more memory. With NetWare version 2.2, you can use the FCONSOLE menu utility from a workstation.

Using MONITOR in NetWare Version 3.x

If you have NetWare version 3.x, use the MONITOR server utility to see if you need to add more memory to your server. Load MONITOR by typing the following command at the file server console:

LOAD MONITOR

If MONITOR is already loaded, press the Alt and Esc keys simultaneously to switch to the MONITOR screen. Alt-Esc is the key combination for switching between program screens when the file server is running more than one program at the same time.

On MONITOR's Available Options menu, move the cursor to the Resource Utilization option and press the Enter key. The Server Memory Statistics screen appears, as shown in Figure 8.5.

Locate the Cache Buffers item and note the percentage listed for cache buffers. This percentage shows the amount of memory being used for cache buffers. If the cache buffer percentage drops to 20% or so, you may need to add more memory to your file server.

FIGURE 8.5

MONITOR's Server

Memory Statistics screen

(version 3.x)

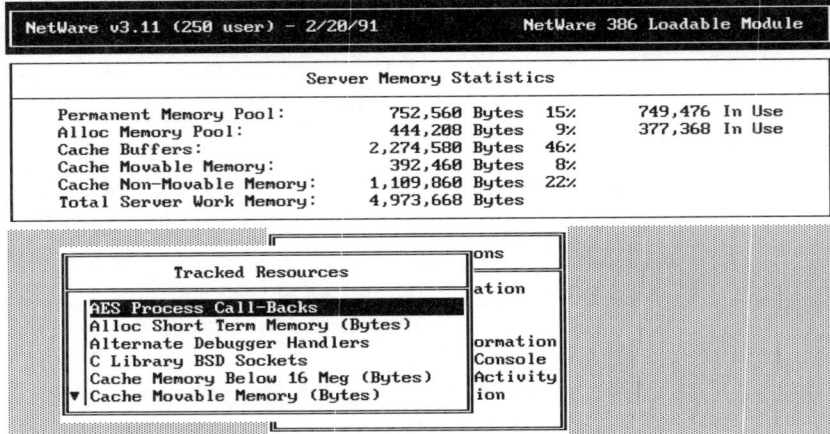

Using FCONSOLE in NetWare Version 2.2

If you're using NetWare version 2.2, run the FCONSOLE menu utility to see the number of cache buffers being used:

I · Run FCONSOLE by typing the following command at a workstation:

FCONSOLE

and pressing Enter.

2 · On the Available Options menu, move the cursor to the Statistics option and press the Enter key.

3 · Move the cursor to the Cache Statistics option and press the Enter key. The Cache Statistics screen appears, as shown in Figure 8.6.

4 · In the Cache Statistics screen, locate the Thrashing Count item and note the percentage listed for cache buffers.

FIGURE 8.6

FCONSOLE's Cache

Statistics screen

(version 2.2.)

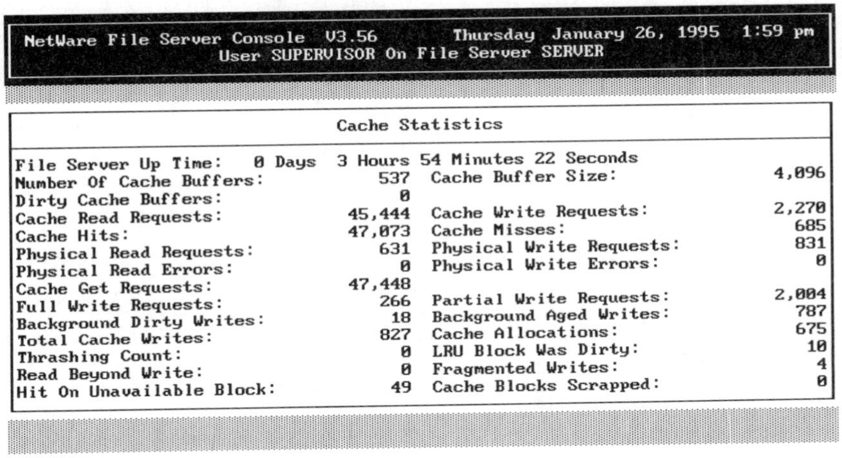

```
NetWare File Server Console  V3.56      Thursday  January 26, 1995  1:59 pm
                     User SUPERVISOR On File Server SERVER

                              Cache Statistics

File Server Up Time:   0 Days  3 Hours 54 Minutes 22 Seconds
Number Of Cache Buffers:          537  Cache Buffer Size:            4,096
Dirty Cache Buffers:                0
Cache Read Requests:           45,444  Cache Write Requests:         2,270
Cache Hits:                    47,073  Cache Misses:                   685
Physical Read Requests:           631  Physical Write Requests:        831
Physical Read Errors:               0  Physical Write Errors:            0
Cache Get Requests:            47,448
Full Write Requests:              266  Partial Write Requests:       2,004
Background Dirty Writes:            18  Background Aged Writes:         787
Total Cache Writes:               827  Cache Allocations:              675
Thrashing Count:                    0  LRU Block Was Dirty:             10
Read Beyond Write:                  0  Fragmented Writes:                4
Hit On Unavailable Block:          49  Cache Blocks Scrapped:            0
```

5 · Divide the thrashing count number by the number of days the server has been running. Ideally, this number should be near zero. If the number is above 1, you should probably add memory to your file server.

6 · To check another statistic, Disk Requests Serviced from Cache, which can help indicate whether you need to add more memory, press the Esc key twice to return to the Cache Statistics screen.

7 · Move the cursor to the Summary screen and press the Enter key.

8 · Locate the Disk Requests Serviced from Cache item and note the percentage listed. If the percentage is less than 93%, you may need to add more memory to the file server.

MONITORING YOUR FILE SERVER'S DISK SPACE AND DIRECTORY ENTRIES

Making sure your file server has enough disk space for all your users' network files is crucial. If your server begins to run out of disk space, you can add hard disks to your file server. Your reseller can help you select the type of external hard disk system that will work with your server.

You can monitor the disk space that is being used by each of the server's volumes using the VOLINFO utility. Monitor the disk space regularly so that you can order a new external hard disk system before you run out of disk space on your existing disk.

VOLINFO also shows the amount of *directory entries* that are in use and how many directory entries are still available. In simplest terms, directory entries are used on the hard disk to help index where information is located. Each directory, DOS file, and trustee list on the network uses up one directory entry. Each Macintosh file uses two directory entries. If you run out of directory entries on your disk, no one will be able to create a new file or directory. This is another reason why it is important to periodically delete and purge unnecessary files and directories from your network.

To see how much disk space and how many directory entries are being used by a volume, type

VOLINFO

and press Enter.

You'll see a screen similar to the one shown in Figure 8.7. This screen shows information about each of the server's volumes. The Kilobytes field shows the total number of kilobytes of disk space allocated to the volume, as well as the kilobytes of disk space that are still free. The Directories field shows the total number of directory entries allocated to the volume and the number of directory entries that are still available. If necessary, you can increase the number of directory entries, as described in the following sections.

Adding Directory Entries in NetWare Version 2.2

In NetWare version 2.2, you can add directory entries by using the INSTALL program's Maintenance option. Back up all your network files (see Chapter 9 for details), and then run the program by typing this command at the file server console

INSTALL -M

and press Enter.

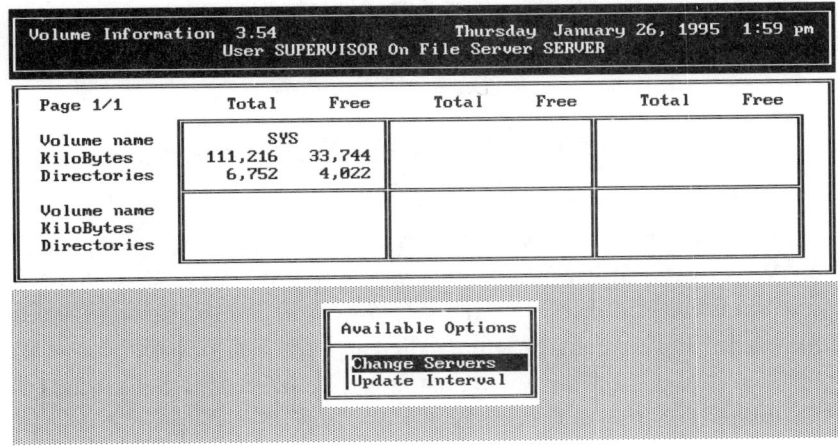

FIGURE 8.7

VOLINFO's disk space and directory entry information

See the NetWare version 2.2 *Installing and Maintaining the Network* manual for specific instructions.

Changing Memory Settings in Version 3.x

In NetWare version 3.x, you can use the SET server utility to change the amount of memory that can be used to hold directory entries. You can increase the SET Directory Cache Buffer Nonreferenced Delay parameter so that cache buffers, which hold the directory entries in memory, store the entries for a longer time. This parameter's default time is 5.5 seconds, but you can set it to any length from 1 second to 5 minutes. For example, to increase the amount of time that directory entries are held in memory to 20 seconds, type

SET DIRECTORY CACHE BUFFER NONREFERENCED DELAY: 20

You can also use the SET Maximum Directory Cache Buffers and SET Minimum Directory Cache Buffers parameters to increase or decrease the maximum and minimum numbers of cache buffers that are available to hold the directory entries in memory. For more information about using the SET server utility, see the NetWare version 3.*x System Administration* manual.

Updating NetWare Software

No matter how thoroughly a software product is designed, tested, and retested before it is shipped, a few little bugs always seem to slip by. This is just as true of NetWare as it is of any other software product. Whenever Novell discovers a bug in a product that has already been released, Novell determines whether it is possible to fix the bug with a small program called a *patch*. If it's possible, Novell will create the patch and make it available to customers. Sometimes, Novell will replace an entire utility or file with a new version.

Some of these updated patches and files may be useful to you. Others may not be as useful because they may affect files you aren't using, such as a LAN driver for a different network board. However, it might be worth it to check periodically for new fixes for files and utilities you're using.

You can get these patches and updated files from Novell in several ways:

- ▶ You can download the patches from Novell's forum, called NetWire, on CompuServe (an electronic bulletin board service). If you subscribe to the CompuServe service, you can access NetWire. For more information about subscribing to CompuServe, call 1-800-848-8990.

- ▶ You can purchase a subscription to Novell's online support and information services, called NetWare Express. NetWare Express is on the GE Information Services teleprocessing network. With NetWare Express, you get much more than just bug fixes; it also supplies new enhancements and software updates, access to bulletin boards and libraries, and access to NetWare Express's electronic mail system. For more information about subscribing to NetWare Express, call 1-800-NETWARE.

- ▶ You can ask your reseller for the updated patches. Your reseller should have access to the patches that Novell distributes for its products and should be able to provide them to you.

Monitoring Network Security

Chapter 6 explained how to set up and monitor your network security. You may want to set up a regular schedule for monitoring your security with the SECURITY utility. You can also take some steps to protect your server and workstations, as described in the following sections.

PROTECTING YOUR SERVER AND WORKSTATIONS

You should occasionally verify that your file server's physical security is intact. Make sure the server is in a room that stays locked whenever possible to prevent anyone from doing damage to the network either intentionally or accidentally.

Another security precaution is to remind your users to log out of the network whenever they leave their workstations. If a workstation is left unattended and the user has not logged out, an intruder could easily access your network files.

LOCKING THE FILE SERVER CONSOLE IN NETWARE VERSION 3.X

In NetWare version 3.x, you can actually lock the file server console so that anyone who wants to use the server's keyboard must first enter a password. Although many file servers have a key lock, locking the console with MONITOR is more secure (an industrious person can get past a computer's key lock).

To lock the server's console, use the MONITOR server utility:

1 · From the file server's keyboard, type the following command to load MONITOR:

LOAD MONITOR

and press Enter.

2 · From the Available Options menu, select Lock File Server Console.

3 · When asked for a password, type in either SUPERVISOR's password or a new password that will be used only to unlock the console.

To unlock the keyboard, type in either SUPERVISOR's password or the password you entered when you locked the keyboard. If the server screen is displaying the *snake*, press any key to clear the screen. Then you can enter the password. The snake is a screen-saver for the server's monitor. It also shows how much traffic the server is handling; the snake moves faster when traffic increases.

Monitoring the Error Log Files

Whenever an error occurs with the file server or the volume, NetWare records the error in error log files. Periodically, you may want to check these files to see what types of errors have occurred. There are three error log files:

▶ SYS$LOG.ERR, for file server errors

▶ VOL$LOG.ERR, for volume errors

▶ TTS$LOG.ERR, for NetWare's Transaction Tracking System (TTS protects files, especially database files such as the NetWare bindery, from being corrupted)

Use a text editor to read and print the error log files. The file server and TTS error logs are both in the SYS: volume. The volume error log is in whichever volume the log belongs to. For example, the VOL$LOG.ERR file for volume VOL1 would be located in the VOL1 volume.

You can also read the file server error log from within the SYSCON utility (the volume error log and the TTS error log can only be opened with a text editor). To see the file server error log, run SYSCON and select Supervisor Options, then select View File Server Error Log. Any errors that have been recorded will appear on the screen. Figure 8.8 shows an example of the display.

If you see any error messages that are not self-explanatory in these files, refer to the NetWare *System Messages* manual for information.

After you review the error log files, you can delete them. New ones will be created if new errors occur. If you use SYSCON to review the file server error log,

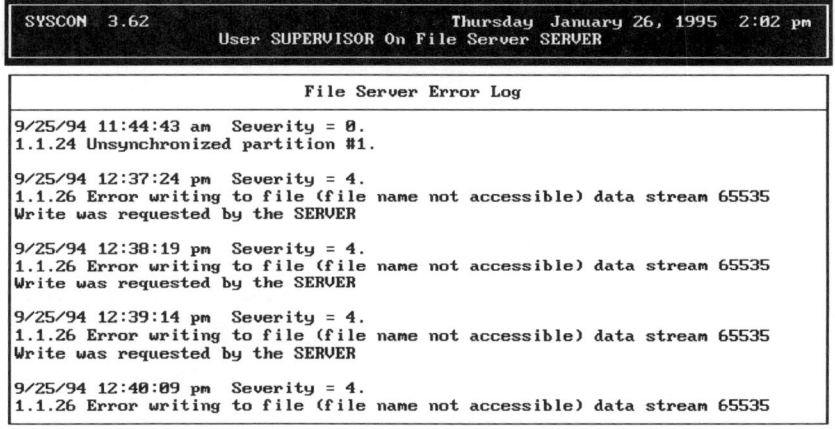

FIGURE 8.8

SYSCON's display of the

file server error log

you can erase the log displayed on the screen by pressing the Esc key. Then answer Yes when you're asked if you want to clear the error log.

Running NetWare Version 3.x Server Utilities with Remote Console

NetWare version 3.x includes Remote Console, which allows you to run server utilities, such as MONITOR, from a workstation. Remote Console can be used by the network supervisor or by anyone who knows the Remote Console password (if you assign one) and has Read and File Scan rights to the SYS:SYSTEM directory.

The utilities you load to run Remote Console depend on how the workstation is connected to the network:

> ► If the workstation communicates with the file server through a modem, load REMOTE.NLM and RS232.NLM on the file server and ACON-SOLE.EXE on the workstation. The RS232.NLM and ACONSOLE.EXE

utilities allow the file server and workstation to use asynchronous communication.

▶ If the workstation and file server are directly connected to the same network and don't transfer information over a modem, load REMOTE.NLM and RSPX.NLM on the file server and RCONSOLE.EXE on the workstation.

To run Remote Console from a workstation, follow these steps:

1 · Load REMOTE.NLM on the file server. You can assign a Remote Console password at the same time. If you don't specify a password when you load REMOTE.NLM, you must use the SUPERVISOR password to run Remote Console. To load REMOTE.NLM and assign a password, type

LOAD REMOTE *password*

and press Enter. If you don't want to specify a password, just type the command LOAD REMOTE.

2 · Load the communications driver on the file sever (either RSPX.NLM or RS232.NLM). For example, to load RSPX.NLM, type

LOAD RSPX

and press Enter.

3 · From the workstation, start either RCONSOLE.EXE (for direct connections) or ACONSOLE.EXE (for asynchronous connections). For example, to start RCONSOLE.EXE, type

RCONSOLE

and press enter.

4 · (ACONSOLE only) Select the Connect to Remote Location option.

5 · Select the server you want to access and press the Enter key. If you are using ACONSOLE, you may also need to specify information about your modem, such as the phone number.

6 · When prompted for the password, enter either the SUPERVISOR password the password you typed when you loaded REMOTE.NLM on the file server.

When the password is accepted, your workstation screen will display the file server's screen. If you previously loaded MONITOR on the file server with the keyboard lock option, MONITOR will appear on your Remote Console screen, and you will be prompted for the keyboard lock password. Otherwise, you will see either a screen showing active file servers or the server console prompt, a colon (:).

You can work with Remote Console as follows:

▶ To access Remote Console's Available Options menu, press the asterisk (*) key on the number pad of your keyboard.

▶ To move between active file server screens, such as between MONITOR and the console prompt, press the minus (−) and plus (+) keys. Note that these keys do not work in the Available Options menu.

▶ To run a server utility, go to the console prompt and type the server utility command.

▶ To exit Remote Console, select End Remote Session with Server from the Available Options menu.

Troubleshooting Hints

Performing routine maintenance on your network will help ensure that your network runs smoothly and efficiently. However, even the best of preventative maintenance can't eliminate all possible network problems. When a problem with your network occurs, where do you start looking for the solution?

On a NetWare network, the possible combinations of networking hardware, networking software, computers, printers, and applications are endless. Therefore, it is impossible to predict every type of problem you might encounter, and equally impossible to predict the solutions. But it may be helpful to know where to begin looking for the sources of problems and what to do after you locate them. The following sections provide some troubleshooting guidelines to follow and point out some common problem areas.

A FEW TROUBLESHOOTING GUIDELINES

When it comes to troubleshooting your network (or almost anything that consists of more than one component), the first step is to isolate the problem. *Isolating* a network problem means trying to identify which component is causing the problem. Only then can you fix it.

Here are some guidelines to follow when troubleshooting a network problem:

- ▸ **Narrow the search:** Were there any error messages? Did the problem occur on only one workstation, on several workstations, or at the file server? Can you pinpoint the problem area? For example, is it a printing problem, a communication problem, an application problem, or a problem in another area of the network?

- ▸ **Check the equipment:** If the problem is with a piece of equipment such as a workstation, printer, or peripheral, try hooking up the machine in stand-alone mode. If it functions correctly by itself, you'll know that the problem has something to do with the connection to the network. If the machine has the same problem when running in stand-alone mode as it did on the network, you can eliminate the network components and concentrate on the configuration of the machine itself.

- ▸ **Check the documentation:** Try looking in the NetWare documentation for ideas. Both the NetWare version 2.2 *Installing and Maintaining the Network* manual and the version 3.*x* *System Administration* manual have troubleshooting sections that point out several common problems and solutions. In addition, the *System Messages* manual explains error messages that may appear.

▶ **Try each solution independently:** After you have narrowed down the search to a particularly suspicious area, begin trying solutions, but *try them one at a time*. Start with the easiest, cheapest solution and work up from there. Changing one element at a time may take longer, but it can save you money. It can also help you solve the problem much more quickly if it happens again.

▶ **Look for patches:** Check NetWire (Novell's electronic bulletin board system) or check with your reseller for any patches that may solve the problem you're having.

▶ **Call a support line as a last resort:** If all else fails, call your reseller or Novell Technical Support for help. Because calling for technical support can often cost you money, make sure you have used every other avenue (especially the documentation) first. Nothing is more frustrating than spending a small chunk of money on a support call, and then finding that the answer was on page 45 of the installation manual.

▶ **Document the solution:** When you find the solution, document it. That way, you or the next person who supervises the network may be able to avoid duplicating efforts if the problem reoccurs later.

By using the one-component-at-a-time technique, you may be able to save both your money and your sanity. For example, suppose you have a workstation that can't seem to communicate with the file server. Frustrated, you change the network board, replace the network cable, and update the network shell files. When you reboot the workstation, it works. Great—but which one of the elements that you changed was the one that caused the problem? If the problem was a corrupted shell file, you just wasted money on a new network board and cable.

COMMON PROBLEM AREAS

The following sections describe a few potential problem areas. They provide suggestions for checking the causes of file server, workstation, application, printing, user, and password problems. See Chapter 2 for more information about installing NetWare and creating boot files. Refer to the section about monitoring your server earlier in this chapter for more information about checking the file server's performance.

File Server Problems

If you're having trouble with your file server, check the following areas:

- ► Are the network boards configured correctly? Are their board settings conflicting with any other boards or printers attached to the server?

- ► Do the LAN drivers loaded on the server match the network boards? If you are using NetWare version 3.x, did you use the BIND server utility to bind the correct protocol (such as IPX) to the LAN driver?

- ► Is the cable that connects the server to the rest of the network functioning?

- ► If you just installed or upgraded your server, did you follow the instructions in the documentation exactly? Check for missed steps, shortcuts you took that may have bypassed an important file, and so on.

- ► Are you using the correct version of files or utilities on this server? You can't use a NetWare version 3.11 VREPAIR utility on a NetWare version 3.1 network, for example.

- ► Does the server need more memory?

- ► Is the server's volume out of disk space or directory entries?

- ► Do you need to reconfigure certain aspects of the server to make it run differently? If you're using NetWare version 3.x, you can use the MONITOR and SET utilities to check the server's parameters and change some if necessary. With NetWare version 2.2, you can use the Maintenance option of the INSTALL program to change some server parameters.

Workstation Problems

If you're having trouble with a workstation, check the following areas:

- ▶ Is the problem with a single workstation or several? If the problem is with several workstations, it may be caused by the network cabling or related cabling hardware.

- ▶ Is the network board configured correctly? Are the board settings conflicting with any other boards or printers attached to the workstation?

- ▶ Does the LAN driver loaded on the workstation's boot disk match the network board?

- ▶ Is the cable that connects the workstation to the rest of the network functioning?

- ▶ If you just installed or upgraded the workstation, did you follow the instructions in the documentation exactly? Check for missed steps, shortcuts that may have bypassed an important file, and so on.

- ▶ Are you using the right NetWare boot files on this workstation? If this workstation is using dedicated IPX drivers, make sure that the boot disk has the correct version of NETx, the LAN driver, and IPX.COM, and that IPX.COM was generated with the correct LAN driver. If the workstation is using ODI drivers, the boot disk should have the correct versions of LSL, IPXODI, NETx, VLMs, and the LAN driver.

- ▶ Is the workstation running on a Token-Ring network that is using source routing? If so, make sure the ROUTE.COM file is on the workstation's boot disk (and is loaded).

- ▶ Is the workstation using the IBM LAN Support program? If so, make sure the LANSUP.COM file is on the boot disk and is loaded from the CONFIG.SYS file.

- ▶ Does the workstation need more DOS environment space? If so, you can increase the DOS environment size by using the SHELL command in the workstation's CONFIG.SYS file.

▸ Is the workstation finding the right DOS COMMAND.COM file? Use
the COMSPEC command in the user's login script or the SHELL
command in the workstation's CONFIG.SYS file to point to the
COMMAND.COM file.

▸ Does the workstation seem to be running too slowly on the network? You
may need to increase the number of cache buffers that the workstation
uses to manage incoming and outgoing network data. You can change the
number of cache buffers by using the CACHE BUFFERS command in
the SHELL.CFG or NET.CFG file.

Application Problems

If you're having trouble with an application, check the following areas:

▸ If you just installed or upgraded the application, did you follow the
instructions in the documentation exactly? Check for missed steps,
shortcuts that may have bypassed an important file, and so on. Often,
just copying applications onto the network isn't adequate. You may
need to run the application's installation program for the application
to function correctly.

▸ Are you using the correct NetWare boot files on the workstation?
If the application required NetBIOS, the boot disk should contain
NETBIOS.COM and INT2F.COM.

▸ Does the workstation need more DOS environment space to run
the application? If so, you can increase the DOS environment size by
using the SHELL command in the workstation's CONFIG.SYS file.

▸ Is the workstation running out of SPX connections, cache buffers, or
file handles? To adjust these items to handle network applications,
specify their new settings in the workstation's SHELL.CFG or
NET.CFG file. For example, to increase the number of SPX connections from the default of 15, type

SPX CONNECTIONS=20

Also make sure that the number of file handles set in the SHELL.CFG or NET.CFG file is the same as the number set in the CONFIG.SYS file.

▶ Does the user have adequate rights to the directory from which the application is executed and to the directory where the application saves files? See Chapter 6 for more information about assigning rights to users.

▶ Is the application file corrupted? Try reinstalling the application.

▶ Is the application installed too deeply in the directory structure? Some applications require that they be installed at the volume level instead of in a subdirectory. If this is the case with your application, you can install the application in a subdirectory and then map a fake root to the subdirectory. For more information about mapping fake roots, see Chapter 7.

▶ Are the application's files flagged with the wrong file attributes? Most applications' executable files should be flagged Read Only and Shareable, but the application's data files should probably be flagged Normal (which is the same as Read Write). See Chapter 6 for more information about file attributes.

Printing Problems

If you're having trouble with network printing, check the following areas:

▶ Is the problem with a single workstation or several? If the problem is with several workstations, it may be a problem with the network cabling or related cabling hardware.

▶ Is the printer configured correctly?

▶ Is the cable that connects the printer to the workstation or file server functioning?

▶ If you just installed or upgraded the printer, did you follow the instructions in the documentation exactly? Check for missed steps, shortcuts that may have bypassed an important step, and so on.

▶ Are the print queues, print servers, and printers all assigned to each other correctly? Use PCONSOLE to see the status of print queues and print servers. See Chapter 5 of this book and the *NetWare Print Server* manual for more information.

▶ Is the application using the correct printer driver for the printer? Check the manufacturer's documentation for instructions on configuring the printer correctly and using the right driver.

▶ Does the workstation hang when the user presses the Shift and Print-Screen keys? If so, make sure the line

```
LOCAL PRINTERS=0
```

is in the workstation's SHELL.CFG or NET.CFG file.

User and Password Problems

If your users are having trouble working on the network, check the following areas:

▶ If the user can open a file but cannot save changes to it, the user may not have enough rights to work with the file. To make changes to a file, the user usually must have the Create, Write, and Erase rights. When saving a changed file, many applications delete the old version. If the user doesn't have the Erase right, the application won't be able to delete the old version of the file, so it will stop the saving process. See Chapter 6 for more information about users' rights to files.

▶ If the user tries to list the files within a directory and the directory looks empty, the user probably has no rights to the directory. Without the File Scan right, a user cannot see the names of any files in the directory. See Chapter 6 for more information about users' rights to directories.

▶ If a user cannot log in to the network, the user may be typing either the wrong password or the wrong username. Only the network supervisor can give a user a new password. Use the SYSCON utility to assign passwords and also to verify the spelling of the user's username. See Chapter 4 for details.

▸ If the user is using the right password and username, but still can't log in, the user's account may be locked. To see if the user's account is locked (and to unlock it), use the SYSCON utility. From the main SYSCON menu, select User Information, select the user, then select Account Restrictions from the menu that appears. The option Account Disabled will show either Yes or No. If the account is disabled, you can reenable it by changing the Yes to No.

▸ If a user's username, password, or rights cannot be changed, the network's bindery may have become corrupted. You can use the NetWare BINDFIX utility to try to repair the bindery, as explained in the next section.

Repairing Corrupted Data

Unfortunately, data sometimes gets corrupted; disks develop faulty spots that corrupt the files that were stored there, a power failure damages a volume, and so on. Or you may encounter problems with your bindery (the database of network information). For example, someone may not be able to change his or her password, or you may not be able to delete a user.

If the problem is a corrupted file, you can probably delete the file and restore an earlier version of that file from a backup copy. See Chapter 9 for more information about making backup copies.

If the problem is with a volume on the server's hard disk or with the bindery, you may be able to use NetWare utilities to make repairs:

▸ VREPAIR is a server utility that repairs minor problems to volumes that may have been caused by a defective disk or a power outage. Keep a copy of VREPAIR on your server's boot disk so that you can use it if you can't get to the SYS:SYSTEM directory (where VREPAIR is copied during the installation process).

▸ BINDFIX is a command line utility that repairs bindery problems. In addition, BINDFIX can clean up your bindery by deleting the mail directories and the trustee rights of users you have already deleted. Make sure all users have logged out, then run BINDFIX. When BINDFIX is finished running, a message will indicate whether it successfully repaired the bindery.

▸ BINDREST is a command line utility that restores an older version of the bindery if BINDFIX was not successful. If you still have problems after you have run BINDFIX, you can try to restore your bindery from a backup copy. However, any changes that were made to the bindery since it was backed up will be lost. For example, users may need to go back to using previous passwords if they changed their passwords since the last backup copy was made.

Refer to the NetWare documentation for specific instructions for using these utilities.

Review

Routine maintenance is an important part of your job as a network supervisor. The following routine maintenance tasks can help keep your network running smoothly and prevent problems:

▸ Documenting the network

▸ Backing up and restoring network files

▸ Deleting and purging unnecessary files

▸ Monitoring the file server's statistics

▸ Updating NetWare software

▸ Monitoring network security

▸ Monitoring the error log files for the server, the volumes, and the
NetWare TTS

When network problems do occur, you'll save money, time, and frustration by
using an efficient troubleshooting approach, such as the following:

1 · Narrow the search.

2 · If the problem is with a piece of equipment, try setting up the machine
in stand-alone mode to see if it works correctly by itself.

3 · Refer to the NetWare documentation for solutions.

4 · Try solutions one at a time. Do not change several variables at the
same time. Otherwise, you won't know which change was the one that
actually fixed the problem.

5 · Check NetWire (Novell's electronic bulletin board system) or check
with your reseller for any patches that may solve the problem you're
having.

6 · If all else fails, call your reseller or Novell Technical Support for help.

7 · When you find the solution, document it.

One important troubleshooting tool is backup copies of your network files.
The next chapter covers the subject of backup copies: how to back up your network, your choices for backup tools, and how often to back up your files.

CHAPTER 9

Backing Up
Your Network Files

Backing up network files is an essential maintenance task. If you routinely back up your network files, you can restore files from a backup copy.

This chapter discusses network backups—why backing up your network is important, what choices you have for backup tools, and how often you should back up your files.

Why Is Making Backups Important?

In a typical day at the office, any of these events may occur:

- One of your users just deleted all the files in a directory and purged them. Then the user discovered that one of the files was still important, and now he wants to get the file back.

- Another user accidentally copied this month's budget report over last month's report, and now the vice president wants to see last month's report again.

- The hard disk in your file server seems to be having problems, and users can't open several of the files. You can replace the disk, but what do you do about the files that have been corrupted?

If you have been a network supervisor for very long, these scenarios probably sound all too familiar to you. How can you recover these lost or corrupted files?

If you have been regularly backing up your network files, you can restore files from a backup copy. On the other hand, if you don't have backups of your network files, you may find yourself in the awkward position of telling your users they need to start over and recreate the files from scratch.

By keeping up-to-date backup copies of all your network files, you can protect yourself and your users against losing days of work in case the original files on the network accidently get deleted or corrupted.

What Does "Backing Up" Really Mean?

When you *back up* your network files, you make a copy of the files onto diskettes, tapes, or some other type of storage media, then store the copies somewhere away from the file server. However, just making copies of your files may not be enough.

Suppose a power spike the size of Rhode Island hits your file server and fries its hard disk. If you have made copies of all your files using a command such as DOS's COPY or XCOPY, you can restore the files to a new disk. Unfortunately, you will then spend several more hours (or days) recreating all the trustee assignments, Rights Masks, file attributes, and directory attributes. What's worse, if the sizzled hard disk also contained the network bindery, you will need to recreate every user, print queue, and so on.

If you want to back up not just the network files, but also all their associated NetWare information, as well as the bindery, you're in luck. NetWare provides backup utilities that you can use to create complete network backups, as explained in this chapter.

Choosing a Backup System

A backup system consists of two main elements: the backup device and the backup program.

First choose your *backup device*, which is the machine that runs the tapes or disks you are using for your backups. The backup device can be attached to either a file server or workstation, depending on the type of device it is.

Then choose the *backup program* you want to use. Backup utilities allow you to back up data onto a variety of storage media, such as tapes, floppy disks, and optical disks. You can choose one of the NetWare backup utilities or software from another manufacturer.

SELECTING A BACKUP DEVICE

Many supervisors of smaller networks use tape backup systems. Tape systems are more economical than optical disk systems, although they may not be quite as convenient to use. Your reseller can help you find the backup product that is right for your network.

Here are some guidelines to keep in mind when you're choosing your backup system:

▶ Make sure that the backup system works with your version of NetWare.

▶ Make sure the backup system can handle the quantity of data on your network. If your network contains a large amount of data, you may want to get a tape drive that can support higher-capacity tapes than other models, for example. On the other hand, if you have a small network with a small amount of data, you probably don't need to spend the money for a high-capacity system when a smaller, less expensive model would be adequate.

▶ Make sure the system has the features you want. For example, some backup systems allow you to run unattended backup sessions, which means you can set them to run in the middle of the night when no one is there.

▶ Make sure the backup system is capable of backing up the NetWare bindery.

After you have chosen your backup system, you need to select which NetWare or third-party program you want to use to back up files onto that storage system.

SELECTING A BACKUP PROGRAM

To select a backup program, you must decide what your backup needs are. Several third-party backup programs work with NetWare, and some backup devices come with their own software. You might find that for your purposes, those programs are the easiest to use. Otherwise, you can use one of the NetWare backup utilities: SBACKUP.NLM (for NetWare version 3.*x* only), BACKUP.VAP (for NetWare version 2.2 only), or NBACKUP.EXE (for both versions).

The following sections describe some of the features and limitations of the NetWare backup utilities. The steps for using the utilities to back up and restore files are explained later in this chapter.

SBACKUP for NetWare Version 3.*x*

If you're running NetWare version 3.*x*, you can use SBACKUP.NLM to back up and restore your network files (SBACKUP did not ship with NetWare versions before 3.11). SBACKUP has the following features and restrictions:

▸ The backup device must be connected to your file server; it cannot be attached to a workstation.

▸ SBACKUP can back up DOS, Macintosh, OS/2, and UNIX files. This is the only NetWare program that can handle long OS/2 and Macintosh file names, so if you have those name spaces loaded on your network, you must use SBACKUP.

▸ If you have more than one file server on your network, you can back up all of them from a single file server.

BACKUP.VAP for NetWare Version 2.2

If you're running NetWare version 2.2, you can use BACKUP.VAP to back up network files onto your storage system. (A VAP is a Value-Added Process.) BACKUP.VAP is a program that runs on your file server. It has the following features and restrictions:

▸ Your backup device must be connected to the file server.

▸ BACKUP.VAP can back up only DOS files. If you have Macintosh files, use NBACKUP instead.

NBACKUP for NetWare Versions 2.2 and 3.x

NBACKUP.EXE is a workstation menu utility that runs on both NetWare versions 3.x and 2.2, but it is not included in NetWare 3.12. NBACKUP has the following features and restrictions:

▶ The backup device must be connected to a workstation; it cannot be attached to a file server.

▶ You can use NBACKUP to back up files onto any DOS read-write devices, such as floppy disk drives, tape and optical disk drives that have DOS device drivers, workstation hard disks, and network drives. You can also use some non-DOS devices with NBACKUP. Drivers for these devices are listed in the DIBI$DRV.DAT file in SYS:PUBLIC. Consult your reseller about the types of devices you can use.

▶ NBACKUP can back up DOS and Macintosh files. If you're running NetWare version 3.x and have OS/2 or NFS (for UNIX files) name spaces loaded, you must use SBACKUP instead.

▶ Individual users can run NBACKUP to back up their own files onto diskettes. (However, most users can make simple copies of their files rather than network backups that also save trustee information.)

Establishing a Backup Schedule

After you set up your backup system, you need to establish a schedule for backing up files. How often should network files be backed up? Does each file need to be backed up every time?

The answers to these questions will be different for every network. You'll need to establish a backup schedule that makes the most sense for your particular network. The following sections provide some basic guidelines that may help you set up an optimum backup schedule.

CHOOSING WHICH FILES TO BACK UP

Most backup utilities present you with a choice of network information to be backed up. You can usually choose to back up the complete network, the Net-Ware bindery, or only those network files that have been changed since the last backup. Figure 9.1 shows an example of the backup choices offered by NBACKUP.

This choice allows you some flexibility and can help you save time. For instance, if you back up only those files that have changed since the last backup, the backup process will be shortened. However, if this is the only type of backup you keep, you will be in trouble if you lose the entire hard disk. All the files that didn't change recently will be gone since they were not copied onto the backup tape.

One solution is to schedule full backups of all the files, as well as interim partial backups of important files, as described in the next section.

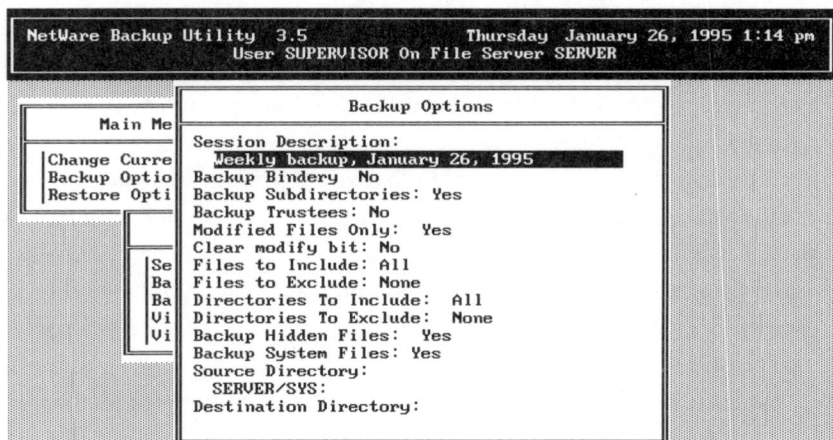

FIGURE 9.1

NBACKUP backup selections

NetWare Backup Utility 3.5   Thursday January 26, 1995 1:14 pm
                    User SUPERVISOR On File Server SERVER

```
                                        Backup Options
           Main Me
                        Session Description:
  Change Curre              Weekly backup, January 26, 1995
  Backup Optio     Backup Bindery  No
  Restore Opti     Backup Subdirectories:  Yes
                   Backup Trustees: No
                   Modified Files Only:   Yes
                   Clear modify bit: No
           Se      Files to Include: All
           Ba      Files to Exclude: None
           Ba      Directories To Include:   All
           Vi      Directories To Exclude:   None
           Vi      Backup Hidden Files:  Yes
                   Backup System Files: Yes
                   Source Directory:
                     SERVER/SYS:
                   Destination Directory:
```

SCHEDULING FULL AND PARTIAL BACKUPS

Many network supervisors set up a schedule for each type of backup so that they get full backups periodically and partial backups more frequently. Here is one common backup schedule:

- ▸ A monthly backup of the NetWare bindery

- ▸ A weekly full backup of all network files

- ▸ Daily backups of only those files that have changed since the last backup

This backup schedule minimizes the time each backup session takes while maximizing the coverage of files. In the event of a total loss of files, you could restore the bindery from a backup that would be no more than one month old. Since changes to the bindery are usually infrequent, a month-old bindery probably would not require much updating. Then you would restore all network files from the weekly backup. Finally, you could restore the daily tapes to update just those files that had changed during that week.

If you make daily changes to trustee assignments, or create and delete several users every week, you may want to back up your bindery more often than once a month.

Similarly, if all your users make backup copies of any files they have changed every evening before they go home, you may decide that you can skip the daily network-wide backups of changed files. In this case, weekly backups of all network files may be adequate. You should encourage your users to back up their own files every night, so that they don't need to rely on the network backup operations.

Evaluate your network and the frequency of changes made to files on the network. Also evaluate the criticality of those files. If you lose a week's worth of work on a file, is it a devastating blow or merely a nuisance? Use these factors to help you decide what backup schedule makes the most sense for your network.

Rotating and Storing Backup Tapes or Disks

In planning your backup system, you also need to consider how many versions of backups should be kept and where you will store your backup tapes or disks.

PLANNING A ROTATION SCHEDULE

Rotating backup media so that you have some older backup versions available is another way to avoid losing network files. For example, suppose the hard disk on Ray's file server is going bad and corrupting files, but he hasn't yet discovered the problem. Ray has only one backup tape which he uses every week, each time replacing the previous week's backup with the new one. Unknowingly, this week he backs up the corrupted files onto his single backup tape. Later, he discovers the bad disk and reaches for his backup tape to restore his files. Unfortunately, the backup tape contains the same corrupted files, and there is no previous tape to which he can return.

To safeguard against this type of problem, you should plan to keep a number of older backup tapes (or disks) on hand at all times. Many network supervisors will use three or four tapes for the same set of files, cycling through the tapes one at a time. Each week, the most outdated tape is used for the new backup. This way, two or three versions of backups are available at any given time. Figure 9.2 illustrates this process.

DECIDING WHERE TO STORE BACKUPS

In addition to planning a rotation schedule for your backup media, you need to decide where you will store the backups. Do you want to keep the tapes or disks on-site or off-site? The advantages of storing backups on-site are that the backups will be handy if you need them and you don't need to worry about transporting or shipping them somewhere else. The advantage of storing backups off-site is that the files will be safe if a disaster, such as a fire or flood, strikes.

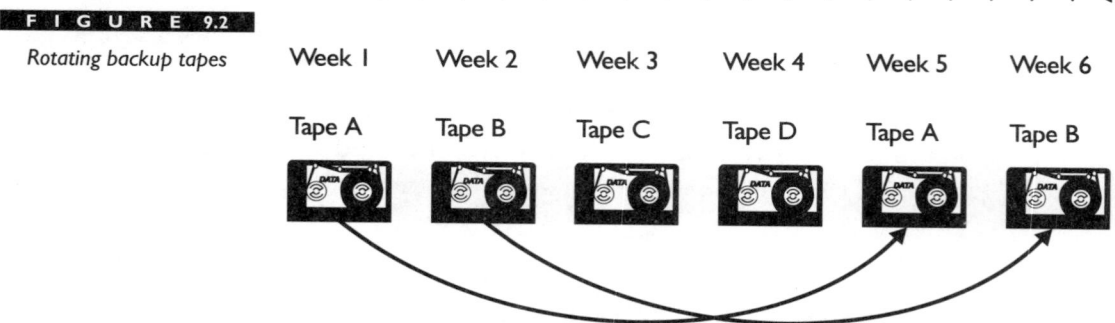

FIGURE 9.2

Rotating backup tapes

Again, you need to evaluate the risk. If your network files are critical to your company's entire business, you should seriously consider storing your backups off-site. Off-site storage could be a bank vault, another office of the same company, or even your own home, depending on how sensitive the information is. However, if your files are not that critical or if they can be reconstructed easily from scratch, you may be comfortable storing the backup copies on-site in a room that is separate from the server. Another option would be to always create two backup copies: one to keep at the office and one to send off-site. Yet another scheme is to keep the current backup on-site, and the older versions off-site. Use the type of storage that will work best for your network.

Are You Sure It's Working?

Keep in mind that backups are useful only if you can actually restore the files when you need them. You would be very unhappy to discover that you can't restore a file because all along you were doing something wrong when backing up your files.

To be sure that your backup system is working, practice restoring files *before* you need them. Make sure you know how to restore them and that the restoration actually happens the way it's supposed to. By practicing, you may identify problems you didn't realize you had. Don't wait until it is too late. If the restoring process works well, you'll have the peace of mind that comes with knowing that your backups are there if you need them.

Backing Up and Restoring Files with the NetWare Utilities

The following sections describe how to use the SBACKUP.NLM and NBACKUP.EXE utilities, which come with NetWare. The instructions for using BACKUP.VAP with NetWare version 2.2 are included in a README file on the NetWare Backup diskette.

USING THE SBACKUP UTILITY WITH NETWARE VERSION 3.X

To use the SBACKUP program, you load the SBACKUP loadable module, a data requester module, and device drivers on a file server, which is called the *host*. You load *Target Service Agents* (*TSAs*) on any file servers whose files you want to back up (called *targets*). Therefore, to back up the host file server, you load both SBACKUP and a TSA on that file server. You can load TSAs on other file servers in your network and back them all up from the host file server. You do not need to run SBACKUP on the other target servers.

You must be supervisor-equivalent to use SBACKUP. The following steps outline the procedure for using SBACKUP to back up and restore your network files:

1 · Attach the backup device to the host file server.

2 · Load the necessary backup device drivers on the host file server. Refer to the manufacturer's documentation and the NetWare *Server Backup* manual for specific instructions.

3 · Load the TSAs on the target file servers you want to back up, including the file server that is running SBACKUP.

4 · Load the data requester module (such as SIDR.NLM) on the host file server.

5 · Load the SBACKUP loadable module on the host file server. You will now begin a backup or restore session.

6 · Enter your username and password for the host file server.

7 · From the main menu, choose the Select Target to Backup/Restore option. If you have loaded TSAs on more than one file server on your network, a list of those target servers appears, and you can select one from the list. If you have only one target server available, you will not see a list.

8 · Enter your username and password for the target file server.

9 · From the main menu, select either the Backup Menu option or the Restore Menu option, depending on which procedure you want to perform.

The Backup Menu option allows you to specify a working directory, which is the directory that will contain the backup error and log files. These files document the backup session. You also use this menu to specify which volumes and directories you want to back up and when you want the backup to start. You can set the backup session to start immediately or at a later time, such as during the middle of the night.

The Restore Menu option lets you specify the working directory that contains the original backup session files. These session files help SBACKUP locate the backed up files. This menu also allows you to specify which volumes, directories, or files you want to restore.

Both the Backup Menu and Restore Menu options let you view the error and log files for the backup and restore sessions.

When SBACKUP is finished backing up or restoring the files, it automatically exits and returns to the console prompt. For more information about SBACKUP, see the *NetWare Server Backup* manual. If you have NetWare version 3.11, also refer to the README file on the NetWare System-1 diskette.

USING THE NBACKUP MENU UTILITY

You do not need to be supervisor-equivalent to use the NBACKUP menu utility to back up your own directories, but only supervisors can back up the entire file server. To use NBACKUP to back up your network files, follow these steps:

1 · From a DOS workstation, start the NBACKUP utility by typing

NBACKUP

and pressing the Enter key.

2 · From the menu that appears, select the type of device you are using to back up your files.

3 · From the next menu that appears, select either the Backup Menu option or the Restore Menu option, depending on which procedure you want to perform.

The Backup Menu option allows you to specify a working directory, which is the directory that will contain the backup error and log files. These files document the backup session. You also use this menu to specify which volumes and directories you want to back up. When you finish making your selections, you specify when you want the backup to start. You can set the backup session to start immediately or at a later time, such as after your office closes.

The Restore Menu option lets you specify the working directory that contains the original backup session files. These session files help NBACKUP locate the backed up files. This menu also allows you to specify which volumes, directories, or files you want to restore.

4 · When the backup or restore session is completed, press the Enter key to return to the Backup Menu or the Restore Menu. From the menu, you can view the error and log files for the backup or restore session, or you can press the Esc key to exit the utility.

For more information about NBACKUP, see the NetWare version 3.x *Utilities Reference* manual or the NetWare version 2.2 *Using the Network* manual.

Review

Backing up your network files means keeping archived copies of files in case anything happens to the originals. Setting up an effective backup system involves the following steps:

- ► Select a backup device, which is the equipment used to back up the files onto tapes or disks.

- ► Select a backup program that will control the backup process.

- ► Establish a schedule for backing up the NetWare bindery, all network files, and only those files that changed since the last backup was made.

- ► Decide how often to rotate the backup media and where to store them.

- ► Test the system by backing up and restoring files before an emergency occurs.

The final chapter of this book is about NetWare for Macintosh, which allows Macintosh computers to operate on a network.

CHAPTER 10

Using NetWare for Macintosh

Novell took an early lead in the drive to allow Macintoshes and PCs to work together. In 1988, Novell released NetWare for Macintosh, and for the first time, Macintosh workstations could connect to a NetWare PC-based network. Since then, Novell has continued to develop NetWare for Macintosh products that work with each new version of NetWare.

With NetWare for Macintosh, Macintosh users can work on the network and take advantage of NetWare's file sharing, security, and printing features. In addition, DOS users can share files with Macintosh users and can access Apple printers, such as LaserWriters and ImageWriters. This chapter explains how NetWare for Macintosh allows Macintosh and DOS workstations to work together on the same network.

What Is NetWare for Macintosh?

NetWare for Macintosh is a Novell product that connects Macintosh workstations to an existing NetWare network. If you have NetWare 2.2 or 3.12, you received NetWare for Macintosh as an additional feature in your NetWare package. If you have version 3.11, you must purchase NetWare for Macintosh separately.

NetWare for Macintosh is not a network operating system by itself. You cannot have a Macintosh file server on your NetWare network, nor can you have a Macintosh-only NetWare network. NetWare for Macintosh only allows you to add Macintoshes to a PC-based NetWare network. Your file server must be a PC, and you must have at least one PC workstation to set up your network.

NetWare for Macintosh includes a set of files that run on the file server. For NetWare 2.2 and 3.11, two utilities run on the workstations:

▶ The *NetWare desk accessory*, which contains modules that allow Macintosh users to work with NetWare rights for their files, view the print jobs in print queues, send and receive messages, and so on.

▶ The *NetWare Control Center* (*NCC*) application, which also runs on Macintosh workstations. NCC deals with NetWare rights, too, but it's more powerful than the desk accessory. As the network supervisor, you can use NCC to create users and groups, assign security, and perform other network administration tasks. Your users probably won't need to use NCC.

For NetWare 3.12, there is one workstation utility, NetWare Tools. This utility is explained in Chapter 11.

In NetWare version 2.2, the NetWare for Macintosh files that you load onto the server are called *VAPs* (Value-Added Processes). VAPs are software programs that run on the file server and add various features to the network. The NetWare for Macintosh VAPs enable the server to store Macintosh files and manage Macintosh communications.

Instead of VAPs, NetWare version 3.*x* uses files called *NLMs* (NetWare Loadable Modules) to add features to the file server. Like the VAPs for NetWare version 2.2, the NetWare for Macintosh NLMs enable the server to store Macintosh files and manage Macintosh communication.

Setting Up NetWare for Macintosh on Your Network

Before you begin to install NetWare for Macintosh, you need to choose which type of network board and cabling you will use. Then you can proceed to install the networking hardware and software.

CHOOSING THE TYPE OF NETWORK BOARDS AND CABLING

Decide on the type of network boards, such as Ethernet, Token Ring, or Local-Talk, and the cabling system you want to use to connect your Macintoshes to your network. LocalTalk is the type of network connection that is already built in to all Macintoshes. If you use LocalTalk, you won't need to install network boards in your Macintoshes. However, you need to buy one LocalTalk network board to install in your file server so that the server can communicate with the Macintosh workstations. You also need LocalTalk cabling.

Using LocalTalk is generally the least expensive option. Its major disadvantage is that network communication is much slower than with other types of cabling. Your reseller can help you select the cabling and network boards that will work best in your situation.

INSTALLING THE HARDWARE AND SOFTWARE

The way that you install NetWare for Macintosh depends on the version you're installing. The following steps outline the basic installation procedure. See the NetWare documentation that came with your NetWare and NetWare for Macintosh packages for specific instructions.

1 · Install the network boards in all Macintosh workstations and make sure the file server has a corresponding network board installed in it. Then cable the Macintoshes (and any printers) to the network.

2 · Create a separate volume on the file server just for Macintosh files. Having this volume often simplifies backing up and restoring Macintosh files separately from DOS files, and it may make it easier to repair volumes without worrying about the different types of files stored on them.

3 · (NetWare version 3.x only) Load the MAC name space module on the file server and add the MAC name space to each volume that will contain the Macintosh files, so that the server and volumes will store the longer Macintosh file names. (Macintosh file names can be longer than DOS file names and therefore take up more disk space.)

For example, suppose you create a volume called MACFILES on your server and intend to store all your Macintosh files in the MACFILES volume. To load the MAC name space to the file server and add the MAC name space to the MAC-FILES volume, type the following two commands at the file server's keyboard:

```
LOAD MAC
ADD NAME SPACE MAC TO MACFILES
```

Then add these two commands to the file server's STARTUP.NCF file so that the Macintosh name space will be loaded automatically every time you restart the file server.

4 · Use the NetWare INSTALL utility to load the NetWare for Macintosh VAPs (version 2.2) or NLMs (version 3.*x*) on the file server.

If you're running NetWare version 2.2, answer Yes when INSTALL asks if you want to install NetWare for Macintosh. If you're running version NetWare 3.*x*, select Product Options from the Installation Options menu, press the Ins key, and insert the NetWare for Macintosh diskette. Then add the LOAD commands for the NetWare for Macintosh NLMS to the file server's AUTOEXEC.NCF file.

5 · Load the AppleTalk LAN driver on the file server.

In NetWare version 2.2, select the LAN driver in the INSTALL utility. In NetWare version 3.*x*, load the AppleTalk LAN driver and bind it to the AppleTalk protocol by using the LOAD and BIND server utilities. Then add the commands to the AUTOEXEC.NCF file.

6 · (NetWare version 3.*x* only) Configure NetWare for Macintosh by adding configuration commands to the AUTOEXEC.NCF and STARTUP.NCF files. The commands you need to add to the files vary depending on whether you are using Ethernet, LocalTalk, or Arcnet and on how your network is set up. See the NetWare documentation for more information.

7 · Load AppleShare workstation software on each workstation's startup disk. This software comes with every Macintosh; it is not supplied by Novell.

8 · Make sure each workstation has the right LAN driver installed for the type of network board it is using. You select the LAN driver from the Network option in the Control Panel.

9 · Install the NetWare desk accessory and its modules on each Macintosh workstation. The desk accessory's modules determine which options users can access through the desk accessory. Install the desk accessory in the workstation's System file, then copy the modules into the System folder or any other convenient folder on the workstation.

10 • Copy the Notify INIT into each Macintosh's System folder. The Notify INIT allows the user to send and receive network messages.

11 • (NetWare version 3.x only) Install the NetWare User Authentication Method (UAM) module in a folder called AppleShare folder on each Macintosh workstation. This software encrypts the user's password before sending it across the cabling (password encryption is a security feature in NetWare version 3.x).

12 • Install the NetWare Control Center (NCC) application on the Macintosh of any user who needs access to it. Because NCC is used primarily by the network supervisor to create users and groups and to change attributes and trustee rights, you may not want to make this application available to all users. Instead, copy the NCC onto your own Macintosh and onto the Macintosh of anyone else who has supervisory rights.

Can PC and Macintosh Users Share Files?

Just because you connected your Macintosh workstations to your NetWare network doesn't necessarily mean your users can share files with each other. NetWare for Macintosh makes it possible for PC and Macintosh users to see the names of each others' files, but whether or not the users can open those files depends on the applications being used. NetWare doesn't control how applications open and create files.

PC applications cannot be used on a Macintosh and vice versa because PC and Macintosh files have different formats. Macintosh files consist of two parts:

▶ The *data fork* contains the text of the file.

▶ The *resource fork* contains information about the file, such as the name of the application that created the file and the icon that should be displayed for the file.

DOS and OS/2 files don't have resource forks. They contain only information that corresponds to the Macintosh file's data fork. However, even though Macintosh and PC files are different, there are still ways to share their files.

Generally, PC and Macintosh users can share the same files if they use an application that has both a PC-based (DOS, Windows, or OS/2) version and a Macintosh version. These types of applications usually can convert files from one version's format to the other version's format.

Another way to share PC and Macintosh files is to convert the files into a format that the other workstation can use. For example, if a Macintosh application allows you to save a file in an ASCII format, you can then open the file from a DOS application that also supports ASCII. However, this process converts only the text in a file; any graphic or formatting elements will be lost.

Another difference between Macintosh and DOS files is the rules that govern file names. DOS files can be up to eight characters long plus an optional three-character extension, such as FILENAME.NEW. Macintosh names can be much longer—up to 31 characters—and can contain spaces and punctuation, which are invalid in DOS names.

When Macintosh file names are displayed on a PC, those names are truncated (shortened) to the DOS format. This is for PC display purposes only; the names are not actually changed, and they will still appear in their original form when displayed on a Macintosh. If your PC and Macintosh users will share files often, encourage the Macintosh users to use DOS-type file names, so that the names are comprehensible to the PC users.

Can PC and Macintosh Users Share Printers?

With NetWare for Macintosh, DOS and Macintosh users can share printers, such as Apple LaserWriters and ImageWriters, on the network. LaserWriter printers cannot be attached directly to the file server, but ImageWriters can.

Macintosh users can take advantage of NetWare's print server and print queue features (so they don't need to wait until the printer is free before they can continue working).

As explained in Chapter 5, when PC workstations send files to be printed on a NetWare network, the print jobs are sent first to a NetWare print queue, which then funnels the jobs to the printer. This process works well for PC workstations because the PCs can recognize NetWare print queues.

Macintosh workstations do not recognize print queues. Macintoshes are designed to send print jobs directly to printers. To get a print job to the queue, NetWare for Macintosh adds a step to the printing process, called an AppleTalk Queue Server (also called a *print spooler*). To the Macintosh, the queue server appears to be a regular Apple printer, so the workstation sends the print job to it. Then the queue server sends the job to the NetWare print queue, where the Macintosh's print job joins any other print jobs from other Macintosh or DOS workstations and waits its turn to be printed. When a printer is available, the print server takes the job from the queue and sends it to the printer.

In NetWare version 2.2, the NetWare print server handles both PC and Macintosh print jobs. In NetWare version 3.*x*, the NetWare print server (PSERVER) handles PC print jobs, and you decide if Macintosh print jobs are handled by the NetWare print server or by a separate AppleTalk print server.

Setting Up Printing with NetWare for Macintosh

The following steps outline the basic procedure for adding Apple printers to a NetWare network.

1 • Use the NetWare PRINTDEF utility from a DOS-based workstation to import the Apple printer's device definition files. These files describe the printer to the file server.

2 • Load NetWare for Macintosh's printing VAPs or NLMs onto the file server. These files create the AppleTalk Queue Server and manage Macintosh print jobs.

3 • Connect the printer to the network. Remember that you can attach an ImageWriter to either the file server or a workstation, but a LaserWriter must be connected to a workstation.

4 • Use PCONSOLE from a DOS-based workstation to set up print queues, print queue operators, and so on, just as you do for a PC-based printer (see Chapter 5).

5 • Make sure that each Macintosh workstation has the correct Apple printer driver software installed in its System folder.

6 • Load the NetWare print server software onto the computer that will be the print server. If you're using the NetWare version 3.*x* AppleTalk print server, load it onto the file server and configure it.

7 • If PC users will be using the Apple printer, use the PRINTDEF utility from a DOS-based workstation to set up a print form called Normal that defines 8.5 by 11 inch sheets of paper.

8 • If the printer is a LaserWriter, use the PRINTCON utility from a PC to set up a print job configuration that PC users can use.

9 • If the PC users have applications that support PostScript printing, create a PostScript print job configuration. If the PC applications do not support

PostScript, you can set up a print job configuration that will allow the users to send jobs to the LaserWriter in Diablo 630 emulation mode.

See the NetWare for Macintosh installation manual for more information about setting up for printing and configuring your print server and print queues for your particular network needs.

SENDING PRINT JOBS TO AN APPLE PRINTER FROM A PC

Sending print jobs to an Apple printer from a PC workstation is no different from sending print jobs to any other type of printer. The user simply selects the print queue to which he or she wants to send print jobs.

If the user has an application that supports network printing, the user selects the print queue from the application. If the application does not support network printing, the user can specify the print queue by using the CAPTURE and NPRINT utilities, as explained in Chapter 5.

SENDING PRINT JOBS TO AN APPLE PRINTER
FROM A MACINTOSH

The steps for sending a file from a Macintosh to a network print queue are the same as the steps for sending the file directly to the printer. To send files directly to an Apple printer, open the Chooser and select the Apple printer you want to use. Then print from your application, and the file is sent directly to the printer.

To send the file to a network print queue, open the Chooser and select a print queue instead of a printer. Make sure the AppleTalk button in the Chooser is set to Active. Then print the file from the application. The file is sent to the Apple-Talk Queue Server, then to the print queue, and finally to the printer. Meanwhile, you can continue your work at the Macintosh workstation.

When you select print queues from the Chooser, you also have the option of setting the Macintosh Background Printing feature off or on. With NetWare print queues, Background Printing makes no difference, so set Background Printing off.

Encourage your Macintosh users to send print jobs to NetWare print queues instead of directly to printers. Sending jobs to print queues is almost always more efficient because it leaves the workstation free for other tasks. In addition, if other users are sending print jobs to the same printer, the print queue manages the printing traffic and ensures that the jobs are printed in the correct order.

In NetWare version 3.x, you can hide printers so that users will see only print queues in the Chooser. To hide a printer, load the ATPS loadable module and specify a configuration command using the option −h.

Using the NetWare Desk Accessory

The NetWare desk accessory is a convenient utility that Macintosh users can run even if they are currently running other applications. Users can use the desk accessory to see information about their trustee rights in files and folders, view the status of their print jobs in the queues, and send and receive messages on the network.

To use the NetWare desk accessory, log in to a file server from the Chooser (located under the Apple menu) and choose NetWare from the Apple menu. When the NetWare desk accessory window appears, the icons for the available modules are displayed in the left panel, and the right panel displays the About module, as shown in Figure 10.1.

The About module briefly explains each of the other modules in the NetWare desk accessory. To close the About module, choose another module from the left panel.

USING THE MESSAGE MODULE

You can use the Message module to send messages to other network users. If you installed the Notify INIT file in your System folder, you can receive messages from other users.

To send a message to a user, follow these steps:

1 • Open the Message module by clicking on its icon in the left panel of the NetWare desk accessory window. The Message window that appears lists the users who are currently logged in to the file server.

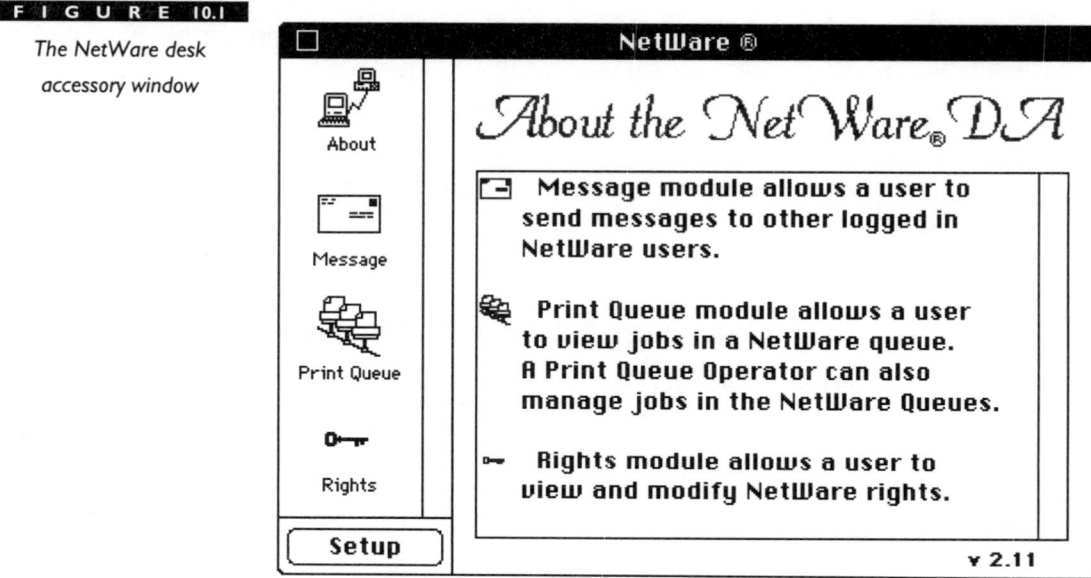

2 · Click on the names of the users who you want to receive your message. To select several users, hold down the Shift key while you click on each user's name. The users you select can only receive your message if they each have the Notify INIT file in their System folders.

3 · Type your message in the Message box at the bottom of the window. Your message must fit on a single line.

4 · Click on the Send button.

An Accept Messages box appears at the bottom of the Message module window. This box allows you to choose whether you want to receive messages from other users, even if you have the Notify INIT file in your System folder. To receive messages, click on the box to mark it with an X.

USING THE PRINT QUEUE MODULE

After you send a print job to a NetWare print queue, you can use the NetWare desk accessory to see the print job's status. If you are a print queue operator or the network supervisor, you can also modify the status of the print jobs in the queue.

To see a list of print jobs and their status, open the Print Queue module by clicking on its icon. A list of all the print jobs currently in a print queue appears. Figure 10.2 shows an example of a print job list displayed by the NetWare desk accessory.

The list indicates each print job's owner and status, as follows:

▶ The Seq column shows the order in which the jobs will be printed. Usually this is first-come-first-served order, but a print queue operator or network supervisor can change the sequence if necessary.

▶ The Name column shows the name of the user who sent the print job if the job is being sent to a LaserWriter. If the job is going to an Image-Writer, the word *AppleTalk* is in the Name column.

FIGURE 10.2

The Print Queue module window

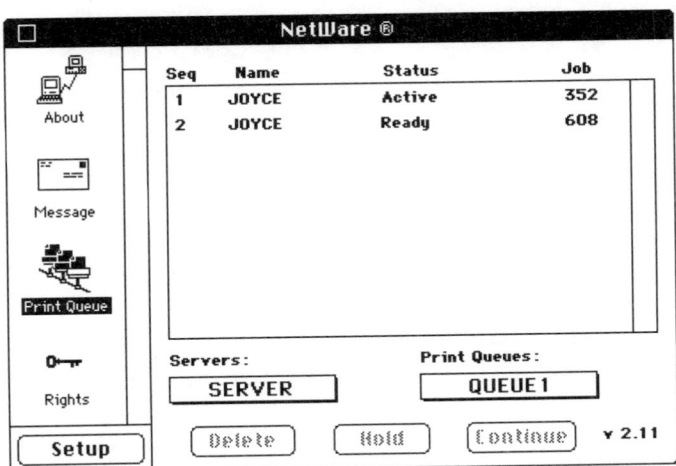

▶ The Status column shows whether the job is Active (being printed), Ready (ready to be printed as soon as the printer is free), or Adding (being added to the print queue). If the print queue operator has specified that the print job should be printed at a different time, the status will be Waiting. The print queue operator can also put a print job on hold, which means nothing will happen to the job until the operator either continues it or deletes it. If the job is on hold, the status will be Held.

▶ The Job column shows the order in which the jobs were added to the print queue.

If additional print queues are available on your file server and you want to see a different one, select it from the Print Queues pop-up menu in the lower-left corner of the window. You can also select a different file server from the Servers pop-up menu.

You can remove, hold, or reorder the print jobs in the list if you are a print queue operator or the network supervisor. (If you are neither, you can only view the status.)

▶ To delete a print job, select the job and click the Delete button.

▶ To put a print job on hold, select the job and click the Hold button.

▶ To continue a print job that is on hold, select the job and click the Continue button.

▶ To change the sequence in which print jobs will be printed, select a print job, hold down the mouse button, and drag the job to its new position in the queue.

USING THE RIGHTS MODULE

With the Rights module of the NetWare desk accessory, you can perform the following tasks:

▶ See your effective rights in a folder.

▶ See a folder's Rights Mask.

▶ Change other users' rights in your folders.

To use the Rights module, follow these steps:

1 · Open the Rights module by clicking on its icon in the left panel of the NetWare desk accessory window.

2 · Choose the volume or folder whose security information you want to view.

3 · Click on either Volume Information or Folder Information.

The top section of the window that appears displays the name of the volume or folder, the file server you are logged in to, and your username, as shown in Figure 10.3. It also contains three buttons you can select to display your effective rights, the Rights Mask, or your trustee rights in that volume or folder.

4 · To see your effective rights, click on the Effective Rights button.

Your effective trustee rights for that volume or folder are those rights whose boxes are checked. Next to the list of NetWare rights, the three AppleShare privilege icons are displayed. These icons reflect the AppleShare equivalent for the NetWare rights that are checked. In normal situations, AppleShare privileges do not have any effect on NetWare trustee rights. They are displayed only for the convenience of AppleShare users who may wonder how they correspond to NetWare rights. However, if you are using NetWare version 3.x, you can set up a user so that he or she operates in Single Trustee Mode. In this mode, the user can use AppleShare privileges.

5 · To see the volume's or folder's Rights Mask, click on the Rights Mask button.

The list of NetWare rights now changes to show the rights that are currently allowed by the Rights Mask. If you have the Access Control right to this volume

The Rights module window

or folder, you can change the Rights Mask by clicking on the boxes next to the NetWare rights.

6 · To see the other trustees who have rights to this volume or folder, click on the Trustee Rights button.

A list of users and groups who have rights to the volume or folder appears in the right side of the window. To see a trustee's rights, click on the trustee's name. The list of NetWare rights changes to show the trustee's rights.

If you have the Access Control right, you can change a trustee's rights, add a trustee, or delete a trustee. To change a trustee's rights, click on the boxes beside each right. To add a trustee, click on the Add Trustee button, select a user or group from the list that appears, click on the Add>> button, and then click on Done. To delete a trustee, select the user or group from the Trustees list and click on the Remove Trustee button. When you're finished making changes, click on the Save Changes button.

Using the NetWare Control Center

The NetWare Control Center (NCC) is an application that you, as the network supervisor, can use to work with network security. You cannot use NCC while you are running another application unless you are running MultiFinder. With NCC, you can perform the following tasks:

- ► Log in to a file server.

- ► List volumes and view their security information.

- ► List folders and files and view their security information.

- ► List users and groups and view their security information.

To use NCC, log in to a file server from the Chooser (located under the Apple menu). Then double-click on NCC's icon. NCC can be run from a folder on the network or from a local disk.

If you are not logged in to a file server when you open NCC, it will display icons for any available servers. You can log in to one of these file servers by double-clicking on its icon and supplying your username and password. When you open NCC, the Server window appears, as shown in Figure 10.4. You can use the Server window to log in to additional servers, list a file server's volumes, list a volume's folders and files, and list a file server's users and groups.

File servers are listed in the left panel of the window. If a file server's name is displayed in italics, you are not logged in to the file server. If the name is in plain type, you are logged in to it.

To log in to an additional file server, double-click on the server's icon, type your username and password, and select any volumes you intend to use. To open a file server so that you can see information about its volumes, users, and groups, double-click on the file server.

FIGURE 10.4

NCC's Server window

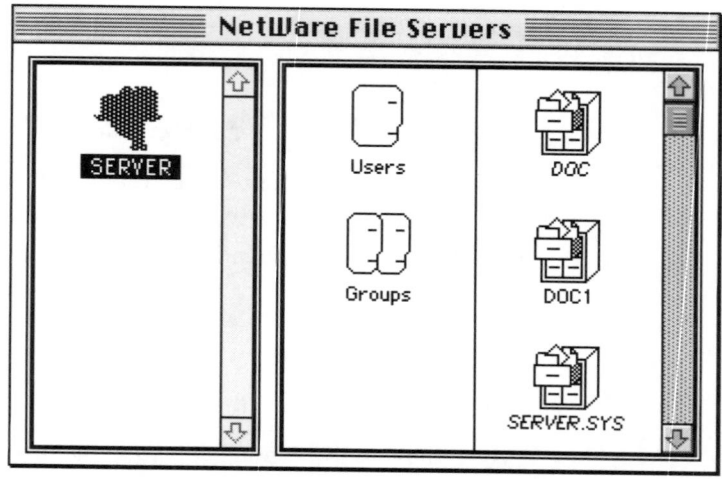

The right panel of the window lists the volumes on the file server that you selected. If a volume's name is in italics, you did not selected that volume when you logged in. If the name is in plain type, you did select it when you logged in. To see information about a volume, click on the volume's icon and pull down the Volumes menu. From this menu, you can select to see volume information (such as its owner, type, and size), effective rights, the Rights Mask, or trustee rights.

To see information about the files and folders in a volume, double-click on the volume's icon. You see a window that lists the files and folders contained in that volume. From this window, you can open folders by double-clicking on them to see the files and folders that they contain. Continue opening folders until you get to the file or folder whose information you want to see. Then click on the file's or folder's name and pull down the Folders/Files menu. Use this menu to see information about the file or folder, such as its owner, size, creation date, and attributes. You can also see your effective rights, the Rights Mask, and other trustee's rights to the file or folder.

To see information about a file server's users and groups, double-click on a file server. Then double-click on either the Users icon or the Groups icon. You see a list of all the users or groups on that file server. To see information about a user or group, select the name from the list and pull down either the Users or Groups menu. If you are the network supervisor, you can also use these menus to add or delete users and groups.

Review

To connect Macintoshes to your NetWare network, you can use a Novell product called NetWare for Macintosh. NetWare for Macintosh includes files you load onto your existing NetWare file server and two workstation utilities: the NetWare desk accessory and NetWare Control Center (NCC).

If you're using NetWare version 2.2, you load the NetWare for Macintosh VAPs (Value-Added Processes) onto your file server. If you're using version 3.x, you load the NetWare for Macintosh NLMs (NetWare Loadable Modules) onto your file server.

NetWare for Macintosh allows PCs and Macintoshes to function on the same network and take advantage of NetWare's security, file, and print services. NetWare for Macintosh does not affect whether or not PC and Macintosh users can actually share files with each other. PC and Macintosh users can share files only if they use applications that can convert files from one workstation's format to the other's.

NetWare for Macintosh allows Apple printers to become network printers. Both PC and Macintosh users can print to Apple printers on the network by using NetWare print queues.

The NetWare desk accessory is a workstation utility that allows Macintosh users to work in a limited way with rights and print queues. It also enables users to send and receive messages. NCC is a more advanced utility that allows the network supervisor to create users and groups, change network security, and monitor information about volumes, folders, and files.

CHAPTER II

Using NetWare Version 3.12

Although NetWare version 3.12 is based largely upon NetWare version 3.11, it contains several important features and enhancements that NetWare 3.11 does not have. These new features include the following:

▸ The ability to install NetWare 3.12 from a CD-ROM

▸ An easy-to-follow menued installation program

▸ Electronic documentation (in the CD-ROM version of the product only)

▸ Updated workstation software

▸ A different product for creating menu programs

▸ A new version of NetWare for Macintosh

This chapter describes these new features of NetWare 3.12 and explains how you can use them.

Preparing to Install a NetWare 3.12 File Server

When you prepare to install NetWare 3.12 on your file server, you will need to know the same information that is explained in Chapter 2. You must take the same security and safety precautions, and you must answer the same questions, such as whether you want to use disk mirroring and whether the file server should boot from a floppy diskette or a hard disk.

With NetWare 3.12, you now have the additional flexibility of installing from either a CD-ROM or from diskettes. (NetWare 3.12 also allows you to use a CD-ROM as a network volume.) In addition, NetWare 3.12 includes a menued installation program, which simplifies the installation process.

There are also two more decisions you must make while installing the file server. First, you must decide if you need to change the default country code and code page on your file server from that of the United States to the type used in your country. Second, if you are using Ethernet on your network, you must decide if you need to change the default frame type that Ethernet uses.

All of these issues are explained in the following sections.

INSTALLING FROM A CD-ROM

If you purchased the CD-ROM version of NetWare 3.12, you will need to attach the CD-ROM reader to the computer that is going to become the file server. The CD-ROM reader's documentation will explain how to attach the reader to a computer and how to modify the computer's AUTOEXEC.BAT and CONFIG.SYS files to load the necessary drivers. Although there are some extra steps involved in installing the CD-ROM reader, installing NetWare 3.12 from a CD-ROM is much simpler and faster than installing NetWare 3.12 from diskettes.

During the NetWare 3.12 installation procedure, you will be asked if you want to create a DOS partition or retain your current partitions. If you want the NetWare 3.12 server to boot from its hard disk, the hard disk must have a DOS partition on it that is at least 5MB (megabytes) in size. If the computer you are using does not already have a 5MB partition on it, you may want to create the partition and format it (using DOS FDISK and FORMAT commands) before you install the CD-ROM reader and before you start the NetWare installation program. (If you create a DOS partition, be sure you leave the rest of the hard disk available for a NetWare partition.) If the hard disk already has a 5MB DOS partition, you can complete the NetWare installation without worrying about this issue.

Formatting a new partition erases all existing files from the hard disk. In other words, if you have already attached the CD-ROM reader to the computer and loaded the reader's drivers, formatting the disk will erase those drivers, and you will have to recreate the AUTOEXEC.BAT and CONFIG.SYS files and reinstall the CD-ROM reader. This is why you may want to create a partition before you install the CD-ROM reader.

However, if you do not want to create the partitions before you start the NetWare 3.12 installation program, or if you are not sure how to do it using DOS commands, you can create or change the size of a DOS partition during the NetWare installation. The only caution is that you will have to reinstall the CD-ROM reader and its drivers half-way through the process.

To let the NetWare installation program help you format the DOS partition, go ahead and attach the CD-ROM reader to the file server and begin the NetWare INSTALL program. INSTALL will ask you if you want to create a new DOS partition, and if you say yes, it will create the partition and reboot the computer. (Make sure the SYSTEM_1 diskette is in drive A: when the computer reboots.) After the computer reboots, format the new partition by typing the following command at the A: prompt:

DOSTOOLS\FORMAT C: /X/S

This command simply tells the computer to use the FORMAT command in the DOSTOOLS directory on the SYSTEM_1 diskette.

At this point, the CD-ROM reader's drivers have been erased from the hard disk. Therefore, you must now reinstall the reader using the manufacturer's instructions. After you have reinstalled the reader, reboot the computer once again so that the CD-ROM reader will be recognized by the computer. When the computer is rebooted, change to the drive that is mapped to the CD-ROM reader, then move to the NETWARE.312\ENGLISH directory on the CD-ROM by typing the following command:

CD NETWARE.312\ENGLISH

Then restart the NetWare INSTALL program by typing the following command:

INSTALL

Then move through the INSTALL program until you get to the point where it asks if you want to create or retain DOS disk partitions. Select "Retain Current Disk Partitions" and continue with the rest of the installation program.

USING A SCSI CONTROLLER BOARD WITH A CD-ROM READER

If you have the first edition of the *NetWare 3.12 Installation and Upgrade* manual, page 19 indicates that you may encounter problems running both a

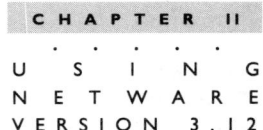
CD-ROM reader and the file server's hard disk from the same SCSI controller board. This is not true. You should have no problems running both devices from the same controller board. This problem was corrected before NetWare 3.12 was shipped.

USING THE INSTALL AND INSTALL.NLM UTILITIES

To simplify the installation of a file server, NetWare 3.12 includes a menu program that walks you through many of the initial steps for installing the server. (In previous version of NetWare 3.*x*, you must type several commands in the correct order at the file server's keyboard to install a file server.)

This new menued installation program, which you run by typing INSTALL, takes you through steps such as creating DOS partitions (as explained earlier), naming the file server, and selecting an IPX internal network number. The final step in this INSTALL utility executes the SERVER.EXE command, which turns the computer into the file server.

When SERVER.EXE executes, the INSTALL utility is finished executing. However, the installation procedure is not yet complete. When the server is running, you will see the server's command prompt, a colon (:), on the screen. At this point, you must load a disk driver on the server. This driver must correspond to the hard disk and its controller that are installed in the file server. Refer to the *NetWare 3.12 Installation and Upgrade* manual or ask your reseller for more information about selecting and loading the correct disk driver.

After you've loaded the disk driver, you must load another installation utility, INSTALL.NLM, to finish the installation. To run INSTALL.NLM, type the following command at the server's prompt:

LOAD INSTALL

The INSTALL.NLM utility will take you through the rest of the installation procedure.

CHOOSING A COUNTRY CODE AND A CODE PAGE

Another decision you must make when installing your file server is whether or not you need to change the default country code and code page used by the server. (A code page determines what numerals, letters, and symbols are supported by the version of DOS running on the computer.) If you are using a keyboard and a DOS code page created for use with United States English, you do not need to change the default values presented by the installation program.

If you are using a different DOS code page and a keyboard designed for use in countries other than the United States, such as a German keyboard with German-specific characters, you can specify the country code and code page that the computer should use. To determine what values you must enter, refer to either your DOS documentation or your reseller.

SELECTING THE RIGHT ETHERNET FRAME TYPE

If you are using Ethernet on your network, you must decide if you need to change the default frame type that Ethernet uses. A *frame type* is the format that Ethernet uses to send packets of data across the network.

In previous versions of NetWare, Novell used an Ethernet frame type called 802.3. In NetWare 3.12, Novell changed the default frame type to 802.2, which is an industry standard.

If you are installing a new network, this change to the default Ethernet frame type won't affect you. Just install your file server and workstations normally.

However, if you are upgrading a file server from a previous version of NetWare to NetWare 3.12, or if you are adding a NetWare 3.12 file server to a network that already has other file servers running earlier versions of NetWare on it, you will need to know how to select the correct frame type.

File servers and workstations can only communicate with each other if they are all using the same Ethernet frame type. If you have an existing Ethernet NetWare network, chances are good that the workstations and file server are all using the 802.3 frame type. Then, if you upgrade the server to NetWare 3.12, the server is automatically given the new 802.2 frame type. This means that now the server is using one type (802.2) and the workstations are using a different type (802.3). Suddenly, the workstations cannot communicate with the file server.

To prevent (or eliminate) this problem, you can use one of the following three solutions:

Solution 1: Update all of the workstations to use the newer, standard 802.2 type. This is usually the best solution. Although it means more work initially to upgrade all of the workstations, changing to the industry standard now may eliminate some of your work later if you expand your network (either by adding new workstations or by integrating your network with other networks).

Solution 2: Change the frame type on the new NetWare 3.12 server to the older 802.3 type. If you do not anticipate expanding your network much in the future and you do not intend to upgrade the NetWare shells on your workstations to the new software included in NetWare 3.12, this may be the easiest solution for you. However, if you install any new workstations or upgrade the NetWare shells on your existing workstations to the new NetWare 3.12 workstation software, you will have to remember to change the default frame type on those new and upgraded workstations to the older 802.3 frame type.

Solution 3: Load both types (802.2 and 802.3) on the file server, so that the server can talk to either type of workstation. This may be a good temporary solution. Loading both frame types will increase the traffic on the network, meaning that network communication may be a little slower. However, this will at least allow both types of workstations to coexist for a while. By using both frame types, you can take your time changing existing workstations to the new frame type. When all workstations finally use the 802.2 frame type, you can then unload the 802.3 frame type from the file server.

To specify the Ethernet frame type that you want the server to use, you include the frame type in the command that loads the LAN driver. For example, if your file server has an NE/2 network board and you want its driver to use the 802.3

frame type, type the following command when you load the LAN driver in the installation procedure:

LOAD NE2 FRAME=ETHERNET_802.3

To make the file server use both frame types, answer "Yes" when the installation program asks "Do you want to add another frame type for a previously loaded board?" Then select the second frame type from the list that appears.

NetWare 3.12 Electronic Documentation

If you purchased the CD-ROM version of NetWare 3.12, you received the majority of the documentation in electronic format on the CD-ROM. Novell's electronic documentation is called Novell ElectroText. ElectroText is not included in the diskette version of NetWare 3.12.

If you have Microsoft Windows 3.1 installed on a workstation, you can access the complete set of NetWare 3.12 documentation online. If you do not have Microsoft Windows 3.1, or if you want printed manuals in addition to the online versions, you can order a set of the printed manuals separately. The printed manuals are identical to the electronic documentation. (If you have Microsoft Windows 3.0, you can copy the DDEML.DLL file from Windows 3.1 into your Windows 3.0 directory. This will allow you to run ElectroText using Windows 3.0. The DDEML.DLL file is located in the WINDOWS/SYSTEM directory on a Windows 3.1 workstation.)

INSTALLING NOVELL ELECTROTEXT

Because the instructions for installing a workstation are in ElectroText, you will first have to install the ElectroText documentation on a stand-alone computer. You can either load the ElectroText files onto the computer's hard disk, or you can run ElectroText directly from the CD-ROM attached to the computer.

Next, follow the instructions in the online documentation to install workstations. After you have workstations set up and running on the network, you can install the ElectroText into a network directory on the server. Then the ElectroText can be accessed from any workstation on the network.

You install Novell ElectroText on the network server as part of the INSTALL.NLM procedure. The following instructions explain how.

1 · From the main "Installation Options" menu of INSTALL.NLM, select "Product Options."

2 · When the "Currently Installed Products" screen appears, press the Ins key. A box appears, asking you to specify the drive or path to the new product's source media.

3 · Enter the drive letter and path to the directory on the CD-ROM that contains the ElectroText files. The directory path to the ElectroText files is NETWARE.312\ENGLISH\DOC.

The INSTALL.NLM program will copy all of the ElectroText files into the directory DOC under volume SYS:. To set up a workstation to view the ElectroText documentation, follow these instructions:

1 · Map a fake root to the directory that contains the Novell ElectroText files. For example, if you want to use drive P:, type

MAP ROOT P:=SYS:DOC

2 · Locate a file called ET.INI in the SYS:DOC\DATA\CONFIG directory, and copy that file to the WINDOWS directory on the workstation's hard disk.

3 · Using a text editor, edit the ET.INI file so that it will look for the ElectroText files in the directory to which you just mapped the fake root. There are several places in the ET.INI file where you must substitute the correct drive letter (in our example, drive P:) for the letter that exists in the commands. In addition, if the workstation you're

using has an LCD display, add the command "DISPLAY=WLCDVGA" to the Preferences section of the ET.INI file. When you have changed all of the appropriate commands to use the new drive letter, save and exit the file.

4 · Using a text editor, edit the workstation's AUTOEXEC.BAT file to include the following command:

SET NWLANGUAGE=ENGLISH

5 · Type the same command (**SET NWLANGUAGE=ENGLISH**) at the command line or else reboot the computer, so that the language setting will take effect.

6 · If this workstation is running Microsoft Windows 3.0, copy the DDEML.DLL file from a Windows 3.1 workstation into the SYS:PUBLIC network directory (where the ET.EXE file is located).

7 · Start Windows.

8 · Select (make active) the program group in which you want to place the ElectroText icon.

9 · Choose New from the File menu, then select Program Item.

10 · Enter a description for the icon, such as "Novell ElectroText."

11 · For the command line, enter the path to the ET.EXE file, which is the command used to execute ElectroText. For our example, enter **P:\PUBLIC\ET.EXE**.

12 · For the working directory, enter the path to the directory that contains ET.EXE (**P:\PUBLIC**).

13 · Select OK. You can now run Novell ElectroText from this workstation.

USING NOVELL ELECTROTEXT

Novell ElectroText is arranged like a set of bookshelves. By clicking on icons, you select the bookshelf you want to access and the book you want to read.

Once you've opened a book, you can read the text from the beginning of the book, using up and down arrow keys or the scroll bar to move through the text. You can also use the book's outline (Table of Contents) to move instantly between chapters and sections of the book.

In the book's text, you can click on icons to see graphics and tables, or you can click on cross-references to move to related information in other sections of the book or even in other books. The search field at the bottom of the window lets you search for specific words or phrases in the book.

Installing DOS and Windows Workstations

NetWare 3.12 includes two different types of workstation software that can be used on DOS workstations. You must decide which type of workstation software you want to use on your DOS workstations.

The original type of DOS workstation software is the NETX shell software, which is described in Chapter 2. The newer type of workstation software is called the NetWare DOS Requester, which includes files called VLM files (for Virtual Loadable Module).

The DOS Requester is designed to allow DOS to handle more local processing directly without having to send all requests through the shell first. This speeds up the workstation's processing.

Deciding whether to use the NetWare NETX shell or the new DOS Requester depends on several factors. Novell has stated that the DOS Requester is Novell's preferred solution for current and future products, so if you anticipate expanding your network in the future, you may want to use the DOS Requester now. In addition, two workstation options are supported only with the DOS Requester: running Microsoft Windows and using "packet burst" (a feature that can increase communication on busy networks).

On the other hand, if you have many existing workstations that are already using NETX and you don't have time to upgrade them to the DOS Requester, you can use the NETX shells in NetWare 3.12 when you install one or two new workstations and you want to maintain consistency. The NETX in NetWare 3.12 has been updated from the version of NETX included in previous versions of Net-Ware. In addition, because the DOS Requester is a fairly new product, not all applications have been tested with it. Therefore, there may be some applications that depend on the NETX software for some reason. If you discover that one of the applications you use depends on NETX, you can use NETX instead of the DOS Requester until a newer version of the application is produced.

Another consideration for installing workstations on a NetWare 3.12 network is that NetWare 3.12 only includes ODI drivers. Dedicated IPX drivers are not shipped with NetWare 3.12.

If you want to install NETX on a workstation, refer to Chapter 2. Installing the DOS Requester is explained in the following sections.

IF YOU ARE USING THE CD-ROM VERSION...

If you have the CD-ROM version of NetWare 3.12, the documentation that explains how to install workstations is located in the ElectroText online documentation. You will have to install the ElectroText on a stand-alone computer to read how to install workstations.

In addition, you cannot install workstation software directly from a CD-ROM. You must first make diskettes with the workstation software on them. To create the workstation diskettes, you can use the MAKEDISK utility, as explained in the following steps.

1 · Install the CD-ROM reader on a standalone computer.

2 · Use the DOS FORMAT command to format and name four high-density diskettes for DOS or Microsoft Windows workstations (three for OS/2 workstations). Use the following names for each diskette:

Diskette	Diskette 1	Diskette 2	Diskette 3	Diskette 4
Label for DOS and Windows	WSDOS_1	WSWIN_1	WSDRV_1	WSDRV_2

Diskette	Diskette 1	Diskette 2	Diskette 3	Diskette 4
Label for OS/2	WSOS2_1	WSOS2_2	WSDRV_1	

3 · Change your current drive to the CLIENT\DOSWIN directory for DOS or Microsoft Windows workstations (CLIENT\OS2 for OS/2 workstations).

4 · Insert the first of the newly formatted diskettes into drive A: or B:. Then type the following command, which will create the diskettes for you (if you used drive B:, substitute "B:" for "A:"):

MAKEDISK A:

5 · When prompted, insert each of the newly formatted diskettes in order.

Now you have a complete set of diskettes, from which you can install all of your workstations.

INSTALLING THE DOS REQUESTER

To install the DOS Requester on a workstation, complete the following steps. If you want to install NetWare workstation software that will support Microsoft Windows, Windows must already be installed on this workstation.

1 · Boot DOS on the computer that you are going to turn into a workstation. If you have Microsoft Windows running on the computer, exit Windows and go to the DOS prompt. You cannot run the installation program from a DOS Box inside Windows.

2 · Insert the WSDOS_1 diskette in drive A:, change to that drive, then type INSTALL.

3 · The first item on the screen that appears asks you for the name of the directory to use for the client installation (client is another word for workstation). The default name provided is C:\NWCLIENT. Accept this default name by pressing Enter. The installation program will create the NWCLIENT directory for you on drive C: (the workstation's hard disk). This directory will contain many of the necessary workstation files.

4 · The second step tells you that the installation program will modify the CONFIG.SYS and AUTOEXEC.BAT files on the workstation. When it modifies these files, it will save the original files as CONFIG.BNW and AUTOEXEC.BNW in case you still need them when the installation is over. Select "Yes" to allow the files to be modified.

5 · The third step asks if you want to install support for Microsoft Windows. If you do, select Yes. The default Windows directory is C:\WINDOWS. If you have changed the name of the Windows directory on this workstation, type in the correct directory name.

6 · The next step asks you to specify the drive for the network board that is installed in this workstation. Press the Enter key. If you are using a driver that is supplied on the NetWare 3.12 diskettes, insert the WSDRV_1 or the WSDRV_2 diskette in drive A: and press the Enter key to see the list of drivers. If the driver you need is not in the list, press the Esc key and insert the manufacturer's diskette in the drive and press Enter. When you've found your driver in the list, press the Enter key to select it. Then change or accept the default configuration settings for the network board.

7 · When all of the selections on the screen are correct, press the Enter key to start the installation process. Insert diskettes when prompted for them.

8 · When the installation program finishes installing all of the files, press the Enter key to Exit the program.

9 · When prompted to "Insert disk with batch file, Press any key to continue…," insert the WSDOS_1 diskette. The batch file that it's looking for is the INSTALL.BAT file.

10 · If this workstation already had previous NetWare shell software (NETX) installed on it, edit the AUTOEXEC.BAT file to remove the files that loaded the IPX or IPXODI driver, the LAN driver, the LSL driver, and NETX file. These commands are now included in the STARTNET.BAT file instead.

BOOT FILES FOR DOS REQUESTER WORKSTATIONS

Because the DOS Requester uses ODI drivers, the list of files described on page 34 in Chapter 2, under "Boot Files for ODI Workstations," also are used on a DOS Requester workstation. The only file that is not used in the DOS Requester is the NETX (or EMSNETX or XMSNETX) shell file. Instead, the workstation uses a set of VLM files.

In addition to the files described in Chapter 2, the DOS Requester requires some new files and commands. The following list describes these additional files and commands.

- ▶ A new directory, called NWCLIENT, is automatically created during installation. This directory contains workstation files.

- ▶ An additional batch file, called STARTNET.BAT, is automatically created by the installation program and is executed by the AUTOEXEC.BAT file. This batch file loads the LSL, LAN driver, and IPXODI files, then executes the VLM.EXE command, which loads all the necessary VLM files. (Most of these commands are put into the AUTOEXEC.BAT file in previous versions of NetWare. If this workstation was previously using NETX, you will need to edit the AUTOEXEC.BAT file and remove any lines that loaded the LSL, LAN driver, IPXODI, IPX, or NETX files.)

- ▶ AUTOEXEC.BAT has a command added to it which executes STARTNET.BAT.

- ▶ CONFIG.SYS has the command "LASTDRIVE=Z" added to it. This command tells the workstation that all available drives can be used as network drives.

▶ NET.CFG is created (or updated if one existed) with some additional sections and commands. These commands configure the requester and the LAN driver to work on the workstation. The original version of NET.CFG (if one existed on the workstation before installation) is saved and renamed as NET.BNW. For more information about NET.CFG, refer to the next section.

▶ If the workstation is using Windows, the SYSTEM.INI, WIN.INI, and PROGMAN.INI files are modified slightly.

CHANGES TO THE NET.CFG FILE

When the NetWare 3.12 DOS Requester is installed on a workstation, the NET.CFG file is created (or modified, if one already existed). NET.CFG is explained in Chapter 2, but there are some additional commands that are added to NET.CFG during the DOS Requester installation.

The commands that are primarily of interest here are the commands that specify which of the VLM files are loaded when the VLM.EXE command is executed from the STARTNET.BAT file. In the NET.CFG file, under the heading called "USE DEFAULTS = OFF," each of the VLM files is listed, as shown below.

```
USE DEFAULTS=OFF
    VLM=CONN.VLM
    VLM=IPXNCP.VLM
    VLM=TRAN.VLM
    VLM=SECURITY.VLM
;   VLM=NDS.VLM
    VLM=BIND.VLM
    VLM=NWP.VLM
    VLM=FIO.VLM
    VLM=GENERAL.VLM
    VLM=REDIR.VLM
    VLM=PRINT.VLM
    VLM=NETX.VLM
```

Every VLM file that is listed is executed, and they are executed in the order that they appear in the NET.CFG file. The order in which the files execute is important, so be sure not to change their order.

If you look at the NET.CFG file after installing a workstation using the installation program that came with NetWare 3.12, you will notice that one line, "VLM=NDS.VLM," has a semicolon (;) in front of it. The semicolon turns off the command. This is sometimes called "commenting out" the command, or making it so that the command appears in the file, but does not actually execute, much like using the REMARK command in a login script.

The NDS.VLM command is turned off because that VLM file is only used when the workstation needs to log in to a NetWare 4.x file server that is using NetWare Directory Services. To log in to a NetWare 3.x server, only the BIND.VLM file is required. Although a workstation will work fine if both the NDS.VLM and the BIND.VLM files are loaded in the NET.CFG file, the workstation will take a little longer to log in to a NetWare 3.x file server. Therefore, to make logging in to a NetWare 3.x server faster, the NetWare 3.12 workstation installation process automatically adds the semicolon to the NDS.VLM command. This way, the workstation skips the NDS.VLM file and goes straight to the file it needs: BIND.VLM.

If you should ever upgrade your network to NetWare 4.x, or if you add a NetWare 4.x server to your NetWare 3.12 network and you want this workstation to be able to log in to the NetWare 4.x server, you will need to edit the NET.CFG file and delete the semicolon. By deleting the semicolon, you will make the NDS.VLM command active, and the workstation will be able to use both NDS.VLM and BIND.VLM to log in to both versions of NetWare servers.

Installing OS/2 Workstations

To install an OS/2 workstation on a NetWare 3.12 network, complete the following steps.

1 · Make sure OS/2 is already installed on the computer.

2 · Insert the WSOS2_1 diskette into drive A: of the computer.

3 · From the desktop, select the "Drive A" icon.

4 · From the "Drive A Tree-View," select the "Drive A" icon.

5 · From the "Installation" menu, select the "Requester on workstation…" option, and follow the instructions that appear on the screen. The default values should be sufficient in most cases.

6 · If you need to configure the workstation after the NetWare workstation software is installed, select the "This workstation" option from the "Configuration" menu.

Creating Menu Programs in NetWare 3.12

NetWare 3.12 includes a different menu-creation utility than the one that was included in previous versions of NetWare. The NetWare 3.12 NMENU utility is actually a trimmed-down version of the Saber Menu System for DOS, created by Saber Software Corporation.

Using NMENU, you can create your own menu programs for your users. If you are upgrading an existing NetWare network to NetWare 3.12, and you already have menu programs that you created using the earlier MENU utility, you can use NMENU to convert those older menus. The following sections explain how to create new menu programs and how to update old ones.

CREATING NEW MENU PROGRAMS

To create a menu program in NetWare 3.12, you first use a text editor to create a text file containing the commands you want the menu program to execute. Then you use the MENUMAKE utility, which takes the text file and "compiles" it into a program file. To execute the menu program file, use the NMENU utility.

The commands you can use in the text file to create your menu program are described below:

MENU	This command identifies the heading of a menu or submenu.
ITEM	This command indicates an option that will be displayed in the menu.
EXEC	This command executes the commands necessary to complete an ITEM option when the user selects it.
SHOW	This command displays a submenu.
LOAD	This command displays a submenu from a different menu program.
GETR	This command requests input from the user that is required for a menu item to be executed.
GETO	This command requests input from the user that is optional.
GETP	This command requests input from the user and assigns a variable to that input so that it can be reused.

Figure 11.1 shows an example menu program as it should appear on a user's screen.

To create this menu, first create two directories to hold the program and the temporary files that the menu program will generate. The temporary directories can be on the network or on the user's hard disk. Then use a text editor to create the following file. The text file has to be named with the extension .SRC or it cannot be compiled by the MENUMAKE utility. In this case, we'll name the file MANAGERS.SRC.

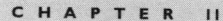

FIGURE II.I

An example menu program

```
Choose a Spreadsheet File
B. Budget
I. Inventory
```

```
Select a Task
S. Spreadsheet
W. Word Processing
M. Mail
E. Exit to DOS
L. Logout
```

```
MENU 1, Select a Task
    ITEM ^SSpreadsheet
        SHOW 2
    ITEM ^WWord Processing
        EXEC WP
    ITEM ^MMail
        GETR Enter your email name: { } 8,, { }
        EXEC EMAIL
    ITEM ^EExit to DOS
        EXEC DOS
    ITEM ^LLogout
        EXEC LOGOUT

MENU 2, Choose a Spreadsheet File
    ITEM ^BBudget
        EXEC COUNT BUDGET
    ITEM ^IInventory
        EXEC COUNT INV
```

Notice that the sections of the file pertaining to each menu or submenu are separated from each other by a space, and the commands for each item within a menu are indented. Each ITEM command, which indicates an option on a menu, is followed by the EXEC command that executes that option.

In this menu, we want users to be able to select an item from the menu by typing the first letter of the option. To accomplish this, add a caret (^) and the letter that should be typed to the beginning of the ITEM command.

Under the Mail ITEM, the following GETR command appears:

GETR Enter your email name: { } 8,, { }

This command asks the user for his or her email user name before the option executes the command to load the email application. The syntax for the GETR command is as follows:

GETR *text {prepend} length, default, {append}*

In this example, the *text* is the statement "Enter your email name:". The *prepend* value is any value that should be automatically supplied to the beginning of the user's input. In this case, no value is needed, so type a blank space inside the brackets. The *length* indicates the maximum number of characters that a user's input can be. In our example, a user's email name can be up to eight characters long, so the supervisor entered the number 8. The next field in the commands lets you enter a default value that the user can select. However, for this menu there is no default user name, so we enter no value here. The two commas, however, are necessary; they show that there is no default value. Finally, the last field, *append* lets you enter any value that should be added to the end of the user's input. Again, in this example there is no value needed, so the brackets contain only a space.

After we finish creating the text file and save it as MANAGERS.SRC, it's time to compile the file. Instructions for compiling the menu file and adding commands to the login script to automate the menu program are explained later in this chapter. For more information about the creating and using menu programs with NMENU in NetWare 3.12, refer to the *NetWare 3.12 Utilities Reference* manual.

CONVERTING OLD MENU PROGRAMS

If you have a menu program that you created using earlier versions of NetWare's MENU utility, you can convert that menu program into an NMENU program. The older menu files have the .MNU extension, such as CLERKS.MNU. To convert a menu file, complete the following steps.

I · Create two directories to hold the program and the temporary files that the menu program will generate. The temporary directories can be on the network or on the user's hard disk. If you already have menu directories for your existing menu programs, you can use those directories.

2 · Use the MENUCNVT utility and specify the name of the menu file you wish to convert. The utility will create a new file with the .SRC file name extension, and will leave the old .MNU file unchanged. For example, to convert the CLERKS.MNU file, type

MENUCNVT CLERKS

3 · Edit the new .SRC file if necessary. For more information about the commands and format for creating .SRC files, see the previous section.

When you have finished converting the old menu file, you are ready to compile it and set up users' access to the new program in the login script, as explained in the next section.

COMPILING A MENU FILE

To compile the MANAGERS.SRC file, use the MENUMAKE utility, and type the following command:

MENUMAKE MANAGERS

It is not necessary to type the .SRC extension in the command. The MENUMAKE utility compiles the file and creates a data file called MANAGERS.DAT. This is the file that will execute when a user runs NMENU.

To allow users to access this new menu program, you must set up drive mappings in the user or system login script to the program and temporary directories. However, if you created the directories under SYS:PUBLIC, you do not need to add these drive mappings to the login scripts, because a drive is already mapped to SYS:PUBLIC.

Next, add DOS SET commands to the user or system login script that provide information about the location of the temporary subdirectories and about the workstation's ID number. For example, if the temporary directory is called MENUTEMP, and you created it in SYS:PUBLIC, you would add the following commands to the user or system login script:

```
SET S_FILEDIR="Z:\PUBLIC\MENUTEMP\"
SET S_FILE="%STATION"
```

Finally, if you want users to enter the menu program automatically after their login scripts have finished executing, add the command to execute the new menu program to the end of the login script. For example, to make a user enter the MANAGERS menu automatically, add the following line to the login script:

```
EXIT "NMENU MANAGERS"
```

Using NetWare for Macintosh 3.12

With NetWare 3.12, a 5-user version of NetWare for Macintosh is included. With this product, you can connect up to five Macintosh workstations to your NetWare 3.12 network.

Installing NetWare for Macintosh on a NetWare server is described in Chapter 10.

However, the utilities used on a NetWare for Macintosh 3.12 workstation are not the same as the earlier versions of NetWare for Macintosh. Instead of a NetWare desk accessory and a NetWare Control Center application, NetWare for Macintosh now has a single application, called NetWare Tools, that consists of five different utilities.

With NetWare Tools, you select a utility, then you select an entity, such as a user, a print queue, or a volume. When you are using a utility with an entity, it's called a *session*.

To use NetWare Tools, double-click on the NetWare Tools icon, then choose one of the utilities from the "Utilities" menu. Then you can select the entity with which you want to work.

Most of the features of the NetWare Tools application can only be used by the network supervisor. The five utilities are explained below:

UTILITY	DESCRIPTION
Print Queue	This utility lets you view the print jobs in a queue, and lets you delete them, delay them, change their position in the queue, and so on.
Users and Groups	This utility lets you create and delete users and groups, change passwords, assign trustees, and assign security equivalences.
Messaging	This utility lets you send short messages to other users on the network.
NetWare Rights	This utility lets you view your effective rights, assign trustee rights to users, and modify the Inherited Rights Mask.
File and Folder Flags	This utility lets you set flags (attributes) for files and folders.

When you first open the NetWare Tools application, a Workspace appears on your screen. This Workspace has two panels: a "Connected Items" panel and a "Saved Items" panel.

The "Connected Items" panel shows the volumes and print queues with which you currently have a session. You can use the "Saved Items" panel to specify entities with whom you often have sessions. If an item appears in either panel, you can double-click on that item as a quick way to reopen the utility session with that entity.

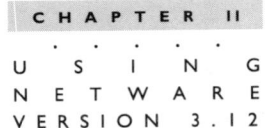
To add a session with a particular entity to your Workspace, choose the "Add to Workspace" option from the File menu. To copy a session from the "Connected Items" panel to the "Saved Items" panel, choose "Add to Saved Items" from the File menu. To delete a session from the "Saved Items" panel, highlight the item and press the Delete key.

You can have more than one Saved Items session file if you'd like. To save items to a different session file, choose the "Export Workspace to File" option from the File menu. Then, to use the new file next time you use the NetWare Tools application, double-click on the new session file's icon to launch NetWare Tools.

Review

NetWare version 3.12 is based largely upon NetWare version 3.11. However, some of NetWare 3.12's additional features include:

- ▶ The ability to install NetWare 3.12 from a CD-ROM. Installing from a CD-ROM is generally faster than installing from diskettes. In addition, with NetWare 3.12 you can use CD-ROMs as volumes on the network.

- ▶ An easy-to-follow menued installation program. INSTALL.BAT and INSTALL.NLM work together to simplify the server installation process.

- ▶ Electronic documentation (in the CD-ROM version of the product only). With Novell ElectroText installed on a network directory, you can access the complete set of NetWare 3.12 documentation from any workstation.

- ▶ Updated workstation software. The NetWare DOS Requester and its associated VLM files provides faster performance at the workstation. The DOS Requester also supports Windows workstations.

► A different product for creating menu programs. The menu utilities
MENUMAKE and NMENU let you create and run a customized menu
program for your users. MENUCNVT lets you convert older menu
programs (creating for the MENU utility in previous versions of Net-
Ware) to a format that can be used by NMENU.

► A new version of NetWare for Macintosh. NetWare for Macintosh version 3.12 contains an administrative application, called NetWare
Tools, which allows you to work with users and groups, print queues,
volumes, and so on.

GLOSSARY

ASCII: American Standard Code for Information Interchange; a standard way of encoding letters, numbers, and punctuation as bits in a file. ASCII is a standard used for moving text files from one computer to another, as well as for printing files without an application.

Attributes: Attributes are assigned to NetWare files and directories. They control such things as whether the file or directory can be shared by several users, whether it can be deleted, and so on. Attributes override any trustee rights a user may have. Attributes are sometimes called *flags*. To set file attributes, use the FLAG utility. To set directory attributes, use the FLAGDIR utility. Note that FLAG and FLAGDIR do not affect files and directories stored on a local disk.

AUTOEXEC.BAT file: A batch file, which is a file that executes several commands automatically for the user. The AUTOEXEC.BAT file located on a workstation's boot disk can take care of several networking startup steps, including loading the necessary NetWare shell files, changing to the network drive, and executing the LOGIN command with the user's name.

Backup: A copy you make of an application or of files. If you lose files because of a system failure or an accident, you can restore the backup copy. Some backup products, such as the NetWare utilities SBACKUP.NLM, NBACKUP.EXE, and BACKUP.VAP, back up trustee information and attributes for files in addition to the files themselves.

Batch file: An ASCII file that contains a series of commands that execute when you run the file. A batch file's name has the extension .BAT. A common batch file on boot disks is AUTOEXEC.BAT, which can be used to execute NetWare workstation files and log the user in to the network.

Bindery: The database of NetWare's network information. The bindery includes information about each object in the network, such as users, print servers, and print queues. Each object has properties that describe it, such as addresses, attributes, or passwords. These properties are also stored in the bindery.

Boot disk: A floppy diskette or workstation hard disk that contains the files necessary for booting the workstation with DOS. Most boot disks for NetWare workstations also configure the workstation's environment, load the NetWare shell files, and log the user into the network.

Booting: Turning on a computer so that its operating system and other necessary files load. See also **Remote reset**.

CD-ROM: Compact disk, read-only memory; a technology that allows for the storage and retrieval of large amounts of data on a small compact disk.

Client: A device, such as a workstation, that requests services from the network file server.

Command line utilities: NetWare utilities that let you perform a network task. You execute command line utilities by typing a command at the system prompt.

Compile: To convert a file into a program, or executable, file. The MENUMAKE utility compiles a text file containing menu formatting commands into an executable program file, so that menu programs can be displayed on a workstation.

CONFIG.SYS: A DOS file that allows you to customize the DOS environment for a workstation so that certain applications run more efficiently under DOS. You also load device drivers from CONFIG.SYS. If you are using DR DOS 6.0 or MS DOS 5.0, this file was created when you installed DOS.

Console: A common name for the file server's keyboard and monitor. For example, you run server utilities by typing commands at the file server console. In NetWare version 3.x, you can use Remote Console to turn your workstation's keyboard and monitor into the file server's console.

Core printing: In NetWare version 2.2, a built-in print server that runs in the file server. With core printing, you can have a maximum of five printers on your network, and they all must be attached to the file server.

Database: A collection of information that is accessible to computer programs. The database can be an integral part of a program, or it can be a separate file accessed by a database program. One example of a simple database is a collection of telephone numbers with names and addresses. The NetWare bindery is a database of network information.

Dedicated: A computer on the network that is reserved for one specific task. For example, you can use a dedicated workstation as a print server.

Dedicated IPX driver: A type of driver used by NetWare workstations. Dedicated IPX drivers understand only the IPX protocol. See also **ODI driver**.

Default: The choice a program makes if a user does not select another choice. Your default directory is the directory in which you are currently working.

Default login script: See **Login script**.

Desk accessory: A small program that runs on Macintosh workstations, appearing under the Apple menu. Desk accessories can be used to accomplish tasks such as running a calculator, setting preferences for the workstation environment, and locating files. The NetWare desk accessory allows you to work with trustee rights, send and receive messages, and work with print queues.

Directory entry: Used on the hard disk to help index where information is located. Each directory, DOS file, and trustee list on the network uses up one directory entry. Each Macintosh file uses two directory entries. If you run out of directory entries on your disk, no one will be able to create a new file or directory.

Disk duplexing: Duplicating network data on two identical hard disks, so that if one goes bad, the other can continue to operate. When two disks are duplexed, they are running on separate disk-controller boards. See also **Disk mirroring**.

Disk mirroring: Duplicating network data on two identical hard disks, so that if one goes bad, then the other can continue to operate. When two disks are mirrored, they are both running on the same disk-controller board. See also **Disk duplexing**.

DOS Requester: See **NetWare DOS Requester**.

Drive mapping: Assigning letters to directories on local disks or to network directories. Mapping drives to directories makes it easier for both users and applications to find files located in those directories.

Driver: Software that allows hardware and software to communicate with each other. For example, LAN drivers allow network communication to travel across network boards and cables, printer drivers allow your printers and applications to communicate, and tape drivers allow tape backup systems to receive network data from the backup program.

Duplexing: See **Disk duplexing**.

Effective rights: The sum of trustee rights that a user can ultimately exercise in a directory or file, taking into consideration specific user and group trustee assignments, security equivalences, rights inherited from parent directories, and the Rights Masks assigned to the directory or file.

ElectroText: See **Novell ElectroText**.

Error log file: Whenever an error occurs with the file server or the volume, NetWare records the error in an error log file. There are three error log files: SYS$LOG.ERR, for file server errors; VOL$LOG.ERR, for volume errors; and TTS$LOG.ERR, for NetWare's Transaction Tracking System (TTS).

Ethernet frame type: The format that Ethernet uses to send packets of data across the network. In NetWare versions 2.2 and 3.11, Novell used an Ethernet frame type called 802.3. In NetWare 3.12, Novell changed the default frame type to 802.2, which is an industry standard.

Executable file: A program file that performs a task. For example, the executable file that runs WordPerfect is WP.EXE. Common executable file name extensions are .EXE, .COM, .BAT, and .NLM.

External router: See **Router**.

Fake root: Some applications require that they be installed at the root of the volume. If you would rather install the application in a subdirectory, you can map a fake root to the subdirectory that contains the application, and the application will think it is located at the root of the volume instead of in a subdirectory.

File server: The computer on the network that has the NetWare operating system running on it. The file server controls file and print sharing on the network and regulates network communications.

Flags: See **Attributes**.

Frame type: See **Ethernet frame type**.

Grace login: When a user logs in after his or her password has expired, a grace login allows the user to finish logging in using the old password without changing it. You can set the number of grace logins a user is allowed.

Group: A set of network users that have been assigned to a NetWare user group so that they all have the same level of security in the same directories.

Home directory: A directory that can be created automatically for a network user. A home directory is named with the user's login name and can be used by the user to store personal files.

I/O address: Input/output address; used by the computer's microprocessor to communicate with peripheral boards. No two boards in the same computer can share the same address, so part of the board installation process is locating an open I/O address.

Identifier variable: A word or phrase used in login script commands that is replaced by a real value determined when the user logs in. For example, the identifier variable LOGIN_NAME is replaced by the user's name when the command that contains that variable is executed. Identifier variables can be used in generic login script commands that become customized for a user when that user logs in.

Inherited Rights Mask: In NetWare version 3.x, a list of the trustee rights that users are allowed to inherit from a trustee assignment to a parent directory. An Inherited Rights Mask is assigned to every directory and file. The Inherited Rights Mask affects only inherited rights, not explicit trustee assignments.

Internal router: See **Router**.

IPX: Internetwork Packet eXchange; a network-level protocol developed by Novell to move communications packets from one computer to another across a network.

IRQ: Interrupt; used by peripheral devices to let the computer know that they are waiting to be serviced. No two boards in the same computer can share the same IRQ, so part of the board installation process is locating an open IRQ.

Loadable module: See NetWare loadable module.

Local area network (LAN): See **Network**.

Local drive: A disk drive on the user's workstation; as opposed to a network drive, which is mapped to a directory located on the file server.

Local printer: A printer that is attached to a file server or workstation that is running the print server.

Log in: The procedure by which a user accesses the network. To log in to a NetWare network, type LOGIN. The LOGIN utility executes a login script, which sets up a user's working environment.

Log out: The procedure by which a user exits the network. To log out of the network, type LOGOUT.

Login script: A file that contains commands that set up a user's workstation environment. For example, a login script may set up drive mappings, display messages on the user's screen, and so on. The login script is executed by the LOGIN utility. The two types of login scripts are the system login script, which executes for all users who log in to the file server, and user login scripts, which belong to individual users. User login scripts execute after the system login script. If a user doesn't have a user login script, a default login script will execute. The default login script is part of the LOGIN utility.

Maximum Rights Mask: In NetWare version 2.2, a list of the trustee rights that users are allowed to exercise in a directory. A Maximum Rights Mask is assigned to every directory. The Maximum Rights Mask can block both inherited rights and specific trustee assignments.

Menu program: A program that allows users to select tasks from a list of options displayed on the computer screen. You can create your own menu programs and execute them using NetWare's MENU utility.

Menu utility: NetWare utilities, such as SYSCON and FILER, that allow you to perform network tasks by selecting options from a list displayed on the computer screen.

Mirroring: See **Disk mirroring**.

Modem: MODulator/DEModulator; a device that lets computers communicate over telephone wires by converting digital computer signals to analog telephone signals and back again.

Name space module: A NetWare version 3.*x* software program that you load on your file server if you are using NetWare for Macintosh or OS/2 and its High Performance File System (HPFS) on your network. Macintosh and OS/2 both support longer file names than DOS does. The name space modules tell NetWare that these operating systems are running on workstations on the network, so NetWare should allow these long names to be stored.

NET.CFG: A file that allows you to customize the NetWare environment on a workstation. You can use the NET.CFG file on workstations with either ODI drivers or dedicated IPX drivers. The SHELL.CFG file is a similar file that can be used only on workstations with dedicated IPX drivers.

NetBIOS: A network basic input/output system; an IBM protocol for network communications.

NetWare: A network operating system from Novell, Inc., which lets you connect a variety of computers together so that users on all these computers can share the same files, applications, printers, and so on.

NetWare DOS Requester: The workstation shell software shipped in NetWare 3.12. The DOS Requester replaces NETX, EMSNETX, and XMSNETX.

NetWare loadable module (NLM): A NetWare version 3.*x* software program that runs on the file server and adds a particular feature to the network. For example, the SBACKUP.NLM loadable module allows you to back up network files from your file server.

Network: A group of computers that are connected so that they can share files, applications, and other resources (such as disk space and printers). The NetWare operating system runs on the file server computer and controls communications across the network.

Network board: A circuit board that allows a computer to communicate on the network. Each workstation and file server on the network must have a network board installed in it. Network cables connect the boards to the rest of the network. Network boards are sometimes called *network interface cards* (NICs) or *network adapters*.

Network drive: A letter (such as F: or Y:) that is mapped to a directory located on the file server.

Network operating system: The software that runs on the file server and controls network communications, including file sharing and print services. NetWare is a network operating system.

Network supervisor: The user who has rights to modify any file on the file server and to install or modify network resources.

Node address: The physical workstation address; each workstation must have a unique node address.

Nondedicated: A computer on the network that is not limited to one task. For example, a nondedicated file server can also be used as a workstation.

Novell ElectroText: Novell's online documentation, included in the CD-ROM version of NetWare 3.12.

ODI driver: Open Data-Link Interface driver; a type of driver installed on a workstation. ODI drivers can handle more than one type of protocol. In addition, ODI drivers can handle different types of Ethernet. See also **Dedicated IPX driver**.

Operating system: A program that controls the way a computer handles communication between data and hardware. PCs can use either the DOS or OS/2 operating systems. Macintosh computers use an operating system called System. NetWare is a network operating system that controls the entire network's communications.

Parent directory: Any directory that contains other directories (which are called *subdirectories*).

Password: A word, phrase, or other combination of characters you type to prove that you are authorized to log in to the network. Each user should have a unique username and password to make sure that the network cannot be accessed by unauthorized people.

Patch: A small program designed to fix a bug in a product that has already been released.

Path (directory): The series of directories you follow to reach a particular file. For example, if you've stored a file called ARTICLE in a subdirectory called LENSES in another directory called PHOTO on the volume VOL1:, the directory path to that file is VOL1:PHOTO\LENSES\ARTICLE.

Path (DOS): DOS allows you to set paths to directories. These paths tell DOS which directories to search through when looking for executable files that are not found in your current directory.

Peripheral: A device, such as a printer, modem, or tape drive, that is attached to the network or workstation.

Port: An outlet on a computer that allows the computer to communicate with printers, modems, or other peripheral devices.

Print job: A file that has been sent to be printed.

Print queue: A directory on the file server that holds a print job temporarily until the print server is ready to take the print job and send it to the printer. Print jobs are held in the print queue in a first-come-first-served order.

Print server: NetWare software that controls how print jobs are taken from print queues and directed to printers. The print server software can be installed on either a file server or a dedicated workstation.

Prompt: The mark the operating system or application puts on the screen to indicate that it's ready to accept another command. In DOS, the DOS prompt usually shows the drive you are currently working in, followed by an angle bracket (>). On a NetWare file server, the console prompt is a colon (:).

Protocol: The method of exchanging data between two systems. The protocol dictates how data is formatted, packaged, sent, and acknowledged between two systems.

Purge: Removing deleted files and directories from the disk. In NetWare version 2.2, when files are deleted, they are not actually removed from the disk until you execute another command that writes to the disk. In NetWare version 3.x, deleted files are moved to another directory, where they are hidden but still available should you need to retrieve them. Purging completely removes those deleted files.

RAM: Random-access memory; the memory used by the computer to manipulate and temporarily store information. This memory is dynamic, which means that any information stored in it will be erased when the computer's power is turned off. Some applications require a large amount of RAM to run successfully.

Remote Console: NetWare version 3.*x* software that lets you run a file server from a workstation. Your workstation screen and keyboard appear to be the file server's screen and keyboard. You can run server utilities from the workstation and they will be executed on the file server. (Remote Console is not available in NetWare version 2.2.)

Remote printer: A printer that is attached to a workstation that is not running a print server. The workstation must be running RPRINT.EXE.

Remote reset: The installation of boot files on the file server so that diskless workstations can boot and access the network. Also called *remote boot*.

Restore: To retrieve files from a backup disk or tape and place them back on the network.

Rights: See **Trustee rights**.

Rights Mask: See **Inherited Rights Mask** (NetWare version 3.*x*) or **Maximum Rights Mask** (NetWare version 2.2).

Router: A software connection between two different networks that allows the two networks to communicate with each other. When a file server contains two or more network boards, each connecting to a different network, the router that connects those networks is called an *internal router*. When networks are connected through a workstation that contains two or more network boards, it is called an *external router*.

Search drive: A special type of drive mapping to a directory. If a search drive is mapped to a directory, the system will look in that directory for executable files if it can't find them in a user's current directory. For example, the NetWare utilities are located in the SYS:PUBLIC directory. A search drive to that directory is placed in the system login script so that the utilities can be executed by users no matter which directory those users are currently using.

Security: The NetWare features that protect your network data. NetWare security includes user passwords, user account restrictions (which limit when users can log in), trustee rights (which are assigned to users to control the tasks they can perform with directories and files), and file and directory attributes (which are assigned to directories and files and limit all users' access to them).

Security equivalence: An assignment that grants one user identical trustee rights to another user. For example, if user Ed is given a security equivalence to user Jane, Ed can exercise the same trustee rights Jane can. However, the security equivalence only lets Ed exercise the trustee rights that are specifically assigned to Jane. Ed cannot exercise any rights Jane received through her security equivalences to other users.

Session: In NetWare for Macintosh 3.12, a session is an instance of using a NetWare Tools utility to work with an entity, such as a user or a print queue.

Shell: NetWare software that runs on the workstation and allows the workstation to communicate with the network.

SHELL.CFG: A file that allows you to customize the NetWare environment on a dedicated IPX workstation. (For an ODI workstation, use a NET.CFG file instead.)

Spooler assignments: Spooler assignments give a corresponding printer number (0 through 4) to a print queue name so that applications that require printer numbers can communicate with NetWare.

Stand-alone: Any device, such as a computer or a printer, that is not connected to a network.

STARTNET.BAT: A batch file that is automatically creating during the DOS Requester installation. This batch file loads the LSL, LAN driver, and IPXODI files, then executes the VLM.EXE command, which loads all the necessary VLM files. (Most of these commands are put into the AUTOEXEC.BAT file in previous versions of NetWare. If this workstation was previously using NETX, you will need to edit the AUTOEXEC.BAT file and remove any lines that loaded the LSL, LAN driver, IPXODI, IPX, or NETX files.)

Subdirectory: Any directory that is contained within another directory.

Surge suppressor: A device that provides some protection for hardware against power peaks that occasionally come through the power-supply line.

System login script: See **Login script**.

Trustee: A user or group who has been granted rights to work in a network directory or file.

Trustee rights: The means by which you control what a user can do to a particular directory or file. For example, trustee rights regulate whether a user can read a file, change it, change its name, delete it, or control other users' trustee rights to it. Trustee rights are assigned to individual users, and one user's rights can be different from another user's rights to the same directory.

TTS: Transactional Tracking System; protects files such as databases, including the NetWare bindery, from being corrupted.

UPS: Uninterruptible power supply; a device that provides alternative power to your file server if the main power supply is interrupted.

User account: The definition of a network user. Every person who wants to log in to the network must have a network user account.

User account restrictions: A means by which you can restrict users' work with the network in various ways. For example, you can limit the hours that a user can log in to the network, the workstations he or she can use, the amount of disk space that user can fill up, or the length of time he or she can use the same password. You can assign account restrictions on a systemwide basis or to individual users.

User login script: See **Login script.**

Utilities: NetWare programs that allow you to perform tasks on the network. There are workstation utilities and server utilities. Generally, you use workstation utilities to work with users, files, directories, and so on. You use server utilities to change the way the file server operates. Some utilities are command line utilities, which you execute by typing a command. Other utilities are menu utilities, which you execute by selecting an option from a menu displayed on the screen. NetWare version 3.*x* contains a feature called Remote Console, which lets you run server utilities from a workstation by accessing the file server from your workstation.

VAP: Value-Added Process; a NetWare version 2.2 software program that runs on the file server and adds a particular feature to the network. For example, NetWare for Macintosh VAPs allow you to connect Macintosh workstations to your NetWare network.

VLMs (Virtual Loadable Modules): Files loaded on a DOS or Windows workstation as part of the DOS Requester workstation software. VLMs replace NETX, EMSNETX, and XMSNETX.

Volume: The top level of NetWare's directory structure. A volume is a portion of the file server's hard disk. The volume contains directories and files. A NetWare file server must have at least one volume, called SYS: (for system), which contains all the files required to run NetWare. You may want to create additional volumes on your file server to contain applications and work files, as well as a separate volume to contain Macintosh files.

Wildcard character: A character that can match any other character; used in specifying file names. The asterisk (*) stands for any series of characters. The question mark (?) represents any single character.

Workstation: A personal computer that users can use to accomplish their daily work. Workstations on a NetWare network can be PCs (running DOS or OS/2) or Macintoshes. A NetWare workstation contains a network board, which connects it to the network cabling, and workstation software, which communicates with the file server.

Index

O

P

T

A Quick Guide to Useful NetWare Workstation Utilities

MANAGING THE FILE SERVER:

BINDFIX (♦)   Repair a damaged bindery.

BINDREST (♦)   Restore the bindery to its original condition if BINDFIX cannot repair the bindery.

CHKDIR (♦)   In NetWare 3.x only, view information about a directory's or volume's storage capacity.

CHKVOL (♦)   View information about a volume's storage capacity, such as the space being used by deleted files, the space available, and so on.

FCONSOLE (*)   View statistical information about the file server and its workstation connections.

SLIST (♦)   List all available file servers on the network.

SYSTIME (♦)   View the file server's time and date.

VOLINFO (*)   View information about a volume's storage capacity.

RUNNING REMOTE CONSOLE:

ACONSOLE (*)   In NetWare 3.x only, establish a Remote Console on a workstation via asynchronous communication.

RCONSOLE (*)   In NetWare 3.x only, establish a Remote Console on a workstation via a direct connection.

LOGGING IN:

ATTACH (♦)   Connect to additional file servers after you've logged in to one file server.

LOGIN (♦)   Access a file server and execute system and user login scripts.

LOGOUT (♦)   End a connection with the file server.

MENU (♦)   Execute a menu program you created.

SETPASS (♦)   Change a user's password.

SYSCON (*)   Create and edit login scripts and change passwords.